JANET DENNY grew up in
Westminster Hospital and we
visitor.

She began writing stories
on restoring a derelict fift
While scraping rot from woo... old brickwork, she was able to let her imagination fly. More tales followed, recounting village life and the unexpected adventures of a bed and breakfast hostess.

After twenty-five years running a busy retail business, Janet returned to "fiddling around with words". In 2014 she graduated with an MA in Creative Writing. Her particular interest is in memoir and biography.

Janet's first book, *The Man on the Mantelpiece*, won The One Big Book Launch Competition and was featured in the main section of *The Daily Telegraph* and on the front page of *The Guardian Family*. She has been invited to speak at prestigious literary festivals. *Andrew's Bonce: A memoir* is her second book and she is currently working on a novel.

Praise for *The Man on the Mantelpiece*

'Meticulously researched and beautifully constructed,
with an imagination expertly deployed to fill in
the gaps between the facts.'

'A moving memoir about the author's search for understanding.
Sometimes funny, sometimes sad, it is a powerful story.'

'A wonderfully rich brew of travelogue, memoir, quest,
and detective story.'

'An important contribution to WWII literature – skilfully written
and deeply humane.'

ANDREW'S BONCE

Janet Denny

SilverWood

Published in 2018 by SilverWood Books

SilverWood Books Ltd
14 Small Street, Bristol, BS1 1DE, United Kingdom
www.silverwoodbooks.co.uk

ISBN 978-1-78132-769-2 (paperback)
ISBN 978-1-78132-805-7 (hardback)
ISBN 978-1-78132-770-8 (ebook)

British Library Cataloguing in Publication Data
A CIP catalogue record for this book is available from
the British Library

Page design and typesetting by SilverWood Books
Printed on responsibly sourced paper

Many tears were shed during the writing of this book, but there were many smiles too. It is written with great love for all my family and dedicated to:

Andrew, my beautiful boy, and Alice, his beautiful girl.

How Long Does a Man Live, finally?
A man lives for as long as we carry him inside us,
For as long as we carry the harvest of his dreams,
For as long as we ourselves live,
Holding memories in common, a man lives.

- Brian Patten

Author's Note

One of the main characters in this book is Polish and uses some Polish words, not always explained in the text. It may be useful to know the following:

The name *Gosia* rhymes with kosher

Cholera jasna – Damnation

O Kurwa – Fuck

Babcia – Grandmother

Kochanie – Darling/love/sweetheart

Dzien dobry – Good morning

Dziekuje – Thank you

Na zdrowie – Cheers

One

The sound screeches through my head. The LCD display reads 1.35am.

Steve fumbles for the light switch, lifts the receiver from its cradle. 'Hello.' Silence. He pulls himself upright, alert, frowning as he concentrates.

It'll be Andrew – it's always Andrew.

It was Andrew, new driving licence in his back pocket, who stared down at his trainers and admitted to us that he'd wrapped his prized old banger round a telegraph pole (no harm done to himself, but a rusting hulk in the garden for months). It was Andrew when a group of carousing young men called after midnight asking to speak to their 'good old mate, Andy', Andrew who called from the southern hemisphere in the early hours: 'Hi Mum, just thought I'd give you a call. Oh – sorry – it's lunchtime here...' And it was Andrew who burst into our bedroom in the middle of the night, fresh from the maternity ward, eyes dancing, face split by a grin, to announce, 'She's here – your granddaughter!'

If it was the middle of the night, it was always Andrew.

'You'd better speak to Janet.' The corners of Steve's mouth turn down as he passes me the phone, the spiral of cream plastic cord pinning him to the pillow.

But this time it's not Andrew. It's his wife. 'Gosia, what's wrong?' I hold the receiver away from my ear and we both listen.

'Sorry Janet if I waked you.' English words are always difficult

11

for her to find but now her voice is twisted, fractured by effort and emotion. 'Andy, he, he make strange noises and he will not wake.'

I take a deep breath. Don't panic, I tell myself, think logically. 'Has he been drinking?' Immediately I am ashamed of the question. He's not perfect, but he's not a heavy drinker.

'No, no, a glass of wine only – with his dinner.'

He's always been a heavy sleeper, he'd sleep through a pneumatic drill digging up the road outside his bedroom. 'Maybe it's a bad nightmare, Gosia. Give him a good shake. I'll hang on.'

A second, two at most, and she is back, sobbing. 'Something is very bad, I know. Please come. I phone –' The line goes dead.

My eyes meet Steve's in alarm before we leap into action. Trousers, sweaters, specs, stairs, coats, keys, car. We roar up the steep, narrow lane and speed along the ridge. Frosted sheep gleam in the moonlit valley. Passing Wick Farm, my eyes turn, out of habit, to find the distant gap in the rolling pasture where a circular moon has turned the sea into a festive silver ribbon.

Ten minutes later our lights cut through the cold streets of Rye, deserted but for one white van with a single headlamp coming towards us. No delay at the level crossing, along Cinque Ports Street, and as we breast the humpy railway bridge we see it: an ambulance outside number one Military Road, lights ablaze, doors open – ready. The bright uncurtained windows of the cottage stare like startled eyes and the door stands wide – an open mouth calling for us.

There is a rational explanation for this. I am the one with medical experience. I will not allow panic to engulf me. We sidestep a green-clad ambulance man as we run down the path. He nods as he sprints to his vehicle. Three bounds and we mount the stairs to Andrew and Gosia's bedroom.

The scene jangles my body. I breathe deeply.

My boy is propped in a sitting position – deeply unconscious. A blood pressure cuff on his arm inflates intermittently and sticky pads and wires connect his chest to an ECG machine. The blue duvet is pushed back and a dark, wet patch spreads across his jazzy boxer shorts. A grey-haired paramedic squeezes Andrew's hand, taps his cheek and repeats again and again, 'Andrew, Andrew can you hear me?'

Gosia stands, staring at the wall above Andrew's head, her pale fingers locked around the brass bedstead. When the young man returns from the ambulance he opens the plastic box he has carried up the stairs and pulls translucent latex gloves on to hands pink with cold.

'What do you think, Joe?'

'Diazepam, Dave. 2mg.' Joe points at the box and Dave selects from the rows of equipment and drugs, unwraps a sterile syringe, attaches the needle, snaps the glass neck of the chosen ampoule and draws up its contents. My distant nursing training clicks in so that I check that he points the needle at the ceiling and gently pushes the plunger far enough to exclude any air before he empties the contents into Andrew's thigh. Then the slow-motion quality of the moment gains momentum and we emerge from our petrified state into one of barely controlled panic. I comb my memory for the uses of diazepam but any residual medical knowledge has deserted me.

'I knew what to dial – 999, that TV programme.' Gosia's eyes glitter at me and I respond with a questioning frown. Doesn't everyone know that? No, not if you have spent most of your life in Warsaw. Thank God for the telly, I think, as I reach for her hand.

'He's waking up.' Steve's brow relaxes as Andrew's hand begins to twitch, his head to jerk.

'Here he goes again,' mutters Joe. He concentrates on our son but tosses a gentle remark to Steve. 'No sir, I'm afraid not.'

I wring my hands together and my eyes widen as I watch my son's body contort, every muscle clenched tight. His legs shake, his arms flex. His hands screw into fists and the knuckles whiten. Eyes roll to the back of his head as if the sky-blue irises have been engulfed by snow and his face scrunches as tight as a baby's about to deliver his loudest, angriest bellow. But the only sounds from Andrew are grunts bubbling through the foam at his lips.

'Oh God, he's fitting,' I whisper. 'Why is he fitting?'

Joe is now working urgently to find a vein. 'This one's no good, Dave – let's try the other arm.'

'Don't know, love,' the man replies to my question. 'We're just trying to stabilise him enough to transfer to hospital.' His measured tones inspire a modicum of confidence, but I detect a sense of urgency in his voice as he instructs his young colleague. Steve and Gosia turn their eyes to me, silently pleading for an explanation.

Meningitis. The word fills my head as it has been filling the media recently. It can kill. It can kill swiftly. *But only other people – not my boy.* At last the paramedics penetrate a vein but the fits still come one after another, almost continuously, despite the medication.

'We'll have to take him now, Dave, and risk it.' *Risk what?*

Dave disappears and returns with a stretcher chair.

'You mustn't wake Alice. You mustn't wake Alice.' Gosia repeats the mantra in a monotone as if thinking about her baby connects her to reality. Steve keeps getting in the way with offers of help which Joe and Dave patiently decline. I stand, drained of the capacity for rational thought, staring at our unconscious son writhing on the bed.

His convulsing body fights against the restraints when they negotiate the chair down the narrow, twisting stairs and we all stand watching as he is lifted in to the ambulance. Before he climbs in beside Andrew, Joe says, 'No point in you coming. You can't do anything, and you'd be much better off staying in the warm with a nice cup of tea. Ring the Conquest Hospital in a couple of hours and they'll tell you how things are.' Dave closes the doors and with a final, 'Try not to worry', they drive off into the night.

Like automatons we troop wordlessly back into the house. As instructed, I switch on the kettle, find mugs, teabags, milk, switch off the kettle, pour in the water... The sight of the tea breaks the spell and Gosia crashes her mug onto the table so that the liquid leaps out and an opaque, brown stream spills like a peaty waterfall to the floor. She yells Polish expletives, *'Cholera jasna*, why do we drink tea? *O kurwa!* We must go.'

She's right. I don't even like tea. 'Come on,' I say. We pull on our coats and, leaving Steve in charge of his granddaughter, race to the car.

In the silent streets behind windows, unlit save for an occasional blinking Christmas tree, sleepers are dreaming. No doubt some are twitching, crying out, only to wake and realise it was a bad dream. *This is just a bad dream*, I think. *I'll wake up soon and it will all be over.*

'What is it that is wrong, Janet? I can't believe in this. I think I am in the TV.' Gosia's broken voice pleads for the reassurance I cannot give. Still, all I can think of is meningitis and I whisper the possibility to her.

'People die with that,' she gasps. 'Tell me he won't die.'

I am silent.

We park on a double yellow line and as we run towards the entrance of A&E at the Hastings hospital we meet Joe and Dave coming out.

'Where is he? Is he all right?'

'They're looking after him,' says Dave and Joe lays his arm on my shoulder and wishes me good luck.

Those two kind words are slivers of ice that pierce my heart.

The relatives' waiting room is meant to be cosy: comfy chairs, yesterday's Sunday Express; but it is all grey. A serviceable charcoal carpet flecked with silver, threadbare ash-coloured upholstery patterned with the stains of others' anxiety, walls the colour of twilight. Even the framed print beside the bare black window is of a stone vase of fading roses. Calming, I suppose. Under the buzzing fluorescent light Gosia's face is paper-white, lined with grey. Both of us shiver despite the stifling temperature. A hesitant male nurse with an acne-ridden face offers us tea, which we accept. At least drinking it might distract us. The en-suite loo is well used by us both; curious how shock affects the bowels.

How is he? Is there any news? Can we see him? Is he conscious? We waylay anyone who passes the open door.

We are waiting for the doctor. Just trying to stabilise him. Try not to worry, are the frustrating replies. Until a young woman of about Andrew's age sits down to talk to us. Pale and weary, her fair hair is drawn back and captured in a red rubber band, save for the few escaped strands she shakes from her eyes.

'The neurologist has seen him and has ordered blood tests and a brain scan for the morning. We can't make a diagnosis before then.'

'Can't you do a scan now?' My boy might... Yes, I think the unthinkable: *he might die before the morning.*

'There are no technicians here at night. I can assure you the delay won't make any difference and it will give us time to stabilise his seizures. All I can tell you is that it does look serious and we're transferring him to the Intensive Care Unit. I will take you to see him now.'

Andrew is lying on a hard couch with cot sides. That scar from the operation when he was six weeks old has grown with him and is visible above the sheet which covers his lower body. A multitude of pads and wires have been attached to his hairless, muscular chest and a drip is delivering fluid and medication into a vein in his right arm. He is still and calm, sleeping perhaps.

'*Kochanie*, my darling, it's me, Gosia. Everything is okay, you're going to be fine.' She squeezes his hand and her voice cracks, her words are more urgent. '*Kochanie*, please can you speak to me? Please...'

The young doctor puts her arm around the young wife. 'He can't hear you. He is deeply unconscious.' Tears fill our eyes, the doctor's too. 'I suggest you go home now and rest. Call again about nine in the morning. Are you all right to drive? I am so sorry.'

I plant a kiss on my boy's brow and dare not contemplate what the scan may reveal. Andrew is wheeled away to the ICU and I make for the payphone. Steve will be anxious, waiting for news.

I turn out my coat pockets – car keys, tissue, sweet wrapper, train ticket. I fumble into the pockets of my jeans. No money. 'Gosia, have you any money? I need money. I must ring Steve.' I can hear my voice shouting. I am banging my fist against the wall, screaming between sobs, 'For God's sake, I must have some money for the phone!'

Someone takes me by the arm and leads me to the desk telephone, hands me the receiver. 'You don't need money for this one, my dear.'

*

16 December 1996

It's December and chilly in the little house, waiting for the winter dawn. The sun went into retreat weeks ago. We are in the small sitting room, shell-shocked, waiting for the child to wake and restore some sort of normality to the world. The clock drags its slow spidery hands through the hours – four…five…six…seven… Steve's eyes droop and he jerks himself awake. The road to nine o' clock is too long. I grab the phone and dial the number on the card the nurse gave me.

'Conquest Hospital, can I help you?' A weary voice yawns.

'Intensive Care, please.' Ring ring, ring ring… Come on, come on, what are you doing? Snoozing? Drinking tea? Or…? Visions of what can happen in intensive care units assault my imagination and I shake myself like a dog emerging from deep water.

'ICU, staff nurse speaking.' At last.

'I'm enquiring about Andrew Denny. I'm his mother. He was admitted in the night. He was unconscious and fitting. And no one knew what was wrong. We were told to ring at nine but we can't wait any longer, we are so anxious you see. Please – is he awake – is there a diagnosis – has a doctor seen him – can we come…?' My voice, hoarse but calm at the beginning of the call, races faster and faster with no pause for reply.

'The doctor would like to see you, Mrs Denny – I am afraid I can tell you nothing else.'

'Oh, I see. Yes, of course, we're coming now.'

Alice is cosy in her fleecy sleeping sack as Gosia carries her down the stairs and her little fists rub the sleep from her eyes.

'We go to see Daddy, *kochanie*.'

Our granddaughter accepts the situation and reaches for the lidded beaker of warm milk I offer. A couple of digestive biscuits are all I can find for her breakfast, so I pop these in my bag and we set off. Steve drives Andrew's car with Alice's baby seat securely attached to the back seat.

*

At the hospital entrance we ask a porter the way to the ICU, then follow directions down stairs and along corridors until we announce ourselves and are shown into another bland, grey room. No words pass between us as we wait. Each of us is in our own private world. Even Alice, sensitive to the atmosphere, sucks silently on her beaker.

A woman in blue opens the door and we jump to our feet. Everyone we have seen in the unit is dressed the same. Is this an orderly coming to offer us the inevitable tea, or a nurse, to apologise for the wait?

'Hello. I am Dr Taylor, the consultant in intensive care.' She smiles at us. 'Let's sit down and I will tell you what I can about Andrew.' She speaks in a professional way, but her eyes have that same compassionate glaze as Joe and Dave's and the young doctor of last night. 'He remains deeply unconscious, but we have stabilised his seizures for the moment. We are delivering fluids and medication intravenously and he is peaceful.'

'Yes, yes, but what –' Steve can contain himself no longer, 'what is the problem?'

Alice is grizzling and I carry her to the window to look at the seagull perched on the opposite ledge, my ears fine-tuned to the conversation behind us.

'I am afraid I can't give you a definite answer yet, but he does appear to have broken his shoulder in several places.'

'What! How?' As I swing round Alice cries for the seagull.

'The seizures, we no longer refer to them as fits, were so severe that the tension of his muscles caused the bone to fracture.'

Bone. Bones can be mended, I've seen it. Hammers, chisels, steel pins. Just bones, not meningitis. The doctor's voice again. 'We have also done a brain scan and I have to tell you, I am afraid, that we have seen a mass in the right frontal lobe.'

'A mass? What is a mass?' Gosia struggles to make sense of the language. I know exactly what a mass means.

'It could possibly be a tumour,' the voice is kind, professional. 'As soon as he regains consciousness we will transfer him to the High Dependency Unit while we organise a bed at a specialist neurological hospital. I am sure you would like to see him now.'

A tumour. A brain tumour. The stuff of fiction and nightmare. People like Andrew don't get brain tumours. No, I won't have it. This is a mistake. A benign cyst, that's what it is. I remember learning about those. Will they still have to open his head though, to get it out? Of course not, they can disperse it with drugs, maybe put in a drain. Thoughts criss-cross my mind like a speeded-up film of a busy rail terminus.

Meningitis would be a relief now.

We cross the corridor to the ICU. No normal hospital ward, this: no bustle, no laughter, no moaning, grumbling or joking patients, but inert bodies of assorted ages and both sexes lying connected to tubes, bags, and flickering machines. Nurses swish and mutter to the accompaniment of bleeps and drips and the intermittent ear-splitting ring of telephones. Our shivering reaction to what we have just been told gives way to sweating in a room where the heating is not set at comfort level for those in winter coats, but for those lying almost naked and uncovered on the beds.

An officious figure in blue looks at her watch, raises her eyebrows, and bars our way. 'Only two visitors at a time please, and it is rather early in the day. Who have you come to see?'

'Andrew Denny. Please let us all stay. We'll be very quiet.'

She smiles and relents a little. 'Could one of you wait outside with the baby?'

'No.' Gosia tugs her daughter from my arms and hugs her so tight that she yelps. 'She must stay with me.'

The woman purses her lips and considers. 'Five minutes then. But keep her well away from the machines. Children are really not allowed.'

I kiss Andrew's blank face, whisper my love into his ear, but who knows what unconscious world he is inhabiting. He is far, far away and shows no reaction. Steve and I grasp hands, unable to comprehend this new reality. I don't notice Gosia carry Alice from the room. After a time, I don't know how long, the nurse suggests that we go home and get some rest. She will phone if there is any change.

*

I have no memory of how we got home, how I collapsed, fully clothed into our bed, what happened to Steve, Gosia or Alice. I just recollect surfacing briefly, only to retreat into a state of near unconsciousness as the pain of realisation approached and my body shut down to protect me.

It is early evening before the soft emollient of sleep has soothed the jagged wound enough for me to wake and remember, and resume my maternal persona. Keep calm, organise, protect. Mummy will make it better. I lie in the dark thinking about Andrew, remembering his birth.

6 April 1967

9.45pm

All through my first pregnancy Steve was convinced we would have a daughter. When I gave that final push and our child slipped into the world he gave a triumphant shout. 'She's here.'

A giggle from the midwife. 'Look again Dad, it's a boy.'

'Whatever it is,' I sighed, 'It's got a bloody big bonce.' As the midwife placed the small, yelling body in my arms, that miraculous rush of new maternal love prevented me from registering that not only was it a big head but that it was also purple, swollen and shaped like an onion. It had been a long labour – forty-eight hours, on and off. Eventually he came in a rush, tearing my flesh. To me he was my beautiful boy.

It took a lot for Steve to be present at the birth. Fathers in the labour ward were a recent innovation and, like all his family, he had an unreasonable fear of hospitals. Anything medical had a touch of black magic about it. In my student days at Westminster Hospital he would never meet me at the door when I came off duty – he said he could smell the disinfectant from the other side of the Thames. So, his visits to the maternity ward were stilted affairs. A self-conscious kiss, a brief, awkward hold of his son, a bunch of daffodils left on the locker and he was gone. An ex-boyfriend appeared, hiding behind a mammoth bouquet. My mother came after school with a card from her pupils, her eyes moist as she beheld her grandson, named

20

for his dead grandfather. My in-laws smiled and hovered at the end of the bed.

In those distant days of 1967 new mums and babies spent ten days in hospital – lots of time for rest and early bonding. But after the late evening feed the babies' cribs were whisked away and lined up in a nursery, any crying silenced by a firmly closed door. At 2am and 6am they were woken or lifted screaming and taken to their waiting mums for a feed, then returned to their isolation.

Steve's relief and pride were palpable when he settled our sleeping bundle and me into the front (beltless) seat of our maroon Cortina with the grey 'gofaster' stripe down the side. Before we reached our house, stops had to be made at his parents', my mother's, and our close friends' homes, to show off this most perfect of all babies.

What a pair we were, this beautiful boy and his young, proud mum. The smell of milk made him grasp my nipple and suck with the urgency of a young lamb. But with every draw of his gums on my hard, inflamed left breast, pain seared through me and I was hardly the picture of the serene Madonna. Breast was best; I knew that. After all, hadn't I been a health visitor? I thought of the advice I had offered with such confidence to mums in my care to breastfeed at all costs – reluctant, overworked, malnourished women, some nearly twice my age, surrounded by scruffy kids in dank south London basements. Now I was ashamed of my arrogance.

The diagnosis, for me, was a breast abscess and when the antibiotics took effect I recovered my youthful energy and a familiar rosy bloom returned to my cheeks. But still, Andrew did not thrive. Skinny limbs became skinnier and his face was carved with wrinkles as the flesh shrank…

Two

'You've got a real sicky baby there, Janet.' Kaye lived next door, a good friend and something of a mother substitute, my own being miles away. With a clutch of five children ranging from teenagers to toddlers, she knew all about babies.

Kaye was right. After a feed Andrew always sicked up a little milk. He fed ravenously from the nasty rubber teat, substituted for my own soft nipple after the abscess, but he regurgitated increasingly large amounts. When he was six weeks old and the vomit hit the opposite wall of our small lounge, I knew what was wrong – I had seen this before. I remembered caring for a baby boy with a pyloric stenosis and looked up an old textbook to be sure. *Most common in the first-born son of a first-born son* (well that figured) – *a narrowing of the pylorus, the sphincter where the stomach opens into the first part of the small intestine – prevents the milk going any further.* What can't go down must come up – and how!

I had trouble convincing the GP. Nurses had acquired a largely undeserved reputation for being fussy mothers and perhaps my over-zealous diagnosis was not tactful. It was not until the vomit was mixed with blood that I managed, after several surgery visits, to persuade the doctor there just might be a problem.

On the bus ride to the hospital, I cradled my precious, six-week-old scrap, wrapped in the snow-white shawl crocheted with love by his great-granny, and I faced the possibility that he could die. *Unlikely*, said my rational self. It was a pretty routine operation for many babies. But this was *my* baby and a general anaesthetic on a malnourished baby could have a devastating effect. I struggled with the prospect of leaving him and my thoughts flew to Julie.

Julie had been in a private room at the hospital. Her baby was born a few hours before Andrew and we met in the nursery, two proud new mums.

'Is he your first? Have you chosen a name? Does he look like you or his daddy?' I chattered on while I tucked my sleeping Andrew into his crib.

An invisible cloud of distress surrounded Julie. Her teenage face, framed by expensively cut black hair, assumed a blank expression but her slim shoulders shook. Blinking could not hold back her tears. Her baby's eyes held hers as she laid him down and bent to kiss him. 'I'm not giving him a name. I'm not keeping him. He is going to be adopted. He will be with me for six weeks and then...' I watched her take a deep breath and straighten her back. Leaving her thumb to linger in the baby's tiny fist, she turned and looked directly at me, 'Then I have to give him away.'

The disgrace of a pregnant, unmarried daughter was too much for Julie's conventional, middle-class family. When her abdomen had begun to swell Julie was sent to live a safe distance from home with her Auntie Mildred. That name always made me think of mildew, so I imagined an old crone with a faint smell of decay about her. After the required six weeks of caring for her baby, Julie would give him to the adoption officer, return home and to school after her 'long illness', sit her exams and go off to university just as her parents expected.

'I am sure it'll be okay,' she said. 'Yes, it will definitely be okay. After all, I was adopted myself and my parents, my adoptive parents, that is, have been great.' I hugged her, and she buried her anguish in my embrace. We didn't meet again in the nursery, but I could not forget her pain.

Now, six weeks on, here was I on the way to relinquish the care of my son for a few days. I wondered if it was today that Julie was giving up her little boy forever.

The bus, delayed by road works, was twenty minutes late when, with Andrew in my arms, I alighted at the foot of the hill leading to the hospital. Why did they build it in such an inaccessible place? I climbed swiftly, anxious to get on with what I had to do. The sooner I left him there, I reasoned, the sooner he would be back at home with Steve and me.

The iron gates made me think of Wormwood Scrubs. Set in the high brick wall was a stone plaque, the lettering half obliterated with yellow lichen. I could just make out the words, *Joyce Green Fever Hospital*. We were within sight of the Thames, the river that has carried so many sailors and passengers to London. Until a few decades ago any unfortunates approaching these shores from foreign parts, who were suffering from suspicious diseases, would be disembarked to institutions like this. Any infection to be contained here before it was carried to the capital. The patients were kept in isolation.

Now my baby was to be left alone. Isolated from me, in what was now a general hospital. I considered running back down the hill, but common sense prevailed, and I walked through the door into a remembered antiseptic smell. My shoes squeaked on polished floorboards as I followed arrows directing me to the children's ward where a large nurse, all starch and efficiency, received us.

'At last – the pyloric stenosis is here,' she announced to the air and patted the grey bun under her plain white cap. 'You're very late, you know, mother. We'll have to be quick with the paperwork.' Without so much as glancing at Andrew she began asking a list of questions, ticking boxes as I whispered my answers.

'Date of birth? Name of GP? Address? Family history?' The woman didn't look at me until she fired the final question. 'Has he been baptised?' I shook my head. 'No? Do you want to do it now, just in case?'

Just in case of what? In case he dies on the table and has not been purged of his original sin – in which case God will not have him in heaven? 'No, thank you.'

She sniffed. 'Well, just as you please. Sign here, mother, to say we can do whatever is necessary when we open him up.'

Open him up. I knew they would, of course. But how could she refer so heartlessly to his smooth little belly? I signed the form, she took Andrew from my arms and dismissed me. 'Don't worry, mother, they do this operation all the time. Phone about four tomorrow afternoon to see how he is.'

I planted a kiss on his soft, downy head, breathing in the smell of milk and Johnson's baby powder, and watched as the nurse laid him in the little cot and wheeled it away. The door closed behind them and I left to trudge down the hill and wait for the bus, as clouds moved across the sinking sun. I felt dismembered, deprived of the body that had so recently been part of mine, the child who relied on me.

The operation was successful but during the half hour visiting time the next evening, Steve held me as we viewed our son at a distance, as if looking at a TV documentary. We had arrived to find the same unsmiling nurse. She jerked her head towards a wooden door with a glass panel etched with the word NURSERY. 'He was having difficulty maintaining his temperature, so we've incubated him as a precaution. He'll be fine, but you won't be able to touch him,' she said, turning back to her medicine trolley.

His face was wizened, but pink. His tiny chest rose and fell with gentle regularity. My shoulders relaxed. 'He's okay,' I whispered to Steve, 'he'll be fine now, I can see.' But I had to restrain my arms from reaching out for him.

After four more restless nights and as many unwelcoming half hour visits to the ward, the day came when we brought home our puny little baby with his tramline scar and I promised him that that was the end of hospitals.

16 December 1996

4.30pm

The ceiling light blinds my eyes and I am jolted from my reverie by Steve's voice. 'I have rung my sister and she'll tell Mum, but I haven't told your mother, Janet, I thought you'd better do that. I can't get hold of Laura.' Steve's tone is efficient, tight, all emotion reined in.

Then it softens as he sits on the bed and hands me a mug of coffee. 'How are you feeling now, love?'

'How am I feeling? How the hell do you think I'm feeling?' I snap. Then I notice the greyness of his skin, the tension round his eyes and I reach for his hand. 'Sorry. I'm okay. I'll go and see Mum when I've drunk this. I'll talk to Laura – break the news gently. You haven't told Matthew, have you?'

'No, I thought he was in Oxford this week?'

'Yes, it's that conference. We won't tell him until it's over – he was nervous enough about his presentation already.'

I must keep calm, organise, protect. *Things fall apart*, the poet said, *the centre cannot hold*. Not true. The mother is the centre of the family and I *will* hold ours together.

I dial our daughter's number. It rings six times.

'Laura.'

'Oh Mum,' she's breathless, 'isn't this weather ghastly? Just got in from town. The High Street's looking really festive, lights everywhere. It's so exciting – Katie's first Christmas and Tony's bought the biggest tree.' Our second granddaughter is chortling in the background. 'I bet Alice is excited. She's just about old enough to feel the vibes this year, isn't she? Mum? Mum, are you there? Sorry, I'm yakking on...'

'Love, I've got some bad news.'

'What? Oh God, Mum, you sound awful. Is Dad all right?'

'It's not Dad. It's Andrew.'

I mount the stairs to my mother's flat nearly opposite Andrew's house. I know he's always been special to her, a prized first grandchild.

When she opens the door, her face is a mask of forced optimism. 'What news? Margaret at number five said there was an ambulance in the night and she thought it was outside number one. I phoned early this morning, but no one answered. I didn't want to bother you, knew you'd let me know if there was any problem...'

'Let's sit down, Mum.'

As I tell the story I watch my mother's face grow pale and crumble, then reassemble itself into stoic bravery.

We have the same genes.

Next day I leave a message at a student house, five hundred miles away in Sunderland, for Matthew to phone, but twenty-four hours pass with no call.

Another message. 'Please tell him it's urgent.'

The phone rings almost as soon as I replace the receiver.

'Sorry, Mum. No one told me you'd rung.'

'Did the presentation go well?'

'Yes, yes, it went all right. Mum, what's wrong? Mark said it was urgent. Is everything okay?'

I deliver my now practiced script, listening to my voice, steadying words I still do not believe.

Andrew's younger brother replies, 'What? Oh God.'

Silence.

'Matthew, are you still there?'

'Yeah Mum. I'm coming home.'

Three

We are back at Andrew's bedside, Steve, Gosia and I, in the High Dependency Unit, a step away from the trauma and unreality of the ICU. In turn, we bend to kiss him. He is conscious. Relief begins at the top of my head and pours through me. I close my eyes, then open them as I feel my mouth curl into a smile. My shoulders loosen, my body relaxes. He's come back to us.

Steve goes in search of chairs and Gosia's hand rests on Andrew's balding head.

'Mum.' His attempt to reach out is thwarted by pain, needles and tubes. He sinks back on the pillow and screws up his face. 'Where am I? What's going on?'

My relief fades, my mind and body tense again. Does he have no memory of what happened or where he is? Has no one explained? I entwine my fingers with his. 'You're in hospital, Andrew. You had a nasty turn last night. You were unconscious for a few hours, but they're sorting you out. You'll be okay, don't worry.' I sound like an echo of the reassuring nurse I was thirty years ago.

Steve returns with two chairs and squeezes them into the restricted space beside the bed. 'It's okay,' he says, 'I'll stand and grow good – isn't that what they say? Not much chance of that though, eh lad?' He is trying to disguise his anxiety with humour and I squeeze his hand to signal that I understand.

Andrew's eyes are glazed, puzzled. He can't process what we're saying. I sense him drifting and fear we are losing him again to that foreign land called coma. I frown at Steve and Gosia, who nod their understanding. We keep talking, trying to hold on to him – telling him Alice is safe with her great-granny, that the staff are coping without him in the shop. He hears us, but I think he doesn't comprehend. Every few minutes he struggles to pull himself up on the cot sides.

'Busting for a pee.'

'There's no need, *kochanie*. They've put in a tube. You don't have to worry.' Gosia touches his shoulder and he winces.

A moment of clarity. 'What? A tube? How dare they fiddle with my dick! Who are THEY? Where am I?'

Again and again we explain the events of the last twenty-four hours. His eyes dilate, a smile plays at the corners of his wide mouth and I am reminded of the eager child who curled up beside me for an exciting bedtime story.

'An ambulance? With a siren and blue lights? Does the whole of Rye know I'm a celebrity?'

I grin. That's my boy. 'Sorry to disappoint you, love, but in the dead of night, with empty roads, they didn't need the siren or the blue lights.'

Flashes of comprehension come and go, but he never faces reality enough to ask for a diagnosis.

The following afternoon, Gosia and I watch as once again he is wheeled into an ambulance, this time bound for the neurological unit on the other side of the county. No room for us in the ambulance so we follow in my car and slowly, stutteringly, my daughter-in-law breaks free from her cocoon of silence.

'What is it… What do you think is wrong, Janet? It is not meningitis?'

'They saw that mass in his brain on the scan.'

I wait for her next question, trying to work out an answer that will not cause panic. But, as if she too needs to avoid the horror, she says nothing.

I switch on the headlights as dusk approaches.

Christmas tree lights are appearing in front windows along our way. Gosia says, 'It was very exciting with the tree. Lights were broke but Andy says it always is like this. He screw in a new, er, what you say?'

'Bulb?'

'Yes, that. And they work. Alice so excited. "Pitty tee, pitty tee," she says, and Andy so happy. He want her to bring in the pudding at the dinner – all in flames, like you do – but I say no, she is too little, and he say next year.'

I explain how there was always a fight with his sister and brother about who would have the pudding honour and we chat about the routine of an English family Christmas.

Gosia turns to look at me, 'It is much work, the dinner and everything, and you always have lot of people.'

'Yes, but I love it. Even though I panic when the Aga isn't hot enough to crisp the potatoes and the pressure cooker nearly explodes.' I smile to myself, taking refuge in memories of normality. When Steve thrusts a glass of wine in my hand and says, 'Don't panic love, it's Christmas', it irritates me even more.

My memories are overtaken by anxiety as the ambulance ahead of us turns right into a busy road and we are left at the junction waiting for the next gap in the traffic. By the time we pull away the ambulance is out of sight. *Oh Lord, which way did it go?* Haywards Heath is foreign country to me.

'Gosia, there's a road atlas in the door pocket. Can you read a map? It's page fourteen, I think.'

'I no good with maps.' She doesn't attempt to open the book but puts it in my lap.

I pull up in the entrance to an industrial estate, find the page, try to memorise the route – *first left, then second exit from the round-about, straight on, fork right, third off next roundabout...* We set off again, but I forget which exit, which roundabout, which fork in the road. In no time, I am lost. After a circuitous detour around mid-Sussex I am at last back on the right road, but Hurstwood Park, the neurological centre, still takes some finding. When we finally arrive, we joke that we can see why they tried to hide it. A gruesome, single-storied, brick building of uncertain age, it is dwarfed behind a new general hospital standing tall and brash in its blue plate-glass and aluminium apparel.

We are only four days short of the winter equinox so when I glance at my watch I cannot see that it is only four o'clock. There is no sign of the ambulance – it probably arrived a good half hour before us. I drive around the car park several times until we spy the reversing lights of a yellow van and pounce on the space it leaves. In the freezing twilight, we search for an entrance to the building. It reminds me of the hospital where I left my baby son twenty-nine and a half years ago. I feared for his survival then, but knew in my heart he would be okay. This time I am not so sure.

Beside a blue and white NHS notice board we find an entrance with dim light evident through the grubby glass panels. We kick aside cigarette packets and a couple of lager cans and the door gives to our push. An unmanned desk on our right is marked RECEPTION. All is silence as we tramp down a long dingy corridor searching for a clue to Andrew's whereabouts.

A notice with a worn, red arrow points to Men's Medical. 'Sounds promising,' I say, attempting to lift the atmosphere of gloom. I slip my hand through my daughter-in-law's arm. 'Let's try it.'

A bustling nurse responds to our enquiry when we push open the door. 'Andrew Denny? We've just settled him in, down there.' She points to the end of the narrow ward.

The long wall on our left is made up almost entirely of metal-framed, glazed doors giving on to a veranda. In the twilight beyond, silhouetted trees surround an area of what might be grass. The balcony would be a pleasant place to sit overlooking green space on a summer's day, but on this December evening the night rolls its menace up to the unscreened windows and I shiver.

Beds are lined up along the right-hand side of the ward, opposite the darkness, and three face us on the end wall. We pass a sleeping figure who has his face turned away. In the next bed, a young man with an expressionless face watches an overweight woman, his mother perhaps, unpacking a bagful of goodies on to the bed table. Her red quilted jacket, its filling emerging through several rips, has obviously not seen soap and water for a very long time, and her grey hair is lank and long. Then there's a boy of about sixteen, head bandaged, apparently asleep, and surrounded by what I assume to be three generations of his anxious-looking family. Beyond him, an old man wearing a striped NHS-issue dressing gown lies propped on pillows. Smiling, eyes closed, he conducts music on his headphones with a waxy arthritic finger. A bright pink furry elephant sits on his locker.

At last we find Andrew in the corner bed at the end of the ward. His shoulder is heavily strapped with adhesive bandages, his wrist is in a sling. I catch my breath with joy at his wide smile of recognition. Gosia flings her arms wide to hug him.

'Don't!' He points his good hand to his shoulder and holds his face up for kisses instead. His head is clearer now, but forty-eight hours of his life have gone absent without leave. All memory of the Hastings hospital and the journey here has been erased.

'So, what's wrong with me then? They say I've smashed up my shoulder. God knows how that happened, but it's no wonder I'm in bloody agony. And they're going to do a scan of my head tomorrow. What's the connection?'

Once more his eyes widen in disbelief as we explain his two lost days.

'So, if it's not just my shoulder, what is it?'

Gosia casts an anxious look at me. Explanations are clearly my department.

'No one seems sure at the moment, love. But in view of these fits you've been having, they think it's something to do with your brain.' I watch his face for a reaction. 'That's why the doctors want to do a scan.'

He furrows his brow and turns the corners of his mouth down. 'What do they expect to see?'

I force a laugh. 'Probably nothing, I always said you were empty-headed.'

Coward. Dodging the issue. I have done my research, looked up lesions of the right frontal lobe in my old medical textbooks, but I am unwilling to even think the word 'tumour'.

I meet Steve at the hospital. He has driven from Rye, I have come from Tunbridge Wells where I have been looking after Andrew's shop. Most of his customers have no idea of our situation and when they ask me where the helpful young man is, I tell them he couldn't come in today, saving myself from explanations, dreading their sympathy. I retain a fixed smile and return their good wishes for a merry Christmas.

In Rye, our hometown, many people know our story. It has been a relief to leave Steve looking after our shop there, to deal with the compassion of friends and customers.

Andrew rouses from sleep when we whisper his name and he regales us with his experience of the MRI machine this afternoon.

'Never doing that again,' he declares. 'You know I'm a bit claustrophobic, so when they told me I had to lie still in this narrow Smartie tube for nearly an hour I was all for legging it out of here.' We smile, appreciating the irony. Even with assistance he can barely walk as far as the loo. 'I was worried about having a fit in there, but they said they'd watch on the screen and get me out at the first sign. Scary, though. "Relax," they kept saying. "It's all right for you," I told them, "you're not the ones going down the tube."'

'Well done, lad,' says Steve and squeezes his hand. 'When will we know the result?'

'The doc says Friday, after I've had an angi thing.'

'An angiogram?' I ask.

He nods. 'Whatever that is.'

'You'll have a dye injected into your groin,' I explain, and he winces. 'Then they'll follow it on a screen all through the blood vessels in your head to see what…'

He sighs, lies back against the pillows and drifts into sleep.

*

The next day, 19 December 1996, is angiogram day and Gosia is visiting this evening while Alice has a sleepover with us.

As usual, I'm late with the Christmas cards. Steve and I had been sitting by the fire writing them the evening before that phone call – a lifetime ago. The carefully categorised piles have since lain ignored on the kitchen table. There are those for hand delivery, a tottering stack of those needing inland stamps, a smaller pile for overseas (airmail is expensive but it's my annual punishment for not thinking about distant friends in October), and the usual sad few still awaiting unknown addresses, that may never get sent. My Christmas letter is written, so I add a final desperate paragraph.

> Stop Press: Early on December 16, with no warning, Andrew became deeply unconscious and suffered some very violent fits, as a result of which his shoulder was broken in four places. While still unconscious in intensive care he had a brain scan, which showed a possible tumour. He was transferred to the specialist neurological centre at Haywards Heath after he regained consciousness. Miraculously, given the position of the lesion, his long-term memory is unaffected. However, he remembers nothing of the last couple of days. As you may imagine the future is frightening and uncertain. Please keep us all in your thoughts and prayers.

Then I print eighty copies and stuff them into the envelopes with cards showing jolly red-cheeked Santas and bells ringing out Christmas joy.

Four

On my next visit Andrew says, 'I've been thinking, Mum, and before you start wisecracking, I do think sometimes, you know.' He grins at me. I grin at him.

'So, what exactly have you been thinking, love?'

The morphine that tames the pain in his shoulder begins to fuddle his head and his eyelids droop. 'Oh, you know...'

Yes. I know this boy so well (despite his twenty-nine years I still can't think of him as a man) that I think I do know what he's been thinking. I can hear his voice in my head saying something like this:

Bloody Hell! What a carry on. One minute I am all set for a busy Christmas and the next... What about the shop? They haven't mentioned it at all. Jenny said she couldn't come in on Saturday. God knows how Angela will manage on her own, now it's so busy, she's hopeless at the best of times. I promised to be in early, straight after swimming.

My thoughts, and his rest, are interrupted by the ward sister. As wide as she is tall in her dark blue uniform, she has a face from a renaissance fresco. An angel's face surmounted by a cloud of gossamer blonde curls. 'Supper time, Andrew,' she says. 'What delicacy do you fancy tonight? Lobster Thermidor and champagne? Oh no, sorry, wrong menu. It's tomato soup and ham sandwich or cauliflower cheese tonight.'

'I'll take the soup and sandwich option, please.' Andrew returns her joke in his characteristic way. 'All the champagne in this place is getting boring. Sister, when is this op going to be? Can they leave my shoulder strapped and deal with it after Christmas? I've got a gift shop to run and, at this time of year, I can't waste my time in here.' He attempts to flail his arm around in the air.

'Ouch! Got a bit carried away there, didn't I? The old shoulder's protesting...'

'Afraid you won't be running the shop for a while, Andrew. We've got a bit of work to do on you first. And we'll need you here to bring a bit of Christmas spirit to this place.' Laughing, she moves on to the next patient.

Andrew's eyes widen, his brow creases. 'Bloody hell, Mum, does she mean I'll be spending Christmas here, in this godforsaken dump? Oh, shit. When is Christmas anyway? No sign of it here – not a strand of tinsel or a fairy in sight. Well, I'm not sure about the fairy, that male nurse is kind enough, but very camp. I hate hospitals, Mum. Always have.'

'I know, love.'

'They split my belly open when I was a baby.' Pushing back the white cellular blanket he pats his scarred torso. 'Then it was tonsils...' He yawns as if to show the absence of the offending glands, then closes his eyes and drifts into sleep.

I sit beside him, holding his hand, thinking about all those other hospital stays, perhaps to blank the reality of this one. A mother's anxiety has etched them deep into my memory.

I'd pulled a few 'this was where I trained' strings when the tonsils needed to come out, and jumped the NHS queue for a bed at Westminster Children's Hospital. I was allowed to sleep in the day room as we were so far from home – there was no accommodation for parents to stay in the old building I knew so well.

Andrew was affronted when he was served cornflakes for break-fast the morning after the operation. 'Don't they understand I've got a sore throat?' he'd complained.

But an exciting trip made up for the cornflakes. There must have been some sort of publicity stunt, or maybe a TV commercial for the Army. Someone from the Duke of York's Barracks phoned the hospital to ask if they could send a suitable young man to review the Life Guards. Andrew, his throat miraculously no longer sore, was delighted to oblige and with an accompanying nurse he set off in a black London cab. His eyes were shining as he recounted the event when he returned. 'I walked up and down pretending to be a King inspecting his troops and had tea afterwards in the officer's mess.' The nurse who went with him was young and pretty. I guess she enjoyed an afternoon away from the ward and she was probably the focus of attention in the officer's mess. Andrew was annoyed that they never got a photo – the kids at school never believed it was true.

Then it was a broken leg. On a Saturday morning in 1979 we'd waved off an excited busload of twelve-year olds as they set off on the long trip to Scotland. On the Monday, we had a phone call from the teacher. Andrew had fractured his left tibia on his first day on the slopes.

'Well,' Steve had joked to cover his concern, 'at least it's not his head.'

In Aviemore hospital they plastered him up and put him in the only spare bed – in the maternity ward – where, he told us, he couldn't sleep because of the noise of groaning women and mewling babies. Discharged the following morning, he spent the remainder of the week sitting indoors at the hostel. He watched the telly and basked in the tea and sympathy dispensed by the staff, while the other kids froze on the slopes during the day and wrote dirty jokes on his leg plaster at night. He's never been skiing since.

Later that year, I began to notice an unpleasant smell when I was near him. Well, he was twelve and boys of that age don't put a lot of value on washing.

'I don't exactly have a soap and water fetish, Mum, but I'm clean enough to get by,' was his response to my nagging.

But I continued to be puzzled and one day I pushed aside his long hair to get a close view of his collar line. I sniffed. 'It's your neck, Andrew,' I said. 'No, it's your ear, you're not cleaning behind your ears.'

As I remember that moment, I feel the guilt wash through me all over again. I should have noticed earlier. I had taken hold of his ear lobe and really looked. A greenish gunge was issuing slowly, smelling of rotting vegetation. 'I'm sorry, Andrew,' I said, 'I've been doing you an injustice, it looks like a nasty septic ear.'

So, then it was a round of doctors' appointments, outpatient visits and, finally, an operation. A virulent infection had busted his eardrum long since and then bored away painlessly into the bone, leaving him with reduced hearing. That's been a great excuse ever since – at school, at home, at work. 'Oh, sorry, didn't quite hear that – I'm deaf in one ear, you know,' he'd say, and any irritation turned to sympathy in no time. But he couldn't use the strategy too often – people got wise to it.

Now he stirs, opens his eyes and asks me what I'm thinking about. I tell him, and after a pause he says, 'Luckily it didn't get right through my skull – no, don't say I've got a thick one – and reach my peerless brain on the other side.' He's joking, but I can't laugh. Shall I mention the brain scan that's scheduled? Has he forgotten?

Yes, he's had more than his fair share of hospitals.

A motherly soul parks her trolley at the end of the bed, reaches down for a supper tray and puts it on his bed-table. Then she pushes the table within his reach. 'Let's sit you up a bit, Andrew.' He flinches as she leans towards him. 'It's all right, dear, I'll be careful of the shoulder.'

'Sorry I'm such a bloody nuisance,' he says, tightening his lips and cuffing his eyes with his fist before he picks up his soup spoon. The woman throws a glance at me, one mother to another.

'Can I get you a cup of tea, love?' she asks and at my silent nod she hurries away to get one.

My boy drops the spoon and reaches to squeeze my hand. As if he has been following my thoughts, he says, 'Don't worry, Mum, I always come through.'

'Indeed, you do, my love,' I say, hoping I sound convinced.

Five

Days of anxious waiting for the dreaded diagnosis are filled with investigations: visits from the junior doctor, the neurologist, the radiologist, the orthopaedic surgeon, and the physiotherapist. Anti-epileptic drugs are keeping Andrew's seizures at bay and a date has been fixed to repair his shoulder. More importantly, the junior doctor has told him the result of the MRI scan.

'It appears to show a venous infarction – otherwise known as a stroke,' he said, 'but I have to tell you, Andrew, that we can't entirely rule out a neoplasm.'

'What's a neoplasm?'

'A tumour, but we think that's unlikely.'

Andrew recounts this conversation when Steve and I visit and find him pale and unsmiling.

'So, I might have a fucking brain tumour.' His tone is as sour as vinegar and he turns away from us.

'They've told you that's unlikely, though. I've always thought so,' I lie.

He rounds on me and I see the tearstains on his cheeks. 'So, you knew? You knew but you didn't tell me? It's *my* head, you know, it's *my* life.' My boy is furious with me, and I recognise my mistake. He's a man now. I can't keep everything from him; he has a right to know.

'I'm so sorry, love. We should have told you.'

Steve's left hand grasps mine, his right reaches for Andrew's. 'Mum was only trying to protect you, lad. Don't blame her. We all knew a tumour was a possibility, but because we love you so much we hoped it wasn't true, that there was no need to upset you. And now it seems it's probably only a stroke and we'll be celebrating very soon.'

Our son nods. Has he forgiven us?

'The doctor's ordered another scan to confirm it,' he whispers.

When? I wonder. *Which doctor? What is his name? Is he the neurologist or the surgeon?* As we leave I ask the sister, who tells me Mr O'D is a consultant neurosurgeon and the scan will be done after Andrew's shoulder surgery. 'No need to worry. It's just to be sure,' she says, 'before he goes home.'

No meningitis, probably no tumour; who would have thought that a possible stroke would be a ray of light in the darkness? But we're not safe yet. There is still that question hanging in the air...

Andrew's joviality returns and quickly enlivens the drab atmosphere of pessimism that hangs over the ward. He is everyone's friend, knows each patient's history and relays it to us when we visit. This is the son I recognise, the boy who has been so frustrating, so loving, so charming, for nearly thirty years. The boy who is always optimistic. The firstborn I love so much.

Andrew turns to the man in the next bed with the pink elephant on his locker. 'Tommy here is eighty-five. He lives in a bedsit and keeps having mini-strokes.' The old man turns to look at us, holding his headphones away from his ears.

'You were really hoping you'd have a little stroke just before Christmas, weren't you Tommy? This is your second home, and you didn't fancy having your turkey dinner delivered to you by a grey-haired WVS lady, did you?' The man laughs and shakes his head.

'Nurses are prettier – and the company's top notch here, eh, Tommy?'

'He's a wag, that one,' chortles the old man and goes back to his music.

Yes, that's what gets my son through life. His humour has made him memorable. A few months ago, when his sister was visiting, they walked through Rye together, the small town where they had been at school. Laura was furious when she returned to our house.

'You wouldn't believe it, Mum,' she said, and I could almost see the proverbial steam coming out of her ears. 'We met Mr Rose, Mr Pearce and Miss Johnson in the High Street. They all greeted Andrew, clapped him on the back and said, "How're you doing, old chap," or "Great to see you Andrew." Honestly, Mum, that brother of mine never exercised one grey cell at school. All he did was make jokes and he was always in detention for something. As for me, I worked my guts out for those teachers, I got high grades, and today they never even recognised me.' Her brother was indeed a memorable wag.

Now, in the ward, Andrew lowers his voice, nodding to the bed where the dishevelled woman we have seen on all our visits is taking Mars bars and biscuits from her bag, packing them into the locker of the blank-faced youth. 'David, over there with his mum – he's had twelve operations – not quite sure what for. His dad left them, so his mum's in here all the time.' He lowers his eyes as he says, 'Thanks, Mum and Dad, for being here.' We are forgiven.

Christmas is nearly here, and I am dismayed at the lack of festive decorations in the hospital. So, I buy an artificial mini-tree complete with tiny white lights, red baubles and silver stars to cheer Andrew and his companions. I take a childish delight in anticipating their reaction, but when I visit this evening I am crestfallen. The ward is decked with garish red and green garlands and a gigantic tree, almost entirely covered with silver tinsel and mirrored baubles of every hue.

Andrew is creased with laughter when he sees my pathetic offering.

'At least this one's got lights,' I say sheepishly, as I place it on his bedside locker. But the only electrical socket within reach is labelled FOR MEDICAL EQUIPMENT ONLY.

Sod it, I think, *failed again*. I can't protect my child and I can't even provide him with a sparkly little Christmas tree.

Andrew sees my despondency and beams his understanding. 'Good try, Mum. Thanks.'

When there are only three more shopping days until Christmas, both our shops are busy with late deliveries and customers searching for last-minute gifts. Despite our exhaustion Steve and I have barely slept. Our emotions are stretched like guitar strings. Keeping up a pretence of optimism, we will not allow ourselves to share our fears with others. *It'll all be fine. He'll be okay, of course he will – he's a strong young man of twenty-nine.* But the strings could snap at any moment.

For the last four days, I have been looking after Andrew's branch of our retail business, leaving Steve in our main shop in Rye, where we have more staff. Today we have changed places so that I can leave early to drive Gosia and Alice to the hospital. Rush-hour headlights blind my tired eyes as we make the hour and a half journey across Sussex. Alice is safely strapped into her little chair in the back seat with her mother next to her. They play games and sing the Teletubby song, leaving me with my own thoughts. What news awaits us at the end of our journey? Has he had any more fits? Will he be as cheerful as he was yesterday?

When we arrive at the ward entrance we see Andrew sitting up in bed, his wrist in a sling, his bald head shining like a beacon under the faintly droning strip-lights. We are hardly through the door before he waves at us with his good arm and shouts, 'It's official. I haven't got a tumour. It *was* only a stroke!' Gosia, scoops her daughter into her arms and runs to hug him – carefully avoiding his right side.

He enfolds Alice with his good arm and lifts his face for kisses. I stand behind them, processing my feelings. Secretly, I have always tended to look on the black side. I've been preparing myself for the worst possibility, strengthening my emotional defences. Now I must rework my mind to accept this confirmation that the worst has not happened.

'Andrew', I say, as I pull up a seat, 'that's wonderful news. Have you had another scan?'

'Not yet, but they're now quite certain.'

If this were a Hollywood movie, orchestras would play, but

I am trapped in a vacuum of silence. Excitement should fizz, but the only tingle I feel is one of fear. Where is the warm glow that should be lighting up a long, beautiful road into the future? Why does my relief feel only skin-deep? A persistent doubt of this diagnosis gnaws away deep inside me. *Relax,* I tell myself, *be happy. This is the good news you dared not believe would come.*

The boy with the bandaged head is awake, chatting to his family whom we have watched coming and going in an endless worried procession over the last few days. They are popping a champagne cork, clearly full of excitement. A young woman, who might be the boy's sister, notices me watching them and calls out, 'We've just heard that they've managed to remove his tumour, so we're celebrating.'

'That is so good. Congratulations,' I reply. I am happy for them, while seeking the relief I should be feeling now that the word *tumour* has been erased from our lives.

Gosia's smile is wide. 'We celebrate, also,' she calls, and leans to kiss her husband again.

There is only so long a nineteen-month-old child can spend at a hospital bedside – however perfect her daddy believes her to be.

'Can we go now?' Alice twizzles her wispy blonde hair around her index finger and fixes big blue eyes on her mother.

'Not yet, *kochanie.* We will stay with Daddy for a bit longer.'

I have an idea. Along the corridor I had noticed something through an open door. 'Alice,' I say, 'shall we go on an adventure?'

She nods her head and reaches for my hand. We leave her parents enjoying the firm prospect of a long life together and go to view the fish tank in the outpatients' waiting room.

With no window and an old-fashioned radiator that gurgles and clanks, the small room is stuffy and stale. Alice climbs onto a chair and steadies herself by pressing her hands against the small aquarium.

'Aren't they lovely, sweetie?' I say, but she does not reply, mesmerised by the brightly lit scene before her. Exotic fish weave silently through waving green weeds while bubbles rise from a little pipe in a corner of the tank. Alice watches silently until she claps her hands and tells me that the fish are playing hide and seek.

We inspect the colours, the shapes, and the patterns on the fish and christen them with imaginative names. 'Do you think that one's called Stripey?' I ask.

'And that one's Fatty,' she shouts.

'There's Goldie.'

Alice stabs her finger at the glass, 'Bulgy-Eyed Monster.' This is fun.

On the wall beside the tank is a poster – once white, now yellowing, curling at the edges and, like everything here, in need of renewal. Useful addresses are printed on it in red. I run my eye down the list. Multiple Sclerosis Society, Muscular Dystrophy Association, Stroke Association – I search my bag for pen and paper to write that one down. I put the pen away and my spirits lift as my eyes reach Brain Tumour Foundation. We won't be needing that. I am beginning to believe it.

Alice is soon bored with the fish. 'They just go round and round, Granny. Can we go now?'

We return to Andrew who can't wait to repeat the story he has been telling Gosia – how the consultant came to see him last night.

'He said he'd seen me when I first arrived, but I couldn't remember, so I asked him when that was. "On Tuesday," he said, but that was no help 'cos I've no idea which day is which. I think he'd been to a Christmas party – I could smell booze on his breath when he shone his torch in my eyes. And I swear his speech was slurred when he asked me the name of the Queen. Then he made me touch my nose with my finger, tickled my feet and said he'd come back and see me today. Sister says he's only here temporarily, filling in for the usual man. I didn't like him, Mum. He never smiled, pompous git.'

I am anxious to hear about the verdict. 'What did he say today, though, about…?'

'He walked into the ward coughing and spluttering. I thought a cold served him right for being so bloody superior.' *Just like my son*, I think, *spinning out a good story*.

'Andrew, spit it out. What did he say?' I need to hear the actual words, to be sure.

'He said he's looked again at the scan and he's certain I've had a funny sort of stroke. I told him I thought only old people got those, but apparently anyone can get them. Mine was a mild one though, and he said when they've repaired my shoulder and I've had some physio, I can get on with the rest of my life. "No tumour then?" I asked, and he said, "No. *Definitely* no tumour."' Andrew's eyes sparkle. He has battled with the dragon and won.

My body softens as I rest my back on the plastic visitor's chair and I close my eyes, absorbing the relief.

'Mum, it's okay, I've got my life back. I haven't got a brain tumour.' His voice is tender, and I can hear a smile. 'When he left,' Andrew is determined to finish with a joke, 'I shouted after him, "Thank you, Father Christmas," but he didn't even look round.'

Six

On Christmas day Andrew holds court in the ward day room. Steve and I arrive first to find that today, it is only for our family. The other patients have either been discharged or are too sick to be out of bed.

Laura and Tony are the next to arrive, with baby Katie. Andrew is glad they're here – It's been a long morning.

'Trust you to be early.' He greets his sister with a rueful grin.

'I couldn't wait to wish my big brother a Happy Christmas,' she bends to kiss him, 'and anyway, I do like to be on time.'

'Tell me about it. All those school mornings when you got into a paddy when you had to wait for me.'

'Not surprising, Andrew, when the rest of us were waiting in the car while you were just pouring the milk on your cornflakes.'

'We always got there, though, didn't we?'

'Only because Mum drove like a maniac and only when the teacher had passed D in the register.'

Andrew turns to his brother-in-law. 'Do you have this trouble with her, Tony? Always knowing best? Sorry to drag you here, though, when we should all be at the farmhouse. Now, let me give my niece a Christmas kiss.' He touches his lips to four-month-old Katie's tufty dark hair.

Soon the rest of the family converge like a chattering flock of sparrows celebrating the dawn: a relieved Gosia, an excited Alice, two determinedly upbeat grannies, one anxious aunt and one brother home from studying bird behaviour in the wilds of Northumberland.

'So, you've heard I'm not dying after all?' Andrew jokes with his two grandmothers.

'Don't say that dear, please,' Steve's mum protests while my mum sighs and shakes her head. They appreciate his humour but find it too black to be amusing.

Alice leaps on to Andrew's lap to a chorus of, 'Mind Daddy's poorly shoulder.' He winces, but no pain can spoil his day.

'Ooh, lovely bubbles,' one granny holds out her glass after Matthew has achieved a satisfying pop uncorking the champagne.

The other granny gives a little giggle and says, 'Just a thimbleful, dear. You mustn't get me drunk.' Fond laughter from us all at the impossible vision of a drunken granny who never takes more than a sip of alcohol before tipping the remainder into the nearest flowerpot. We toast Andrew's recovery and feast on the canapés we have brought with us. Reluctantly, he opts for orange juice. He hasn't been told not to drink but he fears alcohol might trigger a fit. To the accompaniment of Paul McCartney singing 'Simply Having a Wonderful Christmas Time,' we pull crackers, don paper crowns and groan at the answers to silly riddles. Alice is fascinated with her baby cousin and has to be restrained from smothering her with too many hugs and kisses.

'Here comes your lunch, Andrew,' I say, as a nurse with tinsel wound into her blonde ponytail brings in a tray. She lifts the battered metal cover with all the flourish of a maître d' to reveal the NHS's apology for a Christmas dinner. After a valiant effort to eat slices of turkey smothered in gravy to mask the curly edges, soggy roast potatoes and overcooked sprouts, Andrew nibbles at a mince pie and ignores a lump of what purports to be plum pudding, opting instead for the chocolates we have supplied.

'Now it's present time,' I declare.

Alice claps her hands in delight as I place the Santa hat that comes out every year onto her daddy's bald pate. The bell on the end jingles with every turn of his head as he dispenses parcels from the red and green sack we filled at home. His gift to Alice, carefully selected weeks ago, is a soft toy caterpillar, each segment of its body a different primary colour, with black velvet antennae and a smiley face.

Gosia, feigning anticipation, asks, 'What is it, Alice?', as her daughter pulls off the wrapping.

'A pillar, Mummy,' she murmurs and snuggles it into her arm like a baby. Twenty years later this 'pillar', one-eyed and shabby with love, will remain Alice's treasured companion.

Steve carefully drapes our gift of an elegant tartan dressing gown over Andrew's shoulders and Matthew presents his brother with a favourite Elton John CD.

Gosia holds her husband's hand and can't stop smiling.

By two o'clock Alice and Katie are getting fractious and I notice Andrew's eyes glazing over with weariness, his animation flagging. He dreads us leaving but acknowledges that we must.

Gathering up the torn wrapping paper and dismembered crackers, my mind turns to the turkey cooking in the Aga at home – maybe to a frazzle – but that is unimportant. Leaving him is like severing the cord between us all over again. 'Tomorrow, love, I'll bring you a full, homemade Christmas dinner and ask them to pop it in the microwave. I promise.' What else can a mother do but love and feed her child?

We say our goodbyes with kisses, hugs and regret. I look back for a final wave when I reach the door and see my boy wiping a tear from his cheek.

The short winter days following Christmas are lived in a kind of limbo, uncertain of what is to come. Each day family and friends travel from all directions to mid-Sussex. Concerned well-wishers are relieved to hear that Andrew *only* had a stroke.

Only is a relative term. Minor or not, a stroke is a serious medical crisis. When we help Andrew walk to the bathroom on the ward he sways like a drunk and leans heavily on us. What caused this stroke? Will it have lasting effects? Is he likely to have another? Crucially – are they quite sure of the diagnosis?

Over the festive season the hospital seems devoid of senior

doctors and Steve and I finally manage to explain our concern to an overworked junior whose heavy eyes and forced smile indicate that she has not slept for a very long time.

'His unsteadiness is only to be expected after what he's been through,' the raven-haired doctor reassures us. 'We'll do a repeat brain scan to confirm the diagnosis, but you really mustn't worry. As soon as the orthopaedic surgeon has fixed his shoulder, and after a short period of recuperation, Andrew will be as good as new.'

I mean to ask if more seizures are likely, but, by the time I remember, the young woman is hurrying to her next patient.

'Well, that's us well and truly fobbed off,' Steve says.

Monday 30 December 1996

Andrew is the only patient the surgeon will be operating on today. His is considered an urgent case, which can't wait until the routine lists in the new year. We have been warned that the procedure to mend the four fractures in his shoulder will be long and complicated. It will begin at 8am.

Gosia phones me in the shop at ten o'clock. 'Will it be finished, Janet? Shall I call the hospital?'

I look at my watch, calculating, picturing the chain of events: *the anaesthetist's calming words as he places the mask over Andrew's face; the insertion of an airway into his throat; the transfer of his unconscious body to theatre; the positioning of him on the table; the painting of his shoulder and chest with bright yellow antiseptic and the first incision. Then the suction machine, the saws, the hammers, the steel pins, the doctors and nurses laughing and joking as they work, like labourers on a building site. The surgeon doing a final check, satisfied with the result before the smell of burning flesh from the diathermy machine sealing off the severed blood vessels. Then closing the wound to restore his patient's body to something less reminiscent of a butcher's shop; Andrew being wheeled to the recovery room and becoming aware of a voice,* "Andrew, wake up, Andrew. It's all over now."

'It'll have been a long process, Gosia. Leave it another hour, then let me know what they say. Don't worry, I'm sure...I'm sure he'll be okay.' I hope she didn't hear the catch in my voice.

The day wears on. Gosia phones every hour and receives the same response – 'He's not back from theatre yet,' – until at three o'clock a nurse tells her he's in intensive care.

'Intensive care? Why?'

'Just as a precaution. Everything went according to plan.'

Twelve days of driving ninety minutes to the hospital have familiar-ised us with every twinkling Christmas illumination en route. On many of those journeys they barely impinged on our consciousness. The sparkly trees belonged to others, whose lives were normal. Tumourless. The flood of relief that washed over us when the diag-nosis became, 'not a tumour, only a stroke', is now buoyed by the physical repair of his body. This evening, as we travel the familiar roads, the festive decorations are beautiful, and I laugh with my daughter-in-law at the illuminated garden snowmen, and reindeer skidding across roof tiles.

The twilight air of winter bites at our cheeks as we hurry from the hospital car park, so that the heat of the unit is welcome. A small ward, with only four beds, it is less intimidating than the ICU was in the Hastings hospital on that first terrible night. Or perhaps it is to do with our mindset as we walk in, relieved and expecting the best news, rather than frightened and fearing the unknown.

Woozy after the long anaesthetic, Andrew smiles when we greet him but says very little except to mutter, 'Alice okay?' Gosia tells him who is babysitting, and I retreat to the room with the fish tank, to give them some time together. I am shattered, bone-weary, after the roller coaster of the last fortnight. I lean my head against the wall and close my eyes, glad to be alone with my selfish thoughts. *I feel I have been bearing all the responsibility, everyone looking to me for explanations, reassurance – just because I was once a nurse. AND I've had to go to work, wrap the presents, send the cards, and cook Christmas dinner for everyone. It's not fair. And, despite what we've been told, I'm still not sure I believe in this stroke diagnosis. I can't say that to anyone but Steve. And I think he agrees, despite his apparent optimism.*

Why can't all this just go away? Why can't life be normal again?
I open my eyes and shake myself, physically and mentally. *Stop it, Janet. Stop feeling sorry for yourself – stop being so bloody selfish. Think about Andrew lying in intensive care, think about Gosia, frightened in a foreign country. Pull yourself together, girl!* I stand and fill my lungs, straighten my back and return to my son's bedside.

The staff nurse approaches us, pointing to the window that separates the insulated world of the hospital from the vastness that is everything else.

'Look,' he says, 'it's snowing. You'd better think about getting home, you've a long journey.'

'Yes, we shouldn't leave it too much longer,' I say, and as I speak the tiny white snowflakes floating in the darkness become a flurry, then a storm and, by the time we have gathered our coats, a blizzard is raging outside.

Hasty kisses.

'You're in the best place.'

'Love you.'

'See you tomorrow.'

'Bring Alice.'

'Sleep well.'

'Drive carefully.'

I've never liked driving in snow – it terrifies me. But there is no alternative, so we steel ourselves and set out. The country roads are deserted, the snow deep and virginal – not yet compacted into ice. In whiteout conditions we slither in second gear, pausing every few minutes to de-ice the windscreen and summon the courage to continue. The heater is on full and my mouth is dry with fear as we pass abandoned cars, some with their lights still illuminating the falling snow. Does someone need help? Should we stop and investigate? We don't. Self-preservation is top of our agenda and if we stop now we may not be able to start again. Alice is at home with a baby sitter, Steve will be anxious, and we don't have a new-fangled carphone. I hope Andrew is sleeping, not worrying.

'I think, Janet, that if you put your foot on the brake, then off and again on, it helps to stop the skidding.'

'Of course, Gosia,' I throw her a grateful glance, 'how stupid of me not to remember.'

I drive on slowly and doggedly, pumping the brakes on the slippery hills, hardly speaking as we traverse the ghostly, silent landscape. The coloured lights in the trees reflect on the snow-laden branches and the moon shines bright between the clouds. A rare and beautiful sight, but we don't remark on it – anxiety has obliterated aesthetic appreciation. Our safety is paramount. I must not be responsible for more family trauma.

Four hours later, as midnight strikes, I kiss Gosia goodbye and leave her to walk the last treacherous five hundred yards to her door; the drifts look too deep for me to attempt to drive onto their narrow road. When she is out of sight I tackle the final three miles home, and sink, for a moment, into my worried husband's arms. Then I dial Gosia's number.

'Did you get home all right? Is everything okay?' I ask, and her yawning voice tells me all is well. Alice is sleeping and Stella, the babysitter, is staying the night.

I scrabble in my bag for the hospital number and ask the voice who answers on the ICU phone to, 'Please tell Andrew we are safely home.'

The next day is New Year's Eve. The roads have been cleared and we arrive at the hospital to find Andrew back in the general ward entertaining a gaggle of noisy friends. Still enjoying the Christmas break, they listen to his animated description of waking from a snooze this afternoon.

'I opened my eyes and who did I see but John Pyke, the minister from Rye,' Andrew tells his audience. '"Blow me down, it's the old Vic," I said to him, "I must have died and gone to heaven." He liked that, and we had a good old belly laugh.'

'Shush,' I press my forefinger to my lips, as his friends' loud guffaws fill the ward, 'remember there are sick people here.'

'They're loving it, Mum. Don't be a wet blanket – it's New Year's Eve.' Cheers ring round the ward from visitors and inmates alike.

Cheng, a new patient in the bed next to Andrew's is a young Chinese man. He is enjoying the hilarity. He was admitted last night and diagnosed with a possible tumour after suffering a seizure.

'He's at Oxford University – clever, these Chinese,' quips Andrew, in an aside. 'He's having a scan tomorrow, but I told him not to worry – it could just be a funny sort of stroke.'

On 6 January a second scan of Andrew's brain shows the lesion is no worse and confirms an ischaemic attack, i.e. a stroke. The news is delivered by a junior doctor. None of us meets the consultant, Mr O'D, but we are happy to accept this longed-for confirmation. Andrew's left side has almost returned to normal movement, the orthopaedic surgeon is delighted with his shoulder repair and, to everyone's relief, there have been no more seizures – although he is still taking phenytoin as a precaution. Tomorrow, he can be transferred for ongoing physiotherapy to Rye Memorial Care Centre, just a few hundred yards from home.

Andrew is dressed and raring to go when I arrive to collect him. Tommy, the old man in the next bed, insists on giving him his soft pink elephant for Alice. 'Big Sister' gives him a big hug. 'We'll miss you, Andrew,' she says as he waves goodbye to his fellow patients and wishes them good luck. When I ask him where Cheng is, and he whispers, 'Having his head cut open,' I am assailed by emotions: anxiety for that talented young man and his family; hope that his tumour can be removed; profound relief that it isn't Andrew's brain under the surgeon's knife. I am ashamed of this feeling; it must be what they call survivor's guilt.

None of us sees any of these people again but they remain imprinted on our collective memory.

'It's like getting out of jail, Mum,' Andrew says as we drive through the hospital gates. He beams at me. 'Out on the open road at last. Poop, poop!'

The journey home is quiet. Repeatedly I glance to my left to confirm that I am really taking my boy home, that he is recovering. He appears to be sleeping and it is not until we are driving down the hill into the medieval town that he speaks.

'Ah, Rye. I thought I might never see you again.'

When we walk into the Care Centre a nurse in the entrance lobby is talking to a man swinging a stethoscope.

'Andrew, we've been expecting you,' the doctor says. 'Honestly, though, you don't need to stay here. You can go to the clinic in Ferry Road as an outpatient for physio. You'd rather be at home, I'm sure.'

'Too right, I would, Doc.' Andrew grins at him, and we use the desk phone to give the good news to Gosia, Alice and Steve who are waiting at the farmhouse.

Seven

Our son is going to live.

Gosia and Alice cheer when we walk through the back door. Andrew kisses his wife and daughter, hugging them with his good arm. My husband of thirty-one years smiles, and we exchange looks of exhausted relief. Andrew will recover. The month-long nightmare that began with the epileptic fits that caused his flexed muscles to break his shoulder in four places, the ambulance in the night, the brain scan, the news of a possible tumour, the operation to mend his bones, is ended. He is home with his family and he has only (*only?*) had a stroke.

He will recover. *Won't he?*

At the edge of my imagination a little gremlin is dancing, leering, taunting. *Will he? Are you sure of that?*

Yes, I am certain. Yes, yes, yes. I bat away the demon of doubt as I prepare our favourite family meal, until finally the creature is silenced.

'Supper's ready.' This kitchen has resounded to my call most evenings for the last twenty years. Andrew is the first to leave the log fire in the sitting room and appear in the doorway, wrinkling his nose and screwing his face into a smile of anticipation. 'Mmm... I think I recognise that smell.'

Alice bangs her spoon on the tray of her high chair and chortles, 'Daddy home, Daddy home,' as we sit around the old pine table that takes centre stage in the kitchen, tucking into bowls of steaming spaghetti Bolognese topped with a generous grating of Parmesan cheese.

'Dear old house – here I am – back again.' Andrew's eyes roam over the oak beams, the vaulted ceiling, the brick floor, the Aga with its battered chrome lids and he declares it to be the best old house in the world.

I say nothing but catch Steve's eye and I know that, like me, he is remembering that this wasn't always Andrew's view.

'Well, I'm staying here.' Twenty years ago, our nine-year-old son had stamped his foot angrily and jutted out his lower lip. 'So are you, Math, aren't you?'

'S'pose so,' his brother replied hesitantly, glancing at me for reassurance.

Laura ignored her brothers and kept a resolute silence as she continued to enjoy the adventures of Ratty, Toad and their friends in *The Wind in the Willows*.

'Come on, boys, I know you like it here, we all do, but now Dad doesn't have to go to London every day and we don't have much money, we thought it was a good time for a big adventure – and living in the country would be really exciting.' My upbeat tone was as much to convince myself as my children. The dream Steve and I had shared for the last few years seemed to be edging closer to reality and I was scared.

'But this is the country and we can have adventures here,' pleaded Andrew. 'My friends love coming to play 'cos I've got fab Tarzan ropes hanging from those old trees at the end of the garden *and* a gate onto the hill, so we can make camps.'

I understood. I'd smiled with maternal satisfaction as I watched them playing at being real live action men, swinging through the air, shooting toy guns from behind the thorn bushes, rolling down the hill and playing dead at the bottom. I'd loved being the smiling mummy, supplying homemade cakes and lemonade to wannabe heroes. But now that Steve had lost his well-paid but unsatisfying job we could no longer afford to live in this large house, in a desirable commuter village at the foot of the Kentish North Downs.

'And I want to stay with my friends.' Andrew's lip puckered, and he turned away. 'Dad not going to work seems okay to me – at least we don't have to drive to the station every night to meet him.' He faced me again with a mischievous grin. 'Well, we couldn't really 'cos we haven't got the car any more, have we?'

'We've got the Mini,' Matthew muttered.

'Don't be daft, Math, it wouldn't even get as far as the dump. A wheel would probably fall off. Anyway, it would be a bit of a squash for five of us and the dog – specially with Laura complaining all the time.'

Laura looked up from her book, teeth gritted. 'Shut up Andrew. I don't complain, do I Mum?'

'Oh yes you do,' he retorted.

I sighed, ignoring the bickering. 'Tomorrow, you may change your minds about moving,' I spoke slowly and winked an eye, trying to make tomorrow sound like a tempting surprise. 'We're going to see a house in beautiful countryside quite near the sea. It might be just the right one for us.'

I pictured the small fuzzy black and white photo and the blurb the agent had sent: a squat, white, weather-boarded building surmounted by a wide chimney that looked excitingly Tudor. It was affordable and described as *ready for final modernisation.* 'Just a coat of paint then, that's no problem,' Steve had said.

Self-sufficiency was the buzzword of the seventies and we had been seduced by the dream. It was achievable, the books and the magazines told us. All you needed was a decent-sized (preferably characterful) house in a rural location where you could offer Bed and Breakfast. A piece of land for the vegetables and the animals, some outbuildings, and the fantasy could become reality.

'Another couple of years to pay off a bit more mortgage, and then we'll do it.' Steve had been saying this for some time and at the distance of two years it sounded exciting. Now, with no job, it seemed this was our moment. We'd have to sell our house anyway, no way could we afford to stay – so what the hell? As the dream lost distance though, it also lost its romance.

In the meantime, we had to feed ourselves while house-hunting. It was the summer of '76 – interminable weeks of hot, dry weather.

The green of Kent (the Garden of England), withered to yellow, then brown. Parched trees shed their leaves to conserve strength and, as reservoir levels plunged, people queued with buckets and bottles to collect water from standpipes in the streets. Even so, our vegetable spaghetti plants were not to be deterred. The round marrows grew menacingly large, like monsters in a science-fiction novel – Quatermass, we joked. Cut open, they revealed a mass of green edible strands resembling spaghetti. Pretty tasteless, but enlivened with a strong-flavoured sauce, they provided a passable and healthy meal. There was a limit to how many one family could consume, however, and our friends and neighbours, while expressing gratitude for such an unusual gift, viewed them with suspicion and I wondered how many actually found their way to the cooking pot. The local wholefood shop took some on sale or return. They were not returned, neither were we paid.

Other crops survived too, thanks to the recycled washing up and bath water – and the pig manure.

Reminiscing about that time, years later, Andrew found the memory hilarious.

'That was fun, Dad, wasn't it? You ordered it from that pig farm on the Pilgrim's Way and they dumped an enormous trailer load on the drive.'

'It was disgusting,' Laura grimaced. 'I can still smell it now.'

'And Mrs Jackson – d'you remember her?'

'The one we called Margot?'

We'd christened our neighbour after a character in *The Good Life*, the programme that had been part of our Friday routine. We watched it as we ate the fish and chips we picked up on the way home from swimming lessons. Andrew loved seventies sitcoms: *Dad's Army, Reggie Perrin, Fawlty Towers* and, especially, *The Good Life*. He held his sides, convulsed with laughter as Barbara and Tom Good (they were us), experimented with self-sufficiency in their suburban back garden while maintaining an uneasy friendship with their neighbours – Jerry, and his stuck-up wife, Margot (she was Mrs Jackson).

'It was so fresh and stinky it was steaming as we barrowed it up the side of the house to the back garden. "Margot" had her "girlfriends" for tea just the other side of the fence. Oh blimey, they didn't half leg it indoors.' Andrew was enjoying the memory as much as the event. Steve's laughter was edged with discomfort as he recalled his embarrassment.

When we left that house, however, as well as a van full of furniture we had sacks of potatoes, parsnips and carrots to see us through the winter. The pig manure had done its job.

The November afternoon was slipping from still grey to chill dark when we first saw Float Farmhouse. The nameless, deeply cut Sussex lanes were lined with hedges hung with old man's beard. In the fading light, they looked so similar that several times we arrived at a crossroads and chorused, 'We've been here before.'

At last we found the farmer who was selling the old farmhouse, in the new bungalow he had built fifty yards up the lane. No welcoming smile cracked his face when we apologised for our late arrival. 'It's nearly dark, I'll get the torch,' were his only words. We followed in silence as he led us down the lane. Andrew made a face behind the man's back and I fixed him with a warning frown.

The torch battery stuttered and died almost as soon as we crossed the wavy wooden threshold of the back door. 'Watch your feet and duck your heads. There's no electric.' Our guide's voice was expressionless.

We viewed each corner of the kitchen by the light of a match which, when struck, took a second to build up to its full flickering glow. It gave us enough time to gasp at pale light-starved weeds struggling out of foetid puddles in the brick floor, before Steve flung it away with an expletive as the flame scorched his fingers.

Laura's hand tightened around mine as the next match illuminated crumbling walls hosting a coat of mushroomy mould. A cold rusty stove occupied the fireplace at the base of the chimney breast. Ribbons of peeling paint hung from the brickwork like flailed skin.

'Just right for final modernisation,' Steve whispered in my ear and I stifled a giggle. Adjusting to the gloom, our eyes travelled beyond the match-light into the apex of the vaulted roof. A hole in the tiles had provided a convenient nesting site for birds that had deserted months ago, leaving a mini-mountain of guano on the crossbeam below. An ancient brass tap surmounted by a white disc imprinted with black letters optimistically reading 'hot', sprang out of a wall just above bucket height. It carried the house's sole water supply from the spring in the yard.

'Can we go home now? My throat hurts,' Laura whispered.

Today had been the only opportunity to view the house and now I felt leaden with remorse at putting house-hunting above the needs of my little daughter and her raw, recently de-tonsilled throat. 'We'll go very soon, love, but we want to see the rest of the house, don't we?' Her look told me she had discovered her mother to be insane.

The undulating bricks under our feet continued into the 'sitting room' where the life of a match was just long enough for Steve to scrape an oak wall-stud with the serrated edge of a Yale key. The resulting cascade of dust glowed gold in the light of the flame and he muttered, 'this place would collapse if the woodworm weren't holding hands.'

'Worms don't have hands, Daddy,' Matthew whispered.

'Ha ha, clever Dick,' retorted his brother.

Much of our surveying was tactile. Running hands over layers of bubbling wallpaper we detected the shape of a bressumer beam showing promise of a massive inglenook, and a mullioned window, long since plastered over. Steve's eyes blazed with excitement when we found the remains of a king post in the attic and, behind plaster and paint, the lumpy outline of an enormous cruck frame spanning the building from front to back.

'What's that?' Laura stood rigid with fear. I drew her close as our ears were assaulted by the screech of an owl roosting in a tree whose autumn branches, stirred by the wind, scraped a bedroom window like witches' talons.

'It's the demon that haunts this place.' Andrew's fingers loomed out of the shadows and clawed at her cheeks. Laura leapt at him,

Matthew joined in and noisy mayhem ensued until Steve intervened and an uneasy peace was regained. Rodent-like scuttlings in dark corners, however, proved to be the last straw. Our children's patience had been tested far enough. Now they were scared, cold and hungry.

Bim, our faithful Border Collie greeted us with a lick and a wagging tail when we squeezed back into the Mini after a grunted farewell from the farmer. On the homeward journey attempts to cheer our offspring with bags of chips failed dismally. They sulked and argued in the back seat while our conversation in the front was animated.

'That fireplace, Steve. It'll be enormous once we've got rid of that Victorian tiled affair and dug out the rubble.'

'And the little bedroom would make a bathroom. If we took the ceiling down in that middle room it would expose the beams.'

'There's three rooms we could let for B&B and those attic rooms would be fun for the kids.'

'When we've found a way through the cobwebs.' Steve turned a smiling face to me and I patted his thigh. It was a long time since I'd seen that grin.

'*What?*' Andrew's head appeared between us and turned to look first at Steve, then at me. 'You don't mean we're going to *live* there?' The expression on his face was a mixture of incredulity and horror.

'We'll see, Andrew,' I said, 'but just think, if we do buy it, it'll be so exciting. We might even find buried treasure.' Three groans came from the back seat and Matthew told the dog to stop wagging her tail in his face 'cos it wasn't true.

Steve and I were ready for an adventure; what was there to lose? Neither of us was short of imagination. We could see how that building could live again. The kids would come round. They'd love it: fresh air, freedom, kittens, chickens… We had no doubt. We were going to grasp this opportunity with both hands.

We sold our old (new) house and shed a burdensome mortgage, but after paying for our new (very old) house the bottom line of our bank statement was a pathetically small figure and our income nil.

A bone-chilling winter was the quid pro quo for the long hot summer of 1976. The temperature was sub-zero when, before Christmas, Steve moved into an algae-coated caravan in the small field adjoining the farmyard, to oversee the installation of an electricity supply. By night he surrounded himself with hot water bottles under a mountain of blankets and sleeping bags and awoke to find his breakfast egg frozen in its shell. The children and I were grateful for friends' hospitality until we set up camp in the house on 4 January, in time for the first day of term at the village school.

To the last, Andrew vowed he wasn't coming. He planted himself firmly on our friends' doorstep and turned his back. I was beset by feelings of love, regret and shame when I fired up the unreliable engine of the Mini and shouted goodbye. What else could I do when every attempt at persuasion and bribery had failed? I had no real intention of driving off before he climbed into the front passenger seat, dignity affronted, tear-stained face averted. I hugged my boy, turned him towards me and promised him (with wavering inner conviction) that he would grow to love this new home.

Friends were anxious, family horrified. My mother-in-law sank to her knees and called on the Almighty when she saw the wreck we had bought.

Steve and I, however, were floating on a cloud of optimism. 'It'll be fine,' we told the doubters. 'We can demolish walls, dig out fireplaces, lift brick floors, pour concrete, kill the deathwatch beetle. No problem. Yes, it's a big job but we're not afraid of hard work. We'll get an electrician and a plumber, but the rest will be down to us. By the way, we're taking B&B bookings for Easter if you're interested.'

It seemed sensible for us all to sleep in one room, the others being infested with damp plaster and woodworm, and to hope the fumes from the Calor gas heater wouldn't asphyxiate us in the night.

As I had hoped, Andrew was already enjoying the adventure. Tucked into their sleeping bags at night, he told Laura and Matthew they mustn't panic when the giant rats gnawed their way through the floorboards from the next room. Laura, of course, ran downstairs to tell us her brother was winding up Matthew who was lying in bed rigid with fear. When Steve mounted the stairs with a proverbial big stick Andrew was suitably contrite. 'Sorry, Math, I was only joking.'

We'd only been there a few days when we awoke to a white landscape.

Panic ensued over breakfast when a blackbird came down the chimney and appeared three times its normal size as it flapped around our heads. We had to force a window open to let it out and then climb out after it because the snow was drifted against the back door, trapping us inside. It was clear the car wouldn't make it up the steep lane and the children cheered in anticipation of a day off school. But as they pulled their old sledge to the gate a nearby farmer came past on his tractor and offered a lift in his cab.

At the end of the school day another parent deposited our children at the top of the hill and they slithered across the fields, arriving home in good spirits. Snowballing in the playground had been fun. 'We were all trying to "accidentally" hit Mr Stone and then mine hit Mrs Bradley's back and we all ran and hid behind the bike shed screaming with laughter,' Andrew reported.

New skills, new friends, new discoveries enlivened the daily challenge of living on a financial tightrope while we nursed this very old lady of a house back to life, but the only treasures we came across were John, a burly jack-of-all-trades, and Phil, his young apprentice. Together we made a great team. In all the years that followed they responded every time we put out an SOS. Their good humour, strength and friendship – all seasoned with a mellow Sussex dialect – became part of our lives. Neither Steve nor I knew anything about building but were happy to be labourers for John and Phil. We demolished walls which should never have been added, we pulled down ceilings to expose ancient beams, we hugged each other after we had excavated the rubble behind the fireplace and found the massive inglenook and the frame of a salt cupboard engraved with the initials of the maker, R C, and dated 1733. Andrew, reluctant to help his parents, felt very grown-up when Phil and John said they needed an apprentice and would he like the job? After school, he rolled up the sleeves of his blue tracksuit top and shovelled into plastic sacks the rubble and ancient birds' nests found under the attic floor of what would become his bedroom. Then he'd flex his biceps to show what a real man was like.

I scraped the rot from worm-eaten posts, the skeleton of the house, until I felt my arms would detach from my body in protest. The once fat, square beams were reduced to misshapen, knobbly, supports of less than half their original girth. In our initial horror, we asked ourselves if the house would collapse on our heads but were reassured when masonry drills made no impression on these hearts of oak. Bone-weary we fell into bed each night after lifting brick floors and barrowing soil from the kitchen in order to lay a damp-proof course. A second-hand electric cooker stood on an island in the sea of mud, where I cooked the parsnip soup and vegetable spaghetti, harvest of our previous life, which were now staples of our lean diet. On Sundays, we packed the Mini with our dirty bodies and bags of soiled clothes and drove ten miles to dear friends who gladly provided love, lunch, hot baths and a go of their washing machine.

Sometimes, though, our optimism faltered. In March, I wrote a coded letter to my mother. '*HELP*' was the subtext of the cheerful account of how well we were coping with cold, hunger, sleepless nights and an empty bank account. She read the runes and responded with a hundred-pound lifesaver.

Spring sunshine, catkins and greening hedgerows lifted our spirits. The children made friends, witnessed the birth of lambs and bottle-fed the orphans. They waded up to their waists to rescue newly hatched ducklings stranded in the middle of our farm-pond, they fed the chickens, collected their eggs, and searched for sheep in trouble. The farmers in the valley paid them fifty pence for each ewe they reported straying into the river. I hoped my children hadn't given them an extra shove.

Within weeks Andrew declared our house the best place to live in the whole world. Enthusiastically he helped with the restoration and his interest in history and architecture was born. He appointed himself official guide and any visitor was given a detailed tour of the house, whether or not they were interested. He wondered how anyone could consider living in a poncy new house in a posh road when they could have this. I agreed and smothered my smile of relief.

Steve's sparkle, the enthusiasm I had fallen in love with as a teenager, was back. I began to relax my weary muscles, loose my pent-up anxieties and see a future in this place.

Folded into a wide valley of green fields studded with lambs in spring, mushrooms in autumn, the house became the canvas on which we painted our family life. Guests from every continent stayed with us to sample rural England, admire the nearby medieval hill towns, explore famous gardens and castles. And they paid us for the privilege. The sweetest money I ever handled was the ten-pound note our first guests put in my hand as payment for a night's B&B. The most embarrassing moment was finding my two giggling boys taking turns to squint through a crack in the bathroom door to view a German lady's bum.

As the years rolled on, our lives and occupations changed. Six years of giving much of our home over to B&B guests was enough. Steve had set up a business stripping and selling old pine furniture and I learnt to cane chair seats, (the standing joke was that he did the stripping and I did the caning!) In the medieval town of Rye, a couple of miles away, we opened a shop to sell the furniture. Then we sold craft materials and gifts and, much later, we branched out and opened another, in a larger town some miles away.

But the forum for myriad mealtime conversations and sibling arguments was always the kitchen table. Bim, the sheepdog who never thought to chase a sheep, lay curled in her box by the Aga ignoring lively discussions about scout camps, school reports, ambitions, and peals of ribald laughter at the mention of teenage romantic liaisons.

The house and garden were the backdrop to countless celebrations: joyous Christmases, village fundraising events, weddings, anniversaries, birthdays, and the first of the next generation.

Back in the present, with the celebratory supper over, Gosia has driven her husband and daughter to their own home. I am loading the dishwasher when Steve plants a kiss on the back of my neck. 'Okay now, sweetie?' he asks in the exhausted but upbeat tone of a reprieved man.

I nod my head but don't turn to meet his eye. Because the gremlin is back, taunting me, planting doubt, undermining my joy. I hear Steve yawn behind me – it's been an emotional day. 'You go up, love,' I say. 'I'm almost done here.'

Alone in the kitchen I feel the bumpy bricks under my thin slippers. I run my hand over the timeworn cellar door, my eyes over the marks fifteenth-century carpenters made on the crossbeams, my mind over the happiness of two decades here. This house has survived five centuries of life and death and now it seems to wrap its arms around me, reassuring me that I too will survive, whatever the future may have in store.

I turn out the lights and mount the creaky stairs.

Eight

Our boy is home. We can breathe again. A history of seizures has meant surrendering his driving licence, a major blow to his independence that also puts the future of his branch of our family business in jeopardy. If he is seizure-free for two years his licence will be returned. But two years seems like an eternity to Andrew.

Before he left hospital, he was told an outpatient appointment would be sent to him and heavy drinking was not a good idea. Apart from that, he was advised, he could do anything he liked. Anxious about possible seizures, I asked if it was safe for him to be left alone. 'No problem,' I was told.

In an update to the friends who had received my frantic Christmas message I explain the 'good' news that Andrew does not have a brain tumour, he's had a minor stroke. Then I add:

> We would, of course, like more 'definites' regarding the diagnosis, cause and prognosis, but we are thankful for the miracle so far. An event like this makes us take stock, re-assess our values and know that friends, relationships, and other things that money can't buy are the true treasures in life. We are also conscious of the advantages of small-town life. Despite its frustrations and limitations, in a crisis it really does feel like a large extended family.
>
> Thank you for your loving support.

*

A month after discharge from hospital Andrew has still not received an outpatient appointment. His gait is slowly returning to normal, helped by the physiotherapist at the Rye clinic. His shoulder is stiff, his arm remains supported in a sling and he tires easily.

In early February, the annual International Spring Fair takes place at the National Exhibition Centre near Birmingham. Our hotel rooms for this year have been booked for months. The Fair is a vital hunting ground for all gift and design retailers looking for exciting new lines to fill their shops and wow their customers. Visiting all eight halls and thousands of stands at the fair is impossible. Even covering those of interest to us takes three days. Each year we plan our route march of several miles to view the trends, collect catalogues, make notes and place orders for the coming year. Having only just put away the decorations and sold off the remaining Christmas stock in the sale, we must choose the next year's merchandise – even Christmas cards. By the last day, weighed down with information, we have worn our shoe-leather, our bodies and our brains to a frazzle.

Andrew loves this event. Most of all he delights in chatting with suppliers, relishing the bargaining process – 'If I buy a larger quantity, can you give me a better price?' or, 'Sorry, my friend, I've seen the same item on a stand in Hall Five and it's cheaper.' Every encounter ends with a grin and a friendly handshake. It's a shame he will miss out this year.

We should know our son better than that; he is determined to come to the fair. 'Of course, I'm coming, Dad. I'm better now and I'm not having you make decisions on new lines without my input.'

'It's exhausting, Andrew,' I say, 'you know that, and what if you have...' I don't continue. I want him to believe it's all over, that he won't have any more seizures. I want to believe it too, but I know that I don't. I'm not sure I believe any of what we've been told.

'I won't, Mum, I won't have a fit. I'll keep on taking the tablets and I'm coming to Birmingham. I'm ready to pick up the threads again.' He rubs his hands together in anticipation.

With trepidation and cautious warnings, we agree.

Back in the swing of things at the fair, he basks in his newfound celebrity. Noticing his sling and his limp, acquaintances and suppliers assume an injury on the football field or a tumble from his bike, but he has a much more dramatic story to tell.

'What? A stroke!' They are stunned that this can happen to a fit, young man. 'Should you be here, Andrew? Let me find you a seat.'

He waves away their concern. 'No, really, as you can see I'm doing very well as a one- armed bandit.'

We insist he takes frequent breaks and on the second day he doesn't appear for breakfast at the agreed time. Nothing new there; throughout his life he's caused consternation by being late for everything. But in the past, he's not been fresh from hospital after suffering seizures and a stroke.

'Perhaps we should check,' says Steve glancing at his watch, 'It's nearly eight.' I've already thrown down my napkin, abandoned my coffee and am sprinting from the dining room.

Steve is behind me as I knock on Andrew's door and shout, 'Andrew, Andrew, are you okay?', and we both breathe easier when we hear him turning the latch.

'Sorry. Didn't have a good night.' His face is grey, his eyes heavy-lidded and he's still in his boxer shorts. 'I'll be along in a few minutes.'

'No,' Steve says. 'Go back to bed and we'll have some breakfast sent to the room. What do you fancy?'

Reluctantly Andrew agrees to give the Fair a miss and rest in the hotel instead.

I worry about him all morning. He was told not to expect more seizures, just as long as he took his medication, but anxiety is eating away at me. I call the hotel before lunch and there is no reply from his room. I ask if someone will check that he is okay.

'Is he the young man with his arm in a sling?' the receptionist enquires.

'That's right.' *How does she know? Have they had to call an ambulance?* My imagination conjures the worst scenario. *Which hospital will they have taken him to? We should have phoned earlier. How long will it take to get there?*

'He's right here chatting to the chef who's been giving him a tour of the kitchens. Shall I put him on?' the young woman asks, to a background of laughter.

I sigh. 'No thanks, just tell him his fussy mum was checking up on him.'

At the end of the third day we drive home, weary but thankful that Andrew has stayed the course, pleased with our decisions on new stock for the coming year.

Two weeks later we are preparing for bed after a busy day. Steve has been short-staffed in Rye; I have been manning the Tunbridge Wells shop. The phone rings at 10.30 sucking the air from my lungs and triggering a rush of adrenaline.

Gosia tells Steve that Andrew is fitting again, please will we come? He is unconscious when we arrive. Gosia has rung for the on-call doctor but he's in Bexhill, half an hour away. He'll ring back.

We lay Andrew on the floor, wipe his mouth, concentrating on keeping his airway clear, but he continues to grunt and jerk.

'Do you think he needs an ambulance?' the doctor asks me when I pick up his call.

'He's unconscious and fitting continuously. *Of course* he needs an ambulance.' I do my best to control the panic in my voice.

It's a re-run of that December night, three months ago. Still unconscious, Andrew is driven to Hastings by the paramedics. Steve stays with Alice while Gosia and I follow to the same A&E department, the same door, the same curtained cubicle. Emergency medication has controlled the seizures and Andrew is awake but disorientated. A nurse asks us what he had for dinner tonight, and when Gosia tells her it was liver, bacon and onions, she wrinkles her nose and holds up a stained, damp parcel made of his new green sweater. 'Most of it is now in here. I don't suppose you want this back.'

*

When Gosia and I arrive the next morning, a nurse introduces us to Dr McC, whom we have not met before. He shakes us both by the hand and frowns slightly.

'We've done another CT scan which has proved identical to the one done on the sixteenth of December. I'd like to send Andrew back to Hurstwood Park, the neurological centre, to be reassessed,' he says. 'I'll call now and arrange it.'

Alarm bells ring in my head. *He still thinks it's a tumour.* Gosia clutches at my arm and I squeeze her hand trying to convey reassurance.

However, when Mr O'D, the locum neurosurgeon at Hurstwood Park (he of the alcoholic breath) takes the phone call he is having none of it and recommends Andrew should be discharged home. It is not necessary for him to be seen urgently, he says, an appointment will be sent for the outpatient clinic.

'We were told that before – weeks ago,' I tell Dr McC who spreads his palms in a gesture of helplessness.

All the confidence and chutzpah of recent weeks is gone. Andrew, when he is discharged, sits on the sofa, shoulders slumped, devoid of his customary good humour. The future looks frightening. Where is that appointment letter?

After a week, he phones the consultant's secretary. She is still waiting for a discharge letter from Hastings, but will look into it. Ten days later, having heard nothing, I write to Mr O'D, barely masking my anger. I tell him it was only due to good fortune that Andrew wasn't alone with his twenty-one-month-old daughter when he was fitting and unconscious for nearly an hour. We believe the diagnosis of a stroke to be unsatisfactory and demand an urgent consultation. I receive no reply, but Andrew has a phone call asking him to attend an outpatient clinic at Hurstwood Park.

The entrance seems a little cleaner than we remember, and we report to a receptionist who points to a door, saying we can go straight in to see the doctor. The room reminds me of my 1950s school classroom – aged wooden furniture and small-paned, metal-framed windows admitting dim March daylight. The backlit screens on the opposite wall for viewing scans and X ray plates seem like an intrusion of modernity.

A young man introduces himself as Mr K, the neurosurgeon's registrar. 'I'm sorry Mr O'D could not be here today,' he says, and chews at his thumbnail, just as Andrew does when in an uncomfortable situation.

Andrew, Gosia, Steve and I seat ourselves on the line of wooden chairs in front of the desk and the doctor displays Andrew's scans on the illuminated screen. He studies them intently. Then he sits straight-backed in his chair avoiding eye contact with any of us as he shuffles through papers.

'Mr O'D is still convinced, Andrew, that you had an ischaemic attack – a stroke.' Repeatedly he pulls at his left earlobe, then finally looks at his patient.

'Definitely no tumour?' Andrew is hungry for reassurance.

Mr K frowns and glances again at the scans. 'What does Dr R in Hastings say?'

We have never heard of Dr R and tell him so.

More paper shuffling, another awkward silence. 'Oh dear, it seems there has been a clerical error and you were not referred to the neurologist. I'll get onto it.' The doctor offers us an uncertain handshake and bids us farewell without answering Andrew's question.

'He hasn't had a stroke,' I tell Steve as he pours me a glass of cold sauvignon that evening, 'I know it.'

'Mm.' He knows it too, but tries to cheer me. 'It's just a cock-up in communication, sweetheart. All about left hands not knowing what right hands are up to. O'D is a specialist, he must know what he's doing.'

'His registrar doesn't believe him – that was obvious today.' I am convinced Mr O'D is incompetent, if not a drunken incompetent. But who am I to say this? He's a consultant neurosurgeon – although a locum. Maybe he's come out of retirement, maybe his knowledge is a bit rusty. Then so is mine. I was a nurse thirty years ago with little experience of neurology – and I haven't even seen the scans.

Steve has no words. I sip my wine, then turn away to pour it down the sink. 'Tastes like cat's piss,' I say.

Nine

A month has passed since we saw Mr K at Hurstwood Park and we have no idea whether he has referred Andrew to the neurologist.

A pall of depression has settled on Andrew and Gosia's little house. Even Alice seems to feel it – her sunny smile, so like her dad's, is missing. When Steve and I are with her she is compliant, but her face is blank and an unspoken anxiety in her eyes tears at our hearts. All we can offer is love. Andrew tries to remain upbeat, but it is clear to us all that when he walks he is listing more and more to starboard. Rye is a small town with a close social community and we are acquainted with our son's GP. His daughter is in Laura's class at school. However, our friendly feelings toward him cool when Andrew recounts a visit to the surgery.

'I told him I was losing the use of my left side and he told me to stand and lift my right foot off the ground, and d'you know what he said?' I have rarely seen my son so red-faced, tight-lipped, shaking as he fights to control his rage. '"You haven't fallen over, Andrew, you just have to pull yourself together and get on with the rest of your life." Silly sod. I'm going to change my GP.'

However, the doctor did agree to write to the local neurologist, saying, 'This unfortunate young man's follow up seems to have been lost due to administrative confusion.'

Deliveries of the stock we ordered at the Birmingham Trade Fair are arriving daily, in time for the anticipated Easter rush of customers. Each day, mindful of the advice to get on with the rest of his life,

Andrew hobbles across the railway bridge, under the medieval gate to the town and slowly makes his way up the hill to help in the shop. One morning he finds a delivery lorry blocking traffic in the narrow High Street and offers to help unload our consignment as quickly as possible. Carrying a large carton across the road, his leg collapses under him, the box flies onto the pavement and bursts open scattering cardboard Easter eggs, plaster bunnies and fluffy yellow chicks at the feet of an elderly woman.

'Careful, young man,' she shouts, waving her stick, 'that almost hit me.'

He steadies himself as I emerge from the shop to see what's going on.

The woman scowls at him. 'You should be more careful – you might have tripped me up.'

'I'm so sorry, madam,' he says, 'are you okay?'

His customary charm-offensive smile is a dismal failure and a small crowd is gathering. The old lady walks away muttering about the carelessness of the young and a bystander throws a frown at her back, smiles at me and bends to help me retrieve the strewn items. Andrew has disappeared. When I've deposited the damaged box of goods in the stockroom, I search and find him sitting in the office at the rear of the shop, his head resting on folded arms on the desk, his shoulders heaving with silent sobs.

Don't panic, trust the medics, I have kept on telling myself. Now, as I observe my son growing weaker and angrier at his inability to change the situation he finds himself in, I know it is time to act.

'I feel so bloody powerless, just don't know where to start,' I say to Steve that evening. I push my supper plate away, scrape my chair noisily across the floor as I stand to pace up and down the kitchen. My eyes are closed tight to hold back my tears when I feel his arms around me.

'Clearly not with the GP,' he sighs and turns me towards him. 'We'll think of a way, sweetie.'

But when I look into my husband's desolate eyes I know he has no idea of the way forward.

The answer comes to me that night after I have lain for hours staring at the moonlight shining on to our bedroom wall and listening to the bleating of ewes labouring to give birth in the surrounding fields.

'Are you asleep?' I whisper to the silent hump in the bed beside me.

Steve rolls over to face me. 'No, can't sleep. I've been trying to keep still so I don't disturb you.'

I prop myself up on my left elbow to look at him. 'Me too. But I've got an idea. You remember Matthew's old school friend, Dom. Isn't his father a neurosurgeon?'

'Mm, I think you're right.' Steve's eyes widen, he lifts his head from the pillow. Hope is rekindled.

A phone call the next morning confirms our memory.

'Can you ring Dom, Matthew? Ask if he thinks his dad would mind if I call him for advice?'

Two hours later I have the surgeon's home number and Dom's assurance that a call would be welcomed. The day passes with the clock ticking ever more slowly as I give the man time to get home from work and enjoy his supper. I have written down every detail of Andrew's history ready to dictate. At eight o' clock I dial the number and a pleasant female voice answers.

'Mrs Dwyer?'

'Yes.'

'My name is Janet Denny. My son Matthew is a good friend of Dom's.'

She has been expecting my call, but tells me her husband is still at the hospital. She will ask him to phone me. 'I'm so sorry to hear of your son's problems, Janet. I do hope Glen is able to reassure you.'

'Thank you, thank you...' My words tail away. *So do I.*

His operating list is long but to my grateful surprise Glen phones at 10.45pm. I adopt what I hope is a professional, emotion-free voice. He's had a heavy day and it's late. The last thing he needs is a hysterical woman telling him an incoherent story. So, with my notes in my hand, I recount Andrew's history, concluding with a wobbly, 'I'm worried.'

There's a heavy silence before he responds. 'You are right to be worried. I think he needs to be seen urgently by a neurosurgeon.'

'But the guy at Hurstwood Park won't see him.' My voice is steady but I'm shaking my head, stamping my foot in frustration. 'He says he's had a stroke and just needs his medication managed by the GP.'

'There's no need for Andrew to see him again.' Glen's voice is like a cool flannel on my brow. 'I would happily take on his case myself, but you don't want to come all the way to Southampton. I'll give you the home number of a good friend of mine, a respected neurosurgeon in London. I'll tell him to expect your call.'

Someone is taking it seriously. Already my burden feels a little lighter and I summon the courage to ask, 'Glen, do you think it's a tumour?'

'Without seeing him and his scans I can't say for certain. But Janet, I think you should be prepared.' He gives me the number and wishes me good luck.

Hang in there, Janet, I say to myself. *The centre must hold.*

The following evening, I dial the London number and repeat the saga to another sympathetic ear.

'Of course, I'd be only too happy to see Andrew. It seems he's had a very raw deal at the hands of the NHS and I'm very sorry about that. There is one problem, however. I am going on holiday tomorrow. Personally, I'm not bothered about holidays, but after many years without one my wife has finally issued an ultimatum. If I cancel now I will find myself in the divorce court.'

I smile to myself, imagining this domestic situation. 'So perhaps I should contact you again in three or four weeks?'

'Lord, no. He can't wait that long. I'll contact a colleague tomorrow. He is also based at Hurstwood Park but senior to the man who has been looking after...' – he pauses as if to retract – 'the man who saw your son before. I promise you can rely on Paul's diagnosis.'

'But you're going on holiday in the morning.'

'My dear, I am not going until 9.30. Leave it with me. But if you would like an alternative opinion, this is the name of a Professor at the National Hospital for Neurology.'

I scribble the name on the notepad by the phone – just in case.

At nine am the next day, before he leaves for his holiday, Glen's friend calls. 'It's sorted. You should hear within twenty-four hours.'

As I replace the receiver the phone rings again.

'Hurstwood Park Hospital here. Please can Andrew Denny be here at two pm today, with a view to admitting him for a biopsy?'

Who says it's not who you know that matters?

On 18 April 1997, four months after his ordeal began, Andrew is wheeled into the operating theatre at Hurstwood Park.

A few days later he is home with a white gauze dressing taped to his head, near to the front on the right side. The procedure safely in the past, I hear Andrew recounting the experience to incredulous friends. 'First the doc explained what would happen. "Do whatever you have to do," I told him, "just make sure you don't find a tumour, or I'll never speak to you again." I'm not surprised he didn't smile – it was a bit of a weak joke, but I was bloody scared.

'Then they fixed this metal frame over my head, so I couldn't move. It was a bit like that cage thing in Rye Town Hall, the one they strung up that villain in hundreds of years ago.'

'Oh yeah,' Stuart, an old schoolfriend, replies, 'Miss Getley took us to see it on a history trip.'

'That's the one,' says Andrew and hurries on with his story. 'They put some local anaesthetic into my scalp, so I wouldn't feel the knife go in, but then there was the noise of the drill – a bit like Dad's Black and Decker, and I thought, *Bloody hell, how far are you going with that thing? My brilliant brain's in there.* The nurse who was holding my hand told me when they inserted a big needle and sucked out a bit of it – the brain, I mean. Then they stitched me up, released me from my cage, watched me for twenty-four hours and sent me home.'

'Well done, Andy, I think that calls for a celebratory beer,' says Stuart, reaching for a six-pack.

'Sadly, not for me, mate,' Andrew tightens his lips. 'It might set off a fit.' Some of the jollity is sucked from the gathering.

A week after the biopsy operation Gosia, with Andrew beside her and Alice strapped into her car seat, drives to the hospital for the removal of his stitches; and to get the histology result.

Beset by imaginings of what might lie ahead I am unable to concentrate, so I duck out from work early and am retrieving the washing from the line when I hear tyres crunching on the gravel in the yard. I untangle myself from a billowing sheet to see them getting out of the car with the air of those reprieved from death row – exhausted relief.

Andrew holds his thumb up as he lollops towards me. 'It *is* a tumour, Mum, but it's benign. How good is that?'

It could be better, I think, *it could be just a stroke*. But we are where we are, and the word benign is sweet.

'I'll have to have radiotherapy, though,' he adds, almost as an afterthought.

Ten

Andrew's group of friends are an island of reality in a sea of uncertainty, tethering him to a life which has a future. David, his lifelong buddy, visits one day when Andrew is at our house and, over coffee and a large slice of cake (Andrew's appetite is undiminished) I hear them reminiscing about childhood Cornish holidays, and dogs.

I unload the washing machine and, despite the threatening sky, decide to chance pinning the damp clothes on the line. Gusts of March wind swallow my breath as I wrestle with pegs, towels and tee shirts but my mind is with the boys, remembering those distant West Country days, so full of excitement and expectation.

In the early hours before dawn streaked the sky, the Dennys were on the move. It was the beginning of the best week of the year – a holiday at Ivyleaf Farm in North Cornwall. When we'd read the description in The Farm Holiday Guide in 1968 and I heard Rita Stanbury's amiable Cornish voice when I telephoned for more information, I knew we were on to a winner. She was quite unfazed at the prospect of babies and toddlers taking over the farmhouse.

The plan was to holiday with our close friends Ken and Wendy Wilson, their three-year- old daughter Clare and our two 'World Cup' babies, so-called because after watching that famous 1966 final together, I guess we were in celebratory mood, and nine months later Wendy and I gave birth to sons, within three days of one another. Very different boys, these, but David and Andrew were destined to be close lifelong friends. Fecundity knew no bounds and by the time we got to the farm for that first holiday Andrew had a sister, Laura, and Wendy was heavily pregnant with Anna, another sister for David. Thereafter a holiday at Ivyleaf Farm became an eagerly anticipated annual event for both families.

We set off from Kent in the early hours, in order to beat the traffic. The era of the package holiday abroad was in its infancy and summer Saturdays in the sixties and seventies saw countless British families heading for the South West with its cliffs, coves, caravans, and unreliable sunshine. Before the days of motorways (and safety restraints) the journey was long and tortuous, and an early start gave the advantage. When we had two, and later three children I would pack the well between back and front seats of the car with suitcases, picnic bags, toys and Lilos, overlaying it all with soft sleeping bags, pillows and blankets to make a wide, foreshortened bed. Shaking ourselves awake in the chill pre-dawn Steve and I would silently lift our sleeping children from their beds, tuck them into the prepared nest and set out, hopeful of a few hours peaceful driving.

Every year we hoped, and every year we had covered no more than ten or twenty miles before Andrew's head would pop up to ask if we were nearly there. Then he would wake his sleeping siblings to relay the negative answer. The A303 was busy with similarly optimistic parents and wakeful children. A kind of distant camaraderie built up between the mothers in the cars, twisting their spines to soothe, pacify, cajole and finally threaten their little darlings in the back. Steve, like other fathers we observed, drove silently, issuing the odd remark through gritted teeth until, pushed one step too far, he threatened to turn around and go home.

In 1973, we were following the well-worn route for the fifth year. We abandoned all hope of a slumberous journey as the children argued all the way to just before Exeter where there was a 'family friendly' café whose owners had hit on an idea before its time – a themed Red Indian Reserve. This was basically a wooden shed with totem poles, plastic scalps and feathered headgear stuck to the walls. The food was a good old British fry-up with proper corn flakes. The toilets were clean(ish), and the staff not too grumpy, considering the hour. With full stomachs, we resumed the journey with renewed excitement and expectation.

No sign on the road of our friends, the Wilsons, in their smart yellow VW campervan. They were not at the breakfast reserve, so the burning question now was – are they in front of us or behind us?

'I can see the farm', shouted Laura as the excitement mounted when we passed signs to Bude, then Stratton, the closest village to Ivyleaf.

'No, you can't, 'cos I saw it first.' Andrew was not to be outdone.

'No, I did. I did, did, did.'

'Liar, liar, knickers on fire.'

Tears now. 'Andrew hit me'.

'No, I didn't, did I Matthew?'

Matthew, at two and a half didn't much care and continued to suck his teddy's ear. This was the moment Steve's patience snapped and he threatened a return journey. Nobody believed him and anyway, his words were lost in the triumphant shout, 'We're here', as he turned the car into the farm drive at the top of the hill.

Tension was building now. Who had got here first?

'Oh bugger, they've beaten us'. Andrew uttered, sotto voce, as we saw the Wilsons tumbling out of the yellow van parked ahead of us. Bugger was a newly learned word. It had a satisfying sound and he knew it was rude, so you mustn't say it loud. I was mildly shocked at my son's precocious knowledge of bad language, but I ignored it. This was no time for a discussion on the propriety of swear words.

We pulled up in our humble Cortina and David mouthed, *Beat you*. Andrew scowled. All was now hugs and greetings amongst the Dennys, the Wilsons and the Stanburys, our farming hosts. Would we have the pink room with its floral wallpaper and candlewick bedspread? Or the yellow room with the window that overlooked the farmyard and the barn where the cows lumbered in twice a day to be hand-milked? From the blue room, if the mist cleared, you could see Bodmin Moor and the sea.

Rita welcomed us all into her kitchen and produced tea and home-made biscuits. The top of this morning's milk yield was simmering on the Aga in a large open pan. When it was separated she would skim off the top and serve the clotted cream with tomorrow's yummy bread and butter pudding. The week's menu followed a familiar pattern, beef tonight, ham salad tomorrow, pork on Monday, pie on Tuesday – nothing changed and that was why we loved it.

Edwin Stanbury and his almost teenage son Philip were fetching the cows in for milking. Andrew and David shot off to 'help' while the girls were sought out by Judith, the daughter of the house, to admire the trinkets and treasures that ten-year-olds impress younger girls with. The next day after a full fried breakfast the children would, perhaps, search for new-laid eggs in the barn. After that we'd all go into Bude to buy a picnic lunch at the Duchy Bakery. Then we'd be off to Boscastle or Northcott or Sandymouth beach to erect wind-breaks, poke among the rock pools and brave the waves before returning to the motor caravan for pasties, marmite sandwiches, and sometimes a cream lunch of scones, jam and cream.

It was always so good to be back.

In later years when he considered the boys old enough, Edwin took them out on the tractor in the harvesting season. David thrilled to the roar of the engine, alert to any misfiring, anxious to apply his developing engineering knowledge to the problem. Andrew, however, oblivious to talk of carburettors or cylinders, allowed his gaze to wander over the landscape – towards Dartmoor, towards the sea, relishing the beauty. And while Edwin and David fixed the now silent tractor he lay in the fragrant meadow listening to the song of a skylark high above.

In 1973 there was an added attraction. Rosie the farm sheepdog had given birth to pups, six black and white Border Collies. Three of these puppies had been promised to local farms and Edwin was keeping one to train as a working dog of his own. That left two. Andrew and David hatched a plot: the Dennys would have one, the Wilsons the other. Simple.

Ken, David's dad, and I were sold on the idea immediately. Steve stroked his chin and said, 'Steady now, we must be practical and think this through,' but needed very little convincing before he happily complied. Wendy, though, was unsure, protesting she was not a 'doggy' person. Anyway, she was committed to a term's supply teaching in the coming autumn, so couldn't possibly cope with a puppy. I offered to be a daily dog-minder for the term and she was reluctantly won over.

Andrew and David didn't care now if it were to rain all week, preventing days on the beach. They weren't interested in swimming or sandcastles or rock pools. They had more important things on their minds – buying leads and collars and dog bowls, and thinking of names for their new acquisitions.

'Mine's the one with the nearly all black face and she is called Bim, like the dog in that book of Dad's.' There was no doubt in Andrew's mind. The inscription inside the front cover of *The Story of Dog Bim,* read: *To Stephen, on his fourth birthday, from Nana and Grandpa. October 1945.* The glue that had mended the torn pages in the forties had dried and flaked away and been recently replaced with Sellotape. On the black and white pages Andrew had crayoned in a red canine companion for Bim.

Fortunately, David was equally happy with the other puppy, the one with the nearly all white face, whom he christened Scamp.

Bim swiftly became an adored and obedient family member. On the long journey home from Cornwall we stopped for fish and chips and bought a sausage for Bim, which she politely refused, although she must have been tempted. We worried when she turned away from the water we poured into her new bowl but decided that perhaps this clever dog sensed the lack of toilet facilities along the way. On a subsequent long journey to Scotland she lay quietly crammed between the suitcases in the back of our estate car puffing doggy breath over the children.

'Bim, for goodness sake, stop breathing,' Andrew implored, and we all swore that for a minute she did, and sighed with relief when the air became foetid again. Bim was a lady. She knew how to behave.

Most of the time.

Upstairs was out of bounds from the beginning and if she was ever tempted to explore the exciting territory of the first floor of our house we didn't know about it. Until the incident of the chocolate.

Laura had been given a bar of very special Swiss chocolate, which, ever wary of the possible pranks of two brothers, she had hidden safely under her bed. When Bim was home alone one day and bored for long hours, perhaps the aroma of chocolate drifted down to the ground floor and she couldn't resist. She must have bounded upstairs, located the prize, torn the wrapper and begun to gorge on the contents. Did she have a conscience, which got the better of her greed? Did she realise that chocolate could be poisonous to dogs? Or did she hear the family returning, and slink downstairs?

Andrew was concerned to see Bim's tail drooping between her legs instead of wagging with excitement as she greeted us, and not even sniffing at the food he gave her. 'What's the matter, Bim? You're a bit quiet. She won't eat her dinner, Mum. D'you think she's all right?'

A yell from aloft and Laura flew down the stairs, incandescent with rage. She was holding a chewed mess of cardboard, and silver foil.

'You bad, bad, bad dog, you've been eating my chocolate,' she shouted, smacking Bim hard – again, and again. The dog quivered, whimpered, then shook uncontrollably.

'Stop it Laura, stop hitting my dog.'

'She's not your dog, she's all of ours dog. I take her for more walks.'

'Oh no you don't, she's mine and I'm glad she ate your chocolate.'

I pulled my children apart. 'Stop arguing, both of you, you're frightening her even more.'

Laura's anger turned to concern. She sat on the floor, arms around the frightened dog. 'Sorry, sorry Bim, I know you don't understand, please stop shaking, I don't care about the chocolate, really.'

Gradually Bim was calmed and still, subdued for a few hours, then all was forgotten. She never mounted the stairs again.

Andrew and I took Bim to dog-training classes in the local church hall. Our puppy was the new girl and apprehensive when she saw the company – a dozen or so canines from a rangy greyhound to a perfectly groomed Yorkshire terrier with a red ribbon on its head.

'We can't have dogs that pull on the lead.' The female instructor cast a disapproving look at us and pointed a wagging finger at Bim straining towards the door. 'That's why you are here,' she announced to the assembled dog-owners. 'We will teach them to stop that.' Butch and somewhat overweight, she was clad in baggy trousers which had once been navy blue. The ravages of dogs and occasional washing machines had taken their toll. The brown sweater enveloping her ample breasts was apparently knitted with dog hair, or had just acquired a good deal of it during its long life. Her unkempt grey hair was held back with a 1960s Alice band and her whole being exuded a strong canine aroma.

'I don't like that lady, Mum,' whispered Andrew.

Neither did Bim. She didn't see the need for leads. She walked so close to heel without one that, if her fur was wet with rain, her walker's trousers were soon sodden too. But this was a training class, so she had to take her turn walking round the hall on a lead for the teacher to approve. Bim couldn't do it. She sat down, and I was forced to drag her round on her bottom, completing the circuit with some difficulty. Andrew sat at the side convulsed with laughter and I looked back with horror to see, a trail of pee on the wooden floor.

So that was the end of that. Why did we need dog-training anyway, when we already had the near perfect dog?

Bim's life lasted for ten and a half years; not a bad life for a dog. On a walk across the valley one autumn Sunday she struggled to mount a stile she normally leapt with ease and ran for home as soon as she sighted our house, careless of our calls. Something was wrong and on examination I located a small lump on her abdomen.

The vet pronounced, 'Cancer, I am afraid. Breast cancer. We'll do what we can.'

After the operation, she wore a pair of Andrew's underpants to protect the wound from her licking, but she grew weaker and weaker and by mid-November we knew this might be the last visit to the vet's. Andrew, at seventeen, was in his first term at college. He cut afternoon lectures and cradled Bim in his arms on the journey to the surgery. As the lethal injection took effect he held her face in his hands and whispered reassurance in her ear.

We took her home, laid her gently on the beanbag that was her bed, and the five of us held each other and cried together. Our first shared bereavement.

Winter had come early that year. Steve and Andrew could see their breath condensing in the cold November air as they dug Bim's grave by torchlight in the freezing stony soil by the front gate; the spot where she habitually sat to watch the world go by.

Andrew's shoulders shook, and his tightly shut eyes failed to contain his tears. It was his first experience of death.

He was gutted.

Eleven

One afternoon in February 1981 Andrew and Laura jumped off the school bus and plunged into the twilight mist that had settled in the valley. It billowed behind them as they flung open the back door and burst into the kitchen. Andrew's shirt was unbuttoned at the neck, his tie was missing, and I noted that once again his trousers were looking a bit short. They dropped their bags in the customary corner and made to take off damp coats.

'Hang on,' I said. 'Whose turn is it to get the chickens in?'

'Not mine, I did it yesterday.'

'No, you didn't, I did.'

'Well you've been home from school for ages, Matthew, I'm exhausted.' A newly deep voice sighed dramatically. 'You wait till you leave that primary school and get to the grown-up world of the comprehensive, then you'll know what hard work is.'

'Hard work, Andrew? Is that what you've got in that plastic carrier? Just look at all my homework.' Laura indicated her bulging canvas bag. 'We told Miss Getley we shouldn't have history on Thursday but as usual she wouldn't listen so now I've got four subjects and they've all got to be in tomorrow. I bet you haven't got much Andrew – you never seem to have much – so you can do the chickens tonight.'

'Oh, stop trying to be the family swot. I have a very important form to fill in. You just wait until you have to choose a career and then you'll know how important it is not to have to bother with chicken feed.' A grin split his face. 'Oh, that was a bit clever, wasn't it?'

Laura scowled and stomped upstairs muttering, 'At least I might have a few qualifications.' Matthew, ever the conciliator, pulled his coat from the hooks by the back door. 'I'll do it.'

'Cheers, Math, the torch is over there. Do you want a cheese toastie when you come in?' His brother stuck his thumb in the air as he pulled on his wellies and set off across the yard making clucking noises to alert the hens to supper time.

'What's all this about a form then?' I asked.

'We've got to choose options for O level, Mum, and write some ideas of what we want to be. Think I'll put down millionaire.'

I wiped my floury hands and suggested he took it a bit more seriously. 'Let's have a look, Andrew.' I smoothed the scrunched-up paper he pulled from his pocket and ran my eye down the list of subjects, mentally crossing them off. Chemistry? No – not since that incident with the Bunsen burner and the fire extinguisher. And he would not be welcomed in the physics class after being in detention for blacking out some of the letters on the front of the text book so that the title read *P*∗*ys*∗∗*s*.

'It wasn't fair,' he'd told us, 'we'd never have been caught if Paul hadn't passed it round the class for the others to see. It was only when they all laughed that old Beckwith saw what we'd done.'

Toastie smells were coming from the Breville machine and Andrew rescued his hot sandwich before any more cheese leaked on to the worktop.

And perhaps it would be a good idea to give French a miss, I thought, remembering last summer's French holiday. At every toll-booth on the motorway Andrew had insisted on rolling down the window to hand over the francs with a confident, 'Bong jewer, mon sewer.'

'It says you have to take maths and English.'

'Oh pisspots. I'm good at English and a few other things but maybe they'll let me do CSE maths, that's what the thickies do.'

'Andrew you're not a thickie, you just need to work and concentrate a bit harder. What do you think you'll put here where it says career ambitions?'

'Dunno. This cheese toastie is glorious. Think I'll have another. What's for dinner?'

'All you think about is food, boy. Maybe you should be a chef.'

'Good idea, Mum.' So, with molten cheese dripping down his chin he wrote chef and cookery on the form. 'That's that, then.' He threw me a winning smile as Matthew returned, shivering, from the hen house.

That was that indeed. Joan Nunn, always a sucker for his charms, was thrilled to have him as the sole boy in her cookery classes; so were the girls, and so was Andrew, who strutted like a peacock as he regaled them with slightly risqué jokes between the casseroles and trifles.

O levels and CSEs came and went. I cannot recall now all the results – selective memory perhaps. But I remember well my elated son's phone call when he picked them up from school.

'Mum, you won't believe it – I got a B in History and a B in English.'

If he had just announced an exhibition to Cambridge I couldn't have been more proud.

Andrew's school career had been memorable – and not in a good way – to his parents and to his teachers. I have often jokingly described to friends how I needed a large whisky before parents' evenings and another two when we got home. Teachers would lean back in their chairs as we sat in front of them, our eyes pleading for a crumb of hope. They would furrow their brows, scratch their heads as if searching for a positive comment and then, defeated, say, 'Andrew is a great character, but he does need to apply himself to work, concentrate harder', or, 'I've tried separating him from his mates, sitting him with the quieter members of the class. But it makes no difference, he just keeps on chatting. It seems everyone is his friend.'

Not everyone, though. There were playground fights. Sixteen years later his headmaster wrote to us: 'I have often been reminded of the perky, not to say cocky young man who appeared in my study one day with a black eye. He displayed great charm. I feel we forged a friendship because of his style.'

Mrs Bygates, his Hungarian-born French teacher, sensing our frustration, touched my hand saying, 'Vhat does it matter about ze French? He is a luffly boy – he vill always be viz you.'

I laughed and replied, 'Yes, that's what I'm worried about.' How lightly we joke about an assumed future.

We were not a musical family and were surprised when Andrew applied to join the school orchestra. The trumpet was his instrument of choice, but the teacher told him his lips were too thick. 'What about Louis Armstrong?' he asked her, but she wasn't listening. He ended up with the triangle and the cymbals, but his percussion career was short-lived. Every teenager needs music though, so he strummed a few chords on a second-hand guitar and amassed a collection of vinyl LPs: Stiff Little Fingers, The Clash, Joy Division. The rafters of our house shook to the strains of Pink Floyd – *We don't need no education, we don't need no thought control.* He wore faux leather trousers complete with safety pins and chains, he fashioned his hair into a Mohican coxcomb.

Andrew needed no more school, he was ready for life's adventure.

The first step on this adventure, Hastings College, wasn't far away – about half an hour in the two-carriage diesel train that chugged hourly along the valley below our house.

Each morning Andrew set off for the village railway halt on his racing bike with its drop handlebars, minimal mudguards and a narrow, hard saddle that, to me, seemed to threaten his manhood. In his blue rucksack was a canvas roll full of pocketed, expensive kitchen knives and a newly laundered set of chef's 'whites'. My collection of stain removers increased weekly and the washing machine churned manfully to keep his uniform white jacket and blue checked trousers immaculate. To my relief his tall chef's hats went to the college laundry. Stiff with starch they irritated his teenage acne so that the spots itched and became so inflamed that his hat became bloodstained, a clean one was needed, and the cycle began all over again.

The two-year catering course suited Andrew. He'd exchanged

a school uniform for a professional one, a designation of pupil for the trendier one of student. On occasions, he brought home a culinary creation for the family to try, reminding us of how lucky we were that he'd been careful that the treat remained in its dish on the cycle ride home. Crème Bavarois was a particular favourite, with fruits de forêt coulis. 'That's blackberries, raspberries and things, in case your French isn't up to scratch', our emerging chef translated.

The Saturday night disco in the village hall was forgone in favour of a waiting job in a tiny restaurant in Winchelsea, the ancient little town on the opposite side of the valley. Many of the diners were familiar locals. 'Lady M was in tonight,' Andrew announced as he kicked off his shoes and sprawled across the sofa. 'Nearly spilt the soup in her lap.'

'Oh my God.' My hand flew to my mouth. Lady M was the widow of a high court judge and known to be a fierce opponent on local committees, a stickler for efficiency in all things.

'It was okay, though,' Andrew assured us, 'she caught the dish just in time. I got down on one knee and begged forgiveness. Then she patted me on the head and said, "Never mind, dear boy. We all make mistakes." Good night, then,' he said and before he left the room he jingled his trouser pocket, gave us an impish smile, saying, 'and she gave me a big tip.'

'I just hope that boy never runs out of charm,' Steve said.

In the holidays, he worked in the kitchen of The George, Rye's main hotel in the High Street opposite our shop. Hard, hot work for an overbearing, egotistical head chef was relieved by the camaraderie of fellow staff and private jokes behind the boss's back. After a late Saturday night function Andrew was in despair when, after bidding his fellows goodnight he found his front tyre had a puncture. *Sod it, and I'm in at six for the breakfasts.* He sat on the back step of The George, head in hands, contemplating a long, dark walk home. Fred, the night porter was just coming on duty. 'What's up with you, Andy? Been raiding the bar after hours?'

'S'pose you don't have a handy puncture repair outfit in your pocket? I'm on breakfasts tomorrow.'

Fred examined the tyre. 'Nah, but I've got an idea.'

The next day Andrew leaned his bike against the fence and didn't respond to the dog's barking welcome. He came into the kitchen as I was cooking lunch, and sat heavily on a wooden chair.

'Hello, love, you're late. Busy morning?' I said. 'What time did you get home last night?'

'Didn't come home last night,' he replied glumly.

'So where…?'

'Don't ask, Mum.'

He wasn't even cheered by the smell of roast beef as I pulled it from the oven. Over the rhubarb crumble, he explained. Fred had suggested he sleep in an empty guestroom, but one of the chambermaids Andrew had upset with his teasing about her supposed boyfriend had split on him and he had an appointment with the manager that afternoon.

'That'll be the job down the drain. At least there'll be no more early mornings, but no wages either. I hadn't even slept in the bed, Mum, and the cover wasn't creased at all. And I used the Gents in reception.'

'It's a lesson for you, lad,' said Steve. 'Now let's get that puncture mended.'

As fellow traders, we knew the hotel manager, a genial fellow who ran a smooth operation. I imagine he was stern, but perhaps with a hint of amusement, when Andrew appeared in front of his desk. However, we were pleased to hear tuneless whistling and see a smiling face when our son returned from town later. 'It's okay, he just gave me a warning and told me, two more and I'm out. I didn't tell him it was Fred's idea, though.'

Either the charm was still working, or breakfast chefs were thin on the ground.

An annual wheelbarrow race around the streets was a tradition among the seventeen hostelries and restaurants in the town. 'Wheelbarrow' was a loose term for any kind of transport fashioned from all sorts of junk added to old pram bases, buggies, children's scooters – anything with wheels. Large bearded men wearing white bonnets and waving spoons sat in ancient bassinets, keen young waitresses and barmen were cheered on by enthusiastic crowds as they raced down the High Street balanced precariously on Zimmer frames or minute pushchairs, focused intently on staying aboard.

Andrew had struck up a friendship with the new assistant manager of The George, a young Australian – also an Andy. With a couple of other employees, they commandeered a big bottle skip on wheels from behind the bar. Decked out with flags and tinsel and a plastic windscreen, it made a fine vehicle. Members of The George team took turns climbing in and being pushed at speed, careering around the sharp corners of the cobbled streets on two wheels. The castors survived only half the journey, so it then had to be picked up and carried. Andrew, being the lightest, jumped in and took all the glory at the finishing line.

Fired with success, the group decided to enter the annual raft race on the river. A craft was fashioned out of plastic bottles and other empty, floatable food containers that Andrew had been saving for weeks. Taped and tied together with duct tape and baler twine the vessel was launched optimistically with the two Andys on board but, in common with most other rafts, it sank within minutes to the great delight of the crowds lining the bank, who hauled out the dripping sailors.

Two years at college ended with Andrew receiving the prize for *The Student Most Likely to make an Important Contribution to the Catering Industry*. He was ready to take the world of fine dining by storm.

The lowest rung of the catering ladder was a post as a commis chef in a country house hotel in Oxfordshire. Then, after a few months, he stepped up to the position of chef de partie in a smart new London restaurant, *Kensington Place*. The job he enjoyed most, however, was at *Rules* in Maiden Lane. Positioned just off Covent Garden and close to theatre land, it was established in 1798 and is the oldest restaurant in London. Andrew loved the sheer 'Britishness' of the Edwardian décor – deep carpets, red velour seating and silk-shaded lamps, all presided over by paintings and sketches of past patrons, literary and theatrical greats. The food he cooked was quintessentially British, as well – oysters, game and the roast beef of old England.

The camaraderie at *Rules* was very much to Andrew's taste and he made lasting friends there. But the antisocial hours were restricting, and when a summer heatwave hit and the thermometer in the basement kitchen rose to 45 degrees he began to wonder if he had chosen the right career.

David, his lifelong friend, was also looking for a new direction for the coming year before returning to university. 'How about going travelling?' he asked Andrew.

'Fab idea, Dave – I'm in.'

A new adventure was on the horizon.

Twelve

Months were spent scanning the travel sections of the Sunday papers for the cheapest round the world air tickets, poring over maps and guide books and searching out any contact who might be able to offer beds in far distant lands. In January 1989 Andrew bade farewell to his latest girlfriend, and four anxious parents assembled at Heathrow airport to wave off our boys. Even the weight of the enormous orange and red backpacks dragging on the travellers' shoulders couldn't dim the sparkle in their eyes or wipe the grins of anticipation from their faces. The air was alive with excitement. As they were about to go through the door marked *Departures* Andrew felt a tap on his shoulder. When he turned, a smiling young woman offered him a single rose.

'Gill!' Andrew, Steve and I chorused. In turn, we hugged her, the erstwhile receptionist from The George, a good friend and fellow raft-racer who now worked in London. What a kind girl to come and wish him bon voyage – with a rose.

During the next nine months, we received letters (only a few – pen and paper were not Andrew's natural companions) and a couple of phone calls – mobiles and email had yet to enter our lives. So, twenty-eight years later, as I come to fill in this section of Andrew's life, I spend an afternoon listening to David's reminiscences of their backpacking exploits.

The Big Apple was the first stop on their circumnavigation of the globe. Dirty snow was banked up beside the sidewalks on the way from the subway to the YMCA hostel and the boys attempted to warm up by standing over gratings which breathed steam like subterranean dragons. The beds in the dormitory were clean but the windows, encrusted with dirt (and cigarette smoke?) were all but opaque.

Dumping their packs, they set off in search of a phone to call home and report their safe arrival. David's call was short; Andrew's was longer. In 1989, in England, you fed your money into the slot and when it ran out you were cut off. How strange, then, that he could talk and talk, and talk – all for a quarter – twenty-five cents. When he finally replaced the receiver, the phone rang again. He picked it up and was informed that he owed twenty dollars. Apart from small change all their money was in traveller's cheques. Andrew replaced the handset, spread his palms, pursed his lips and pronounced, 'Come on, Dave, we'll have to leg it.' So, they did – and when there were no repercussions they felt they were well up to dealing with New York.

They viewed the city from the top of the World Trade Centre, the Empire State building and from a helicopter-flight which made a big hole in their dollar reserves but, according to Andrew, was worth every cent. They found their way to Wall Street, laughed at Trump Tower in its brash gold finery, took the subway to Brooklyn, poked around shops in Greenwich Village and, using Andrew's well-thumbed guide, identified the birds in Central Park. A tour of the United Nations headquarters was a must, and despite being stopped and searched for setting off the alarms (how, I wonder?), they viewed the chamber where the people seen on the TV news actually sat. David yawned but Andrew, always keen on politics and current affairs, was full of questions for the guide.

David quotes from the journal he kept on that trip and tells me how puzzling he found this serious aspect of Andrew's character at the time. But now, with the passage of nearly three decades, he acknowledges his nineteen-year-old friend's maturity; the flip side of the expansive, humorous personality he usually showed to the world. I remember how, after watching Blue Peter or other children's programmes, Laura and Matthew would abandon the TV for more interesting pursuits. But Andrew would remain, waiting for news of what was going on in the world. Soon after his eighth birthday he ran to me in the kitchen as I prepared the evening meal, a smile of innocent joy spread across his face. 'It's over, Mum. The war – there won't be any more killing now.' The end of the Vietnam War had just been announced on the BBC News and Andrew was jubilant. It was his best birthday gift.

New York was perfect for celebrity-spotting too. When he and David came across a large crowd gathered on Fifth Avenue near FAO Schwartz, the iconic toy shop, and heard a rumour that Princess Diana was coming, Andrew insisted they should hang around to see her. Sure enough, after a long delay, she arrived to do her constitutional duty – promoting Thomas the Tank Engine. Andrew cheered loudly and felt the lack of a Union Jack to wave. David tucked his freezing hands inside his anorak and stamped his feet hard on the sidewalks when the crowd broke up, but Andrew was warm with satisfaction.

A flight to California was the next leg. They were met at Los Angeles airport by my cousin Jill and her Texan husband, Joe. They fed the boys and did their laundry, then lent them a car to explore the opulence of Hollywood, the fun of Disneyland and the outrageous excesses of Las Vegas where the food was free in the gambling halls – the expectation being that punters paid with their losses. The boys allowed themselves twenty-five dollars each to gamble with. As they fed in their last few coins Andrew hit the jackpot on a one-armed bandit and, as the quarters came tumbling out, he did a victory dance at the derisory pay-out, to the puzzlement of serious gamblers nearby. Frank Bruno, the British heavyweight boxing champion was staying in one of the swankier hotels, preparing for his upcoming world championship fight with Mike Tyson. David tells me how they hung around the entrance waiting for a glimpse of Bruno, but he never appeared. Andrew, however, insisted on passing on his good wishes, via the big man's entourage.

In a bar in Pasadena Andrew, who smoked occasionally, and had not quite got the hang of American slang, climbed on to a barstool at the end of a busy day and, raising his voice above the general hub-bub, said, 'Cor, Dave, I could really do with a fag right now.' A hush fell and all the eyes in the room turned to Andrew. David chuckles at the memory and tells me they had some difficulty explaining to the barman and persuading him to serve them. Some of these anecdotes Andrew had recounted to us – but not that one.

After flying over the Grand Canyon in a five-seater Cessna, their next stop, Hawaii, was a disaster; no beds in the hostel and the floor wasn't inviting for more than a night so the next day they changed their flights and flew to New Zealand.

Back home in Rye we had been following their progress on the map and exchanging news, garnered from the odd phone call, with David's parents. We were all relieved when they reached Auckland, knowing they were to be met by Brian Adcock, an old schoolfriend of Steve and Ken's. They set out to hitch their way around the North Island. Cheap hostels had to suffice; they were saving money for superior accommodation with a TV, so they could watch the Bruno v Tyson fight. The room in the motel they chose had a hot tub on the balcony and the boys dragged the TV into the open air. Well prepared with cans of beer and bags of unhealthy snacks, they settled themselves in the warm bubbly water for a long evening's enjoyment. Sadly, Bruno was overcome in round five, so they shrugged their shoulders, pulled the telly indoors, and went out for a pizza.

According to Andrew, the geysers at Rotorua made the place smell like one gigantic fart, and the laid-back atmosphere in the country didn't have the get up and go that he was looking for. When he returned home he told us he'd enjoyed the beauty of New Zealand. It was just a pity they'd arrived while the country was closed.

As pre-arranged, this was where the boys parted. David stayed to gain work experience on a sheep farm while Andrew made for the high-life of Australia. In Sydney, he was offered a bed by Phyllis, a kind, but proper single lady who had been a friend of his grandparents during their days living in Oz.

He told us he should have known it wouldn't work – even for four nights. He went off for a day's sightseeing with a couple of blokes he'd met on the bus from the airport. Phyl maintained that he'd said he would be back for supper. Well, perhaps he had, but the boys had a great day and ended up with a burger and a good few cans of Four X. On his return Phyl was thunderous when she opened the door, but he gave her a smacking kiss and apologized for being a bit late. Three other elderly ladies were sitting around the dining table expectantly.

'We have waited supper for you, Andrew,' Phyl's words were clipped, 'but I am afraid it's now past its best. These ladies have been waiting to meet you. They all knew your father when he was small. In fact, Beth here was his Sunday school teacher.'

With perfect timing, the gas from the Four X could be contained no longer and he belched loudly.

'Terribly sorry,' he said with a lager-induced smile. Phyllis harrumphed and turned to the kitchen but dear little Beth, who looked like Mrs Tiggywinkle and was not much bigger, winked and took his hand.

'Sorry, Andrew dear, I am afraid she insisted. We know you don't want to spend your time with us oldies. But it's so lovely to meet you and, my, you do look so much like your dad – and your granddad.'

As he kissed them all goodbye, Margaret, whom he described as 'a really game old bird', whispered in his ear.

'You can't stay here Andrew. Come over to us tomorrow. Stay as long as you like.'

He did go and she and her husband, Alan, were very welcoming, but he made sure he soon found a bed in a hostel.

He worked on the dodgems and sold candyfloss in the funfair at Luna Park. Then he left to make his way to the Whitsunday Islands to meet up with an old mate, Andy Carter, his colleague at The George, in Rye. Andy had returned to Oz to be head waiter at The Dolphin Room, overlooking Cat's Eye Bay on Hamilton Island. Andrew had sent his CV to the head chef who offered him a position as sous-chef.

The two Andys shared a flat with three others – all called Andy. Maybe the name was a condition of employment.

The restaurant had a pool curving around it, containing two dolphins. Andy remembers when, relaxing by the pool with a beer after work, Andrew nearly convinced him that they could release the dolphins, Speedy and Buttons, back into the sea. He never liked the fact that they were 'locked up'. Fortunately, for the sake of their future employment (and possibly the welfare of Speedy and Buttons), they never pulled it off.

After a while, Andrew saw a postcard in a shop window advertising for a chef/crew member to join a yacht about to sail for Brisbane. That was on the way to Sydney where he was planning to return, so he waved goodbye to Andy and the dolphins and sailed south. 'Sun and sea were a great combination,' Andrew recounted when he finally arrived back home, 'but most of the time I was imprisoned in the galley.' At least he worked his passage and, after hitching from Brisbane, had a bit of cash in his pocket when he arrived back in Sydney.

The restaurant at the top of the Sydney tower offered a job in its late-night kitchen and David, recently arrived from the sheep farm in New Zealand, got a job requiring a very early start so the boys paid for one room and 'hot-bedded'. 'In fact,' says David, 'we shared many beds on that trip – a real testament of friendship.'

I'm sure there were many high jinks in the flat they shared with several others, but David doesn't elaborate. Would I be shocked? Better not to know. The Hard Rock Café was a regular hangout, they took in a WOMAD concert and, anxious to experience the Sydney Opera House, sat through a performance of The Yeomen of the Guard, although Gilbert and Sullivan was not their thing at all.

The time came to move on, although the head chef at the Tower restaurant did his best to persuade Andrew to stay, offering to sponsor him for citizenship. But there were more places to go, more people to see and, at heart, Andrew was always a home-bird. He and David welcomed new travelling companions. Alistair, a friend from home, flew in to join them and in Queensland they linked up with a German couple, Peter and Anke, who were spending an extended honeymoon in Australia. Together they explored the desolate lands of the Northern Territory. Andrew was always keen to point out the wildlife, especially the crocs and the redback spiders whose webs hung from the trees overhanging the narrow rivers, terrorising the friends paddling their canoe.

'Goodbye Oz, I'll be back.' Andrew told us these were his words as he looked down at the coastline on his way to Bali. The boys travelled separately to Indonesia, not knowing exactly where they were bound. But wandering along a beach in Bali one morning, David and Alistair were amazed to hear a familiar voice shout, 'Oi!' Andrew was skint, so they smuggled him into their two-bed cabin in the Logie Gardens 'hotel'. They explored the island on scooters, passing many roadside traders. Andrew, never one for small souvenirs, was taken by a five-foot high wooden banana tree. He bargained with the vendor and was delighted when they agreed on a low price. Then he had to work out how to transport it. Detachable leaves and fruit were wrapped in Balinese newsprint and stuffed into rucksacks and pockets, and tied to handlebars. What to do with a tree trunk on a scooter, though? Yards of string and much ingenuity resulted in it being insecurely attached to Andrew's saddle so that every time he hit a bump in the rough road it bashed against his unprotected head. David laughs as he relives the memory, but I am thinking about my boy's head.

On an escalator in the airport on Java (I've no idea how he got there) he met three American girls battling with their luggage. Offering assistance, as was his way, he got into conversation. I'm not sure where they were bound or what happened to the other two, but Kathy decided to accompany Andrew to his next destination, Koh Samui. Serendipity cast its spell and they met up, not only with David and Alistair, but, a few days later, with Peter and Anke who appeared on the same beach – friends reunited.

In the eighties Koh Samui, an island off the coast of Thailand, was a quiet, tourist-free paradise. 'A little piece of heaven, with lovely people,' was how Andrew described it to us and they spent a couple of perfect weeks exploring its beauty and relaxing on the sand by the gently lapping water. But the insects were less than friendly and a bite on Andrew's buttock became increasingly swollen and painful. He was convinced spiders were breeding in his bum. They all left the island, and arrived in Bangkok where they were to part and pursue their varied itineraries, Kathy back to her Indonesian au pair job, Andrew to India, David and Alistair to Kuala Lumpur, Peter and Anke to who knows where? But before that, Andrew's friends decided a surgical operation on his backside was called for. David describes to me how they cut a hole in a sheet 'like proper surgeons' and laid it over Andrew's naked form, to expose the hot, purple, angry lump. Then they held the blade of a penknife in the flame of a match 'to sterilise it,' and made the incision. A few painful minutes later the patient stopped screaming and no baby spiders were found in the resulting pus. Andrew reported that on his flight to Delhi the next day he was forced to sit uncomfortably on one cheek only.

I don't know how long he intended to stay in India, but the symptoms of Delhi belly began soon after the taxi driver who took him into town cheated him of most of his rupees. The next morning, he boarded another plane, glad to leave the sub-continent behind. That flight was to land in Warsaw.

While he was still in London, our son had met an attractive, young Polish lady whose name was Malgorzata, shortened to Gosia. She'd been working in England on a six-month visa and in those days of strict immigration laws and border controls there was no way of extending it, so she had reluctantly returned home. Andrew, who always fancied himself in shining armour, rescuing damsels in distress, was determined to help, and anyway, it wasn't only the armour he fancied. He took a taxi from Warsaw airport to Gosia's address but, although he was expected, there was no reply to his knock on the door. Had they got the dates mixed up? Or didn't she want to see him? A sign-language conversation with the taxi-driver ensued (Andrew was good at those), and he ended up spending the night at the driver's home. The next morning the man drove him to Gosia's address and cheered when he watched the pair kissing on the doorstep.

On a late October evening Steve and I were getting ready to attend a concert in Rye Parish Church. I was standing in front of the full-length bedroom mirror rubbing a mark on my skirt when the door opened, and I felt arms around my waist. I looked up and I saw behind me in the mirror, not my husband's smiling face, but Andrew's. 'Hello Mum,' he said, 'I'm back.'

We missed the concert and opened a bottle of champagne instead.

Andrew had two ambitions when he returned home: to obtain a visa for Gosia and to never work as a chef again. Sick of the anti-social working hours and the poor pay, he was done with catering. It so happened that we were short-staffed in our shop at the time, so it was mutually convenient to employ him on a temporary basis. Temporary soon became permanent when he had the chance to interact with suppliers, staff and customers – and to emulate his dad.

Many hours were spent on the phone to Warsaw. How many ladies on the Home Office phones he sweet-talked I don't know, but finally, seven months after he kissed her goodbye in Poland, Gosia was granted a visa.

We first met her when Andrew proudly introduced her at a party to celebrate our silver wedding. It must have been a difficult occasion for this slim, blue-eyed blonde who had a limited command of English. But her friendly smile charmed us all and in 1991, she became our daughter-in-law.

Thirteen

The radiotherapy centre is in Brighton, fifty miles from home. This means a drive of an hour and a half each way and he is to have treatment every weekday for six weeks.

Andrew is offered the opportunity of staying in the old St Dunstan's hostel, built as a rehabilitation facility for blinded servicemen returning from World War Two, and travelling by taxi to the hospital each day. We consider this option.

'You don't want to drive all the way to Brighton every time,' Andrew tells us in a flat, heavy voice. The treatment and taxi rides would take only a couple of hours of each day. How would he fill the remainder? No. We decide that Steve, Gosia and I will share the daily drives.

We must be patient, however. The appointment to see the radiologist is over four weeks away.

Another month.

Another month for that malevolent mass to grow. Silently its minute cells will divide, each one producing two daughters. (Why, in medical parlance, do cells only produce daughters?) How swiftly will this happen? How rapidly will it snowball, compress good healthy cells, suffocate them like crowds of prisoners herded into a small room and deprived of oxygen until they are unable to function?

Why must we wait a month?

Meanwhile, we all cheer the election of New Labour under Prime Minister, Tony Blair. The long years of Tory rule are over, and we've even won the Eurovision Song Contest. 'Cool Britannia' is here and nothing can prick Andrew's balloon of cautious optimism. He may have a brain tumour but 'they' say it's benign and we have Alice's second birthday to celebrate.

On the tenth of May, the small semi-basement room that opens on to the back garden of number one Military Road is crowded with Alice's family – her parents, aunt, uncles, cousin, grandparents, great aunt and two great grandmothers. Rain spatters against the window but inside, determinedly jolly, we sit on the floor, the stairs, even in the tiny tent that is a birthday gift. Alice hugs her proud daddy, and reaches to kiss the scar on his head, *his injury*, she calls it. Two pink and white candles are lit on the cake Andrew has made for her – 'I am a trained chef, after all'. We sing Happy Birthday and exhort the little girl to blow out the flames. At two she is more adept at sucking than blowing so there is much hilarity (and a few sprays of saliva) before she finally achieves her goal and camera shutters click as for a royal princess. She claps her hands in delight and Katie, her baby cousin copies. They are the only ones without a cloud fogging their joy.

'Make sure you get plenty of pictures of Andrew,' I whisper to Steve. He touches my hand and, almost imperceptibly nods his head. He knows why.

Four weeks have never taken so long to pass. It is as if a pernicious force is pulling back the hands of the clocks, the dates on the calendar, taking pleasure in our torture.

When the day of the first appointment is finally in sight Andrew, Gosia and Steve agree that I should be the one to accompany him. 'You'll understand all those medical terms,' they say. *Will I? After all these years? Don't they realise how quickly things move on in the world of medicine?* I need to be there, though. I want to be there. But secretly, I resent the burden of responsibility shifted on to me.

A curtain of heavy grey cloud advances across a milky sky as we approach Brighton for the long-awaited meeting with the radiotherapy consultant. We are directed to a small room crowded with pale-faced people – patients and carers, we decide. Everyone looks strained but those here for treatment can be distinguished from their anxious companions by skeletal limbs, heads bereft of hair or with a few lank strands holding on to life. The women sport jolly headscarves, doing their best to imitate normality. Some sit in wheelchairs, some are silent, others talk in low voices. There are a few watery smiles but no laughter rings in the stale air.

The consultant radiologist rises to greet Andrew when we are called to her office. Probably in her fifties, her face, under a severely cut dark fringe flecked with grey, is scrubbed and unsmiling. She could be a bank manager who has summoned a customer to discuss a badly overdrawn account, dressed as she is in a business-like navy-blue suit and white blouse. She does not acknowledge me but indicates two chairs and we sit down.

After running her eyes swiftly through the file on her desk she confirms that Andrew has been referred for a course of radiotherapy and explains the procedure for the delivery of the radiation to his brain.

'You will have a mask made of your head and face which will be marked with the specific points where the beam is to be delivered.'

'Can they make the mask today?' Andrew asks eagerly.

'Oh no.' The woman's tone is withering, intimating her disdain at such a forward request.

'When, then?'

'You will hear in due course. The procedure for making it is not particularly pleasant, but essential. Then you will be required to attend each day from Monday to Friday for the six weeks of the treatment. There should be no side effects except that you will feel tired. Do you understand?'

'Yes, It's all quite clear. I just want to get on with it.'

The doctor has not looked at me, but now I lean forward and smile at her, in an attempt to lighten the atmosphere, to try to unlock this tight-lipped woman. I wonder what problems she might have at home to cause her to present this unsympathetic face to a young man recently given a devastating diagnosis. Her expression remains unchanged.

Andrew grins. 'Don't worry, Doc. I'll put up with anything, now I know it's not malignant.'

'Who told you that?'

'Mr W at Hurstwood Park.' Anxiety has crept into Andrew's voice, his smile has faltered.

'I can tell you that that is not the case,' the doctor says. 'You have a glioma, which certainly is malignant. Not too bad at present, but likely to get worse. We hope the radiotherapy might slow it down a bit.'

I reach my hand out to my son, but the word 'malignant' has winded me and I am unable to form the words I want to say, the questions I want to ask. Time is suspended and, as I try to process this new information, I am transfixed by the sight of rain battering on the window behind the desk and bouncing off the top of the brick wall beyond. The doctor rises and offers her hand to Andrew, who ignores it. 'Goodbye, then,' she says, then sits, picks up a pen and begins to write. We are dismissed.

Like zombies we tramp the corridor to the front door of the unit. As it closes behind us Andrew leans on my arm. 'Don't say anything, Mum.'

The rain has abated a little, so we are merely damp when we reach the car two streets away. I break our loaded silence by remarking how lucky we were to find this space as the unit has no car park. My words are trite, and I regret them, so I add, 'Sorry, love.'

Andrew's face is turned away from me as I start the engine and pull out into the stream of traffic. He sits beside me with eyes closed as we travel along Marine Drive. The sea to our right is shrouded in misty rain and, as we proceed along the A259, the drizzle explodes into giant drops, hitting the windscreen like shrapnel. We pass through the soulless, bungaloid, developments of Rottingdean and Saltdean that were a vision of Eden for developers between the wars. By the time we reach Peacehaven our progress is reduced to fifteen miles per hour and even with the valiant windscreen wipers on full speed our view of the road ahead is diminished to a few yards and

I judge it unsafe to drive. I draw to a halt beside sodden figures scurrying to seek shelter.

Andrew's eyes remain closed, but leak tears. What can I say? I can't make it better. So, I vent my anger on that stupid, insensitive, fucking doctor. In my fury, I grip the steering wheel so hard that my knuckles turn white. Then my boy puts his arm around my shoulder and comforts *me*. The rain eases and, trembling with emotion, we hold each other close in a long embrace. Then we dry our eyes and drive on.

Google has only just been born in 1997, in fact all search engines are mere newborns, and anyway, we are techno Luddites. I search the library, look up medical tomes, and call on friends with computer skills to find all I can about gliomas – benign and malignant. I discover that those categorised as grade I and II are indeed classified as benign, portending a better prognosis. But, inevitably, they increase in size and grade, and when they reach grade III they are said to be malignant. What grade is Andrew's? No one has told us.

Whatever the grade, it was not a kindness to mislead Andrew into believing that he didn't have cancer, and it was cruel of that taciturn radiologist to dispel that belief so harshly.

I find Andrew, a couple of days after Brighton, sitting on the sofa in the little cottage with his head in his hands. I explain what I have found out (downplaying, but not deleting, the inevitable progression). 'Yours must be only grade I or II, love. That is what they class as benign.'

'She said it would grow.'

'She also said radiotherapy will slow it down – it might stay as it is for years and years.' I try, and fail, to lift his spirits. My own are locked away within my emotional armour plating.

He lifts his gaze to mine, eyes bleary, as if shutting out a world too full of horror to view it clearly. 'Gosia's taken Alice to the surgery, she's got a lump on her head. Could it be a tumour, Mum?'

My arm curls gently around his still tender shoulder. 'Sweetheart, it's probably only a cyst or something. Nothing to worry about.'

But what do I know? It could be sinister; the forces of nature seem to be aiming more and more arrows in the direction of this little family. No wonder the word *tumour* is dominating their life.

Three days later, on 25 May, Andrew suffers two more grand mal (severe) seizures and loses consciousness. I arrive, breathless, in response to Gosia's phone call to find her whispering soothing words to her writhing, twitching husband, wiping the foam from his lips. A doctor from the local practice, whom we have not met before, follows me through the door and reassures us. She crouches beside the sofa where Andrew lies and holds his hand as the convulsion subsides. He blinks at her as he re-enters the world. 'Who are you?'

'My name is Lelly,' she says. 'I am a doctor, Andrew, and I am going to change your medication so that these seizures can be better controlled.'

'Thanks, Welly,' he replies, 'you're a great girl.'

My anger with the radiologist is still red hot and I write to her detailing the history of incompetence, which delayed Andrew's diagnosis, pleading for treatment to begin without further delay.

Alice and her lump have been referred to a paediatrician who diagnoses a fatty cyst, which he will remove in his next clinic. When the day arrives, Andrew kisses his daughter before Gosia and I set out with her to the hospital, and he tells her to be brave. She responds by kissing his *injury*, saying, 'Like you, Daddy.'

She hugs her beloved soft toy caterpillar and winces silently as the surgeon injects the local anaesthetic, and then offers her a big juicy strawberry as a reward for courage. Deftly he removes the swelling and tells her she is a very brave girl – something to relay to Daddy when she gets home.

At last a date is proposed for Andrew's mask-making – a full month after the harrowing consultation with the radiologist, who has not replied to my letter.

As predicted, the making of the mask is not a pleasant process.

'I had to lie absolutely still,' Andrew explains, 'and this pretty girl put cream all over my face and neck. Then she started laying strips of plaster of Paris bandages all over, leaving space for me to see and breathe, thank God. She told me it would get hot as it dried and I mustn't move. Blimey, she was right, I thought my head would explode. It seemed to last forever, but she said it was actually only about five minutes before she lifted it off. I told her I felt like a cooked mummy. They're going to make a Perspex mask from the mould and next week the radiotherapy begins. So, at last I'm on my way.'

It's a relief to see him positive again.

We develop a routine for our thirty trips to Brighton, always stopping in the High Street for one of Rye Bakery's warm, aromatic cheese and onion flat breads. Andrew has always enjoyed food and now that the steroid medication – to reduce swelling around the tumour – is kicking in, his appetite is increasing. He relishes this late morning snack as we sit in A27 traffic jams or as we drive past Kemptown racecourse where, in the grass beside the track, swathes of scarlet poppies show their faces to the sun.

On the return journey, we pass through Ashburnham and know we are only half an hour from home. In the grounds of the Christian Conference Centre on our left two umbrella pines tower above the carefully manicured shrubs.

'See those trees, Mum. The branches have grown into the shape of brains and the trunks are like the spinal cords.'

I nod my head and trust he hasn't noticed the brown foliage encroaching on the right-hand tree. That tree is dying.

We are normally back home by mid-afternoon. Then he falls asleep.

Fourteen

When will we know if the radiotherapy has had any effect? Not yet. Again, we must be patient, wait until the local swelling caused by the treatment has subsided, in order to get a clear picture. A scan is scheduled for late September – more than six weeks away.

A friendship forged with two Dutch sisters when they stayed with us as bed and breakfast guests, helps to fill those weeks. Both now married with children and living in Maastricht, they have welcomed us to their homes in the past. Over more than twenty years our relationship with Reit, Ine, and their families has deepened and matured. There is pleasure on all sides at the serendipitous decision that led them to pick our farmhouse from their tourist guide to Sussex, all those years ago.

Andrew and his friend, Dick, when they were only fourteen, crossed the channel from Dover and cycled through Belgium, overnighting in youth hostels, to stay with the sisters in their ancient home town, situated on the little tail of Holland that snakes into the very heart of Europe. Now I look back and wonder at our courage (or was it irresponsibility?) in allowing these young boys to set off on such an adventure in 1981. They had nothing but their bikes, a map, and, safely stowed (we hoped) in their panniers were their clothes, passports, ferry tickets, emergency phone numbers and a handful of guilders.

Knowing of Andrew's current plight, our Dutch friends are keen to help and urge us to visit whenever we can. Now that we must wait so long for news, time will pass slowly. Why not fill some of those days with a European sojourn?

'Of course, I'm up for it.' Andrew jumps at our suggestion. 'You'll love Holland, Booboo,' he tells his daughter. 'Everyone wears big wooden clogs with pointed toes and funny lace hats that stick out at the sides.'

I pull my face into a frowning question mark.

'Well, maybe not everyone,' he admits, 'in fact hardly anyone. But never mind, we'll have a brilliant time, clogs or no clogs.' Alice looks at him quizzically, then laughs, because he laughs.

The Chunnel is recently completed, so for the first time we can enjoy the novelty of travelling beneath, rather than over, the waves.

Bruges is a convenient place to break the journey, to eat our picnic and big Belgian ice creams. We explore the canals on a tourist boat, trailing hands in the cool water and savouring the cooking smells floating from street stalls and open-air restaurants. Why did we bother bringing sandwiches? Before returning to the car we treat ourselves to hot dogs and Alice and her dad clown around painting their mouths and cheeks with tomato ketchup.

At the end of the long day Andrew, Gosia and Alice, together with bags full of medication, are welcomed into the home of Reit and her family while Steve and I relax in the warm hospitality of Ine, her husband Martein, and their children. Unwinding after the evening meal, we are glad of the opportunity to discuss our fears with friends. At home we feel that, for the sake of Andrew and the rest of the family, we must be continually upbeat and optimistic. In our shops, we sell a poster of an emu with frantic, staring eyes. The short sparse white feathers on its head and long stretched neck stand on end like that picture of Einstein's hair reacting to a bolt of electricity. The caption below the picture reads: *It's only my tension that's holding me together.* I have felt like that emu for the last eight months. It's exhausting, but if I let myself relax too much I might fall to pieces and that must not happen. Nevertheless, this stay with friends is welcome.

In Maastricht, this last weekend in August is the time for the Preuvenemint, an annual food and music festival that raises large sums for charity.

Leaving Alice in the safe hands of Reit and her small daughter, we plan to set out from their house, which lies within ten minutes walking distance of the festivities. Ten minutes for us, but surely Andrew can't make it.

He refuses the offer of a lift. 'No thanks, I'll walk. Can't let the bloody tumour win, can I?' Steve supports him as he drags his left leg on the slow passage across the park, along cobbled streets and past ancient buildings that might have jumped from a Vermeer master-piece.

The Preuvenemint takes place in the great medieval central square. Open-fronted marquees house mini pop-up restaurants, temporary outposts of eating houses and bars from a wide surrounding area. In the body of the square are beer tents, burger bars and all manner of international street foods. Around the perimeter, though, are five-star establishments, manned by white-gloved waiters attending customers at tables laid with starched linen, silver cutlery and fine glass. Even chandeliers sparkle with light reflecting off myriad crystal pendants.

No money changes hands within the square. Visitors buy books of tokens as they enter and exchange them for dishes of their choice – oysters requiring rather more vouchers than pizzas.

As the sun sinks, a jewelled necklace of coloured bulbs bursts into life, illuminating the trees around the market place. Good-natured crowds stream from narrow streets and music-makers mount the capacious, temporary stage to play jazz, opera, and rock, Strauss or Beethoven.

Andrew's face is drained of colour as we reach the entrance, his breathing laboured. The nearest seats are in a tent hung about with Chinese lanterns and we sink, gratefully, into them. Andrew leans back in his chair, eyes closed and doesn't respond when we ask if he is okay. Gosia strokes his hand and we ask the waiter to bring us a jug of water and glasses. Time is suspended as we knit our brows and silently wonder what to do next.

The minutes tick slowly by until Andrew opens one eye and sits a little straighter. His pallor has left him, his animation has returned and the spring of anxiety in my chest begins to unwind. Our son curls his wide lips into a smile and lifts his water glass, as if toasting us all. 'So,' he says, 'looks like it's dim sum for starters. Let's get this party under way.'

Tempting culinary smells waft from neighbouring booths and we consider the options to follow our small Chinese openers. We view their menus – Indian, Thai, French, Swedish, Italian – even Polish. We try taster portions of gravadlax here, pierogi there, a mini beef wellington, paella, lemon and lavender mousse, crepe suzette… Andrew, the erstwhile chef, tastes, considers, makes a judgement and laughs with the cooks. He's loving it.

When we are making our way through the crowd towards the stage, where a band is playing *Things Can Only Get Better*, Andrew clutches Gosia's arm and mutters, 'Fit coming.' A pre-seizure aura has given him warning. He sits on a low wall nearby with Gosia and me supporting him. His arm twitches, his eyes roll. Steve tries to clear a space for him to lie down, but Andrew recovers.

'No Dad, it's okay.'

For once it was a mild seizure, but the relaxed feel of the evening has evaporated. He rests in the first-aid tent, joking with paramedics, before we take a taxi back to Reit's home.

Andrew has been studying a map of the area, bordered closely by Belgium and Germany and on the third morning of our trip he phones us at Ine and Martein's house.

'Fancy a trip to Germany, Dad?' He sounds excited. 'Anke and Peter live just over the border and it'll only take an hour and a half to get there. I've already phoned them, and they've invited us for tea tomorrow. How about it?'

Peter and Anke, the couple he had met on his Australian travels, now have two small children and run an architectural practice attached to their home near the German city of Aachen.

We are delighted to accept the invitation and the next day make the convoluted journey to Huckelhoven.

The twenty-first century house Peter has designed for his family is stunning. Bedrooms with glass roofs so that the family feels it is sleeping among the stars, blinds that close at the touch of a button, loos that flush automatically and a central laundry chute to deliver soiled linen directly to the door of the washing machine in the basement. Vast areas of glass open on to an extensive, child-friendly garden where Alice and her new German friends frolic with the family dog while the rest of us enjoy tea and strudel.

Our day is bathed in warm, caring hospitality and I am gratified that our son's life is so enriched by his gift for friendship.

The thirty-first of August is the day of our departure from Maastricht. When we come down for breakfast Martien intercepts us on the stairs.

'It is bad news for you,' he says, and my shoulders tighten.

'Andrew?' Steve voices my fear.

'No, not Andrew. It is your princess – she is dead, they say.' Martin indicates the television and translates the unfolding news as images of police motorbikes, tunnels, ambulances, hotel doors and wrecked cars flick across the screen.

Diana, Princess of Wales has been killed with her boyfriend, Dodi al Fayed, in a car crash in Paris. I acknowledge the news to be tragic and shocking, but it leaves me impassive. The pressure in my emotional boiler is building daily and I can't admit the distant tragedy of others, even the grief of two motherless little boys. If I do, I will lose control. But when we arrive at Reit's to pick up the rest of the family we find Gosia and Andrew distressed to the point of tears.

Having made our farewells, we crawl through the heavy traffic as we leave the town. Noticing our British number-plate men and women with moist eyes knock on our car windows to offer their sympathy. All these folk from a foreign nation, crying for our princess, while I am dry-eyed, saving my tears for my son.

Fifteen

Since we returned from Holland, Andrew has been quiet, morose even, following the dramatic aftermath of Diana's death. I think he would have liked to lay his own floral tribute at the gates of Kensington Palace. Instead he has become increasingly morbid in front of the television and brooding on the result of the forthcoming scan.

Gosia and Andrew bring Alice to the farmhouse and she comes with me to gather runner beans from the vegetable garden. Andrew leans against the wall of the old pigsty watching. 'Bet Dad's pleased with them this year,' he comments as my basket begins to overflow.

Alice has been hiding between the rows and re-appears, fallen bean flowers caught in her hair, a scarlet crown. 'Look what I've picked, Daddy.' She proudly holds out an armful of long green pods.

'Fantastic, Booboo, we can take them home later and cook them for our tea.'

We try to adopt a cheerful air as we eat our lunch of quiche, runner beans and ice cream. 'Wish me luck,' Andrew says, and I hug him before he climbs into the car. Gosia starts the engine and they set off for Brighton and the baseline CT scan. Eight weeks since the last radiotherapy session – the swelling around the tumour should have diminished enough to give a clear image.

Please God, I offer a silent prayer to a deity I haven't believed in for years, *please let that mass of malevolent cells be shrunk so small it is incapable of pressing on his healthy brain. And don't let it grow again. Please.*

Alice and I walk through the sheep pastures below the house to the river to check on the cygnets. A flapping and rustling in the reeds and four young swans emerge. We have followed their progress since Andrew discovered the nest last summer, when they pecked their way out of six big white eggs. Through the months we have watched four of them shed their ugly, stubbly, grey feathers and replace them with snow-white plumage. We wonder what happened to the others, the two tiny creatures we saw for only a couple of weeks.

'Do you think they died, Granny?'

I hesitate to reply, not wanting to contemplate any sort of death. 'Possibly. Or maybe they joined another family of swans.'

'If they died, where are they now?'

Coward that I am, I rattle the tube of Smarties in my pocket, knowing the sound will divert her interest in the afterlife to the prospect of sugar-coated chocolate.

The air is unseasonably hot and humid, so we sit on the riverbank watching for ripples as fish break the surface of the water.

'Tell me about the big fish, Granny.'

'Again?'

Snuggling up close to me she nods, 'Again.' She loves the oft-repeated tale of when her daddy landed a mammoth pike.

'One day, when he was eleven years old,' I begin, 'Andrew and his friend Simon who lived at the top of the lane, decided to go fishing. Simon brought his fishing rod and they searched under the big stones in the orchard for wriggly worms which they picked up with their fingers and put in a little box.'

'Urgh.' Alice pulls a face and continues, 'Then Andrew got a bucket and you made them a picnic, and they went down to the river.' She knows the story by heart and we share the telling of the tale. How the boys hooked the wriggly worms on to the end of their line and cast it out into the water; how they ate their Marmite sandwiches while they sat patiently for a long time; how they took it in turns to hold the rod, until Andrew felt something tugging on the line.

'They pulled and pulled, but it was very hard.' Alice knows the script.

'It was so hard, Alice, that Simon had to stand behind Andrew and put his arms around his waist and the two of them pulled together.'

'And a big fish came out.'

'Yes. On the end of the line was an enormous silver fish twisting and turning until they pulled it on to the bank and Simon took the hook out of its mouth.'

'So it couldn't escape.'

'It was much too big for the bucket and it thrashed around on the grass until big, brave Simon put it out of its misery.' Alice never asks about the nature of this misery or how Simon ended it.

'Then you put it in the freezer.'

'I did. When they brought it home, Simon said it was a pike and his mum didn't like pike, so we could have it.'

'And one day you cooked it for your dinner.'

Alice stands, jumps up and down, clapping her hands while I think about those times when I watched anxiously from the kitchen window. If they kept within prescribed limits I could just see the boys sitting by the river. Every few minutes I checked for a blue anorak and a red sweater and only relaxed when I saw two figures trudging back up the field towards the house, usually with an empty bucket.

I wish I could see my boy now. Is the scan over? Are the doctors looking at it? Has it shrunk? What have they told him?

Back in the kitchen, Alice helps me prepare lasagne, a favourite meal. She wrinkles her nose and wipes her eyes as I chop the onions, then stands on a chair at the sink, sleeves pushed above her elbows, and declares that she is a good washer-upper, as I drop wooden spoons and saucepans into her bowl of sudsy water.

A drowsy sun is dipping below the horizon when Steve comes home and raises his eyebrows into a question. I shrug, shake my head and spread my palms.

At last Andrew and Gosia arrive, both faces blank, there is no joy. They relay the verdict – no change. The tumour is the same size, with some associated oedema.

'What's oedema, Mum?'

'Just a bit of fluid, nothing to worry about.' But I am worried. Six weeks of radiotherapy has had no effect at all.

'So where do we go from here?' Steve asks.

'They say we have to watch and wait.' Andrew sits heavily on to a kitchen chair and stares at the floor. Alice stands beside him and pats his thigh. With his right arm, he pulls her onto his lap and buries his face in her fine golden hair.

What do I feel? My legs are leaden, immobile; my tongue is still, silent; my eyes are closed, pricking with trapped tears.

'Wait for what?' Steve is genuinely puzzled and stifles a gasp as Andrew points his thumb toward the floor.

This will not do.

I fill my lungs, blink my eyes, straighten my slumping shoulders and paint a smile on to my lips. 'Well, that's *good* news, isn't it? They've stopped the bugger in its tracks.'

'S'pose so.' Andrew shrugs.

'Now, who's for a big plate of lasagne?'

Twenty-four hours later despair has morphed into anger. I will not accept this verdict after all my boy has been through. My left-handed writing is all but illegible, so I try to adopt an aura of formality by writing a letter to the hospital on the third-hand computer Matthew has passed on. I have no typing skills and all technology is a mystery to me, so the result is far from professional. I send it anyway, demanding Andrew's scans are sent to him as we are seeking a second opinion. It is time to contact Professor L, the neurosurgeon recommended by Glen Dwyer's friend.

Andrew phones Hurstwood Park Hospital but is refused the scans. When he remonstrates, the voice on the line tells him she is sorry, but those are the rules. This news makes me seethe like that cauldron in Macbeth, fire burning inside me. I will get those scans. Never mind the toil of the long journey to Hayward's Heath, I jump into my car determined to make trouble for that witch.

I pull up illegally outside the hospital door, thrust it open, and bang my fist on the reception desk. 'I want my son's scans, and I will stand here until I get them.' The startled receptionist asks for more information. I bark my replies at her and feel my face and neck reddening.

'Please wait here, Mrs Denny. I will see what I can do.'

She stands and makes for the office behind her and my balloon of anger deflates. 'I'm sorry,' I call after her, 'I was rude, please forgive me.'

She turns, and noting my distress, she smiles. 'This may take a while. Why don't you get a cup of tea from the machine and have a seat in the waiting-room?'

All energy wrung from me, I drag myself to the airless room with the fish-tank, sink on to a plastic chair and talk to the fish. 'Hello, bulgy-eyed monster. Still swimming around in circles, I see. Just like Andrew.'

Fifteen minutes later the receptionist opens the door, holding a large, brown envelope with X Rays stamped on it in bold letters. I'm afraid we can't release the scans to you, Mrs Denny, but I have permission to send them to Professor L at The National.' I narrow my lips, straighten my shoulders and breathe in noisily as I prepare to protest. The woman taps the envelope and her voice is gentle as she says, 'I promise I will put these in the post tonight before I leave. I do understand the urgency. The prof will have them tomorrow, I promise.' I believe her and follow her to the desk, repeating profuse apologies for my earlier outburst. 'No worries,' she tells me in her Antipodean accent and touches my hand, saying, 'Goodbye and good luck.'

With relief, I note the car has no penalty notice stuck to it and I drive off.

Mission accomplished. I feel re-energised.

I've already phoned the professor's secretary and badgered her for an early appointment. I call her the next day to check the scans have arrived.

'Yes, I have the scans. The professor has looked at them and feels surgery is not indicated. If you still want to see him I can arrange an appointment at the National Hospital for Neurology on Tuesday the seventh of October at nine.'

This is not the news I've been hoping for. 'Surgery is not indicated' could mean it's unnecessary, but more probably that it is of no use. I assume it is the former when I tell Andrew. 'Thanks for arranging that, Mum. I should have done it really, but…' He is feeling worthless, marginalised, but I make light of his concern.

'It's easier for me – I know about hospitals.' (Well, I did thirty years ago.)

Sixteen

Steve has to be at work on 7 October, the day of the appointment, Gosia will only drive on familiar routes and I balk at the idea of driving in the capital.

A plan is laid. I'll drive Andrew to Steve's mother's flat in south London where we will spend the night of the sixth and a taxi will take us both to Queen's Square for the nine o'clock appointment the next morning.

My mother-in-law's sofa cushions on the floor of her sitting room make a less than comfortable bed for me and my fitful sleep is punctuated with dreams: the doctor tells us it was a stroke after all; the scans have not been sent from Hurstwood Park because they've never had a patient by the name of Andrew Denny, it must have been a dream (a dream within a dream); then, as we sit in the London consulting room listening to a string of explanations neither of us understands, Andrew's already large head begins to swell. The doctor doesn't appear to notice, just continues to look at notes and talk nonsense as my boy's head grows as big as an oversized Disneyland character, then bigger still, until finally it bursts open and I wake, blood thundering in my ears, my body weak with shuddering. I rise before the sun and calm myself back into reality. I have breakfast prepared and Andrew's drugs ready earlier than necessary and have resumed control of myself when he and his granny appear. I am watching from the kitchen window when the white Mondeo taxi pulls into the shrub-fringed car park in front of the flats, prompt at seven-thirty.

Granny's face contorts with anxiety as she waves us off. Andrew sits in the front passenger seat chatting to Graham, our driver, and their conversation interrupts my thoughts as I sit behind them.

'What takes you to London today, then?' Graham asks, employing chirpy, cabby small talk.

'Got an appointment at the hospital in Queen Square,' my son replies.

'No problem, I hope?'

'Well, yes, actually. A small matter of a brain tumour.' His voice is light, jokey, but the words are a conversation-stopper. I open my mouth to chip in, ease the driver's embarrassment, but Andrew gets there before me. 'Don't worry, mate. I'm hoping for good news.'

The car weaves expertly through rush-hour traffic and I listen in to Andrew's cheerful answers to the driver's questions – yes, he hopes the tumour will be smaller. No, he doesn't live in Eltham, just been staying here for the night, so we can make an early start. He's from Sussex, loves the countryside and wouldn't live anywhere else.

'Main entrance?' Graham, our driver, jolts me back into the moment.

'I guess so. You will wait? Don't know how long we'll be.'

'It's never quick. What if I find somewhere to park and meet you here in two hours?'

'Fine. That'll give us time for a coffee.'

This is not a new building. It cries out for a face-lift. A well-respected centre of excellence though, so I have no misgivings. Caged in the ancient elevator, the diamond latticed cube reveals to us the stained concrete of the lift shaft walls as it clanks up to the second floor where we escape our confinement and ferret along dingy corridors for Professor L's clinic. Someone has had the idea of dressing the walls with a few unframed canvases of primary coloured flowers and geometric patterns, hoping to lift the spirits of anxious patients. They do nothing for ours. We check in and wait with a dozen silent souls to be called into 'the presence'. Our nine o'clock slot slips to ten o'clock.

'Shall I see if I can find a coffee machine?'

Andrew shakes his head.

'Shouldn't be long now,' the receptionist calls to us. 'It's a busy clinic this morning.'

At ten-thirty a nurse calls for Andrew Denny and shows us to a small consulting-room lit by a strip-light buzzing like a demented fly. The professor is the epitome of the suave consultant: fifty something, clean-shaven with well-cut copper-coloured hair, the edges of his linen jacket straining to meet over his well-fed stomach. He offers a genial but somewhat distracted welcome, repeatedly glancing at his watch as he runs through the case history. Then he inspects a whole line of negative plates pinned to the light-box on the wall, a series of walnut-shaped images filled with amorphous grey and white smoke. I could identify a fractured femur, a newly pinned hip, a crushed ankle, but soft tissue confuses me. I know the tumour is in the right frontal lobe and yes, I can see a puff of white, but where is the edge of it? It is like a cloud, merging into a murky sky. The doctor runs his finger over the plate talking of enhancement. What does he mean by that?

Pursing his narrow lips, the professor turns and makes eye contact with Andrew. 'I'm sorry to tell you, Mr Denny, that the tumour is growing.' He points to the image on the left of the screen, using his forefinger to circle a pale area, then draws the invisible ring on the image to its right, then on the next, and the next... 'This is the tumour, and you can see that each image shows it increasing.' Both Andrew and I have stood to get a closer look. Now we are blown back on to our chairs as if hit by an oncoming hurricane. 'Surgery will be no help, I'm afraid. The tumour is in such a position that any physical intervention risks damaging healthy brain tissue beyond repair.'

'They, they – said it hadn't changed,' Andrew is the first to find words, but they are left hanging in the air.

'Chemotherapy would seem to be the next step.' The professor looks back at his notes. 'I'm sorry. I see you have been dissatisfied with your treatment in Sussex,' I nod my head vigorously, 'so I am going to refer you to my colleague Dr B in the next room. He is an oncologist working at the Royal Marsden, our foremost cancer centre. He and I run a joint clinic here. I regret that I can't give you better news.' He calls a nurse and asks her to take us to Dr B.

'Thank you,' Andrew whispers as he shakes the professor's hand.

Thank you for what? Thank you for shattering any hope he had left? Thank you for giving him a death sentence?

Stunned and shocked, we follow the young nurse into the corridor, into another airless room. A cheerful middle-aged man rises to greet us. He has a well-tended beard, striped shirt – sleeves rolled, top button undone, blue and green zigzag tie, loosened. 'Hello Andrew, good to meet you.' Take a seat and let's see what we can do about this.' I am greeted with a firm handshake as I introduce myself. Dr B pins up the scans, studies them, and then turns to beam at us. 'I have good news for you.' A slight touch of Yiddish clings to what sounds like a minimal European accent.

Andrew lays his forehead on the desk in front of him as if he can ride this roller coaster no longer.

Slowly I move my head from left to right in disbelief. Inside, my brain is dizzy, as if I am on a carousel. I've been riding it for ten months now and it's been rotating with gathering speed. It has spun us through meningitis, tumour, stroke, tumour again, benign, malignant, bigger and now, perhaps, smaller. I am giddy with absorbing tragedy, then relief, followed by yet more conflicting information. I have glimpsed thunderclouds over a dismal scene, then been dazzled as I've spiralled into sudden sunshine, before twirling back into darkness.

My eyelids snap shut. I won't believe this man. I won't risk another descent into the dark.

Dr B walks around his desk, squats down beside Andrew and speaks softly. 'Professor L has made a mistake. He has looked at the scans in the wrong date order, beginning with the most recent. The tumour is not increasing in size. Any increase in size took place before the radiotherapy.'

'You sure?' My son lifts his head very slowly.

'Quite sure.' Dr B looks up into my re-opened eyes and gives me a reassuring nod before returning to his seat.

'Watch and wait' is the way forward, he ordains. The frustrating way forward. Dr B explains that repeated scans would be of little help, causing more anxiety than useful guidance. Briefly, he alludes to the possibility of tumour progression in the future, but without using the actual words, he succeeds in making it sound like a distant future.

'You are a young man, Andrew, your left side is getting back to normal strength. My advice is to get on with your life and live it to the full.'

So, we must learn patience and cling to the hope that the status quo will continue.

'Do you have any questions?' Dr B asks.

'Yes,' Andrew is quick to reply. 'Can I pass this on to my daughter?'

A wide smile lights up the doctor's face. 'Absolutely not. Tumours of the brain are never hereditary. Your little girl is quite safe.'

'Phew, that's a relief. What about the fits? I'm still having one or two a week and it's really embarrassing to have them in public. Oh, and will you take on my case? I'm not going back to that shower in Sussex.'

'Of course, Andrew.' Dr B understands. 'You can come to see me at the Royal Marsden – the Surrey branch will probably be more convenient for you.' He glances at me for confirmation and I incline my head in agreement. 'I will write to your GP and suggest some possible changes in your seizure medication and ask her to monitor it.' He stands and pumps Andrew's hand vigorously. 'You can call at any time if you are concerned or need advice, but I really hope I won't be seeing you for a very long time.'

The news is good, but the tumour is still sitting smugly in the frontal lobe of my boy's brain. It's on hold, but for how long?

I see the humanity in Dr B's eyes and realise that I trust him to be there for Andrew, whatever the future holds. Already the burden feels lighter.

'Mum, it's gone twelve – the taxi.'

On the pavement outside the National Hospital for Neurology, our eyes scan the parked cars to the left, to the right, searching for Graham and his minicab. A motorbike roars past, the sign on the back of his machine announcing it is delivering essential blood supplies, but there is no sign of our taxi.

'Perhaps he's parked in the next street,' I say, but I glance at my watch and it reads 12.10. He said he'd meet us at eleven o'clock. I am thinking, *Oh God, what do we do if he's given up on us, can Andrew cope with public transport?* We turn the corner into Great Ormond Street and Andrew shouts, 'There he is,' and steps into the road between a builder's van topped with ladders and a Porsche with clamped wheels. He waves both his arms at the white Mondeo cruising slowly, the driver's eyes searching the pavements for us.

'Thank you. Thank you *so* much for waiting. So sorry. Never thought it would take so long, and we had no way of contacting you.' I am breathless with relief as we pile into the car.

'You're lucky. I was going to do two more turns around the block and then give up.' Graham turns to Andrew in the front passenger seat. 'Anyway, how did it go?'

'All right in the end. But that bloody professor. I'm going to write a letter...'

'Can't he give us any idea at all of the prognosis?' Steve paces around the kitchen table when I report on our consultation with Dr B. 'I understand he doesn't want to dash Andrew's hopes, but we need to know. We need to prepare ourselves to manage the situation,' his voice breaks and he pauses, swallowing his emotion, 'and then there's the business, will he be able to return to running the shop?' I know he is deflecting his thoughts from the pain of what may lie ahead for Andrew by putting on his business head.

I rest my head against his soft, green sweater, loving his safe familiar smell. 'I'll write to him,' I say, 'and ask for the truth.'

Nine days after our trip to London Andrew phones me and reads out the reply to the letter he wrote to Professor L, pointing out the distress caused by the mistaken reading of the scans:

I discussed you with Dr B after he had seen you in the clinic. He has convinced me that the recent scan does not show a real change in the tumour since before radiotherapy. I agree with him that the change in the size and nature of the tumour took place before radiotherapy and not afterwards. As he told you the scans were out of sequence. I am sorry you have been troubled by doubt and anxiety. Please accept my apologies.

Dr B is prepared to see you at The Royal Marsden Hospital if you wish.

'Then,' Andrew's words are thick with rage, 'then he signs it, Yours sincerely. Well, he'd bloody well better be sincere, after what he put me through. Bastard.'

'I know how you feel, love, but anyone can make a mistake,' I attempt to cool his anger, while I am thinking – *but not a professor, and not such an elementary blunder, not one to cause so much anguish. Couldn't he even read the dates?*

Seventeen

I too have had a letter, but I don't tell Andrew. In reply to my request for a full and frank discussion about Andrew's prognosis, Dr B says he really should have the patient's permission to discuss his case with us. But he understands our concerns about the future, is happy to explain the position, but would prefer to talk face to face.

Another long journey, this time negotiating M25 traffic, to another unknown hospital, the Surrey branch of the world-famous Royal Marsden Hospital.

Once again, I sit facing Dr B, but this time it is not my frightened son, but my husband by my side, ready to share the burden of what we are about to be told.

After the initial pleasantries Steve and I clamour to pour out the history of our anxieties.

'First the diagnosis was a stroke, then there was no follow-up.'

'Finally, but only after pulling personal strings, Andrew had a biopsy.'

'He has a benign tumour, they said – and benign to most people means it's not cancer.'

'Then we found out that a grade two neoplasm is classed as benign but, inevitably, it would grow at some future date and when it reaches grade three it is classed as malignant. How illogical is that? How misleading? How cruel?'

'Where is Andrew along this line of progression? Are you sure it can't be removed?'

'Please tell us the plain, unvarnished truth. We need to know, even if Andrew doesn't.'

Our anxiety, our desperation, our frustration is clear.

Dr B leans forward, fixing us with an expression of compassionate concern. 'I understand, and I will be as honest as I can be.' He narrows his lips and raises his eyebrows as he flicks through the paper work in front of him. He closes the file and looks at us. 'Andrew's treatment does seem to have been a series of cock-ups. Now that he is under my care I will do all I can to see that none occur in future.'

He knows of our business dilemma and is also conscious of our personal feelings. Mindful of our request for frankness, he is gentle but truthful. As I suspected, we are about to face, if not darkness, increasing gloom.

'I agree with professor L that because of its position, surgery is not an option. The tumour is too close to vital areas of the brain, which would almost inevitably be compromised if we attempted to operate. He could be left completely paralysed – or worse.' *Worse, what is worse?* I dare not imagine. 'And anyway,' the doctor continues, 'we can only ever remove some of the tumour.' I throw him a puzzled look. 'Imagine the tumour as an octopus,' he explains, 'with a body and lots of thin tentacles made of strands of cells that reach into the tiny fissures of the brain. In suitable cases, we can cut out as much as possible. This is known as debulking, it relieves pressure, but we can never get to every cell. And, sooner or later they will always multiply.

'It is important for patients, especially young patients, to retain hope. Indeed, there are those who survive gliomas, symptom-free, for many years. I have studied Andrew's history and his scans carefully and, although he was told his tumour was a benign grade two – and I do understand your confusion about the classification – I believe it has now moved on to grade three. It's impossible to estimate the rate of progression, but it is certainly a life-limiting condition.'

He cannot give us any timescale, he doesn't know himself how long Andrew may live. It could be several years, but... That 'but' is a verbal punch to our stomachs.

'What caused this, doctor?' Steve asks.

'I wish I could tell you that, Mr Denny. There is a theory that a blow, or blows to the head might trigger abnormal cell division, or may awaken a dormant tumour that has been sleeping there for years. But these are just theories, absolutely no cause has been proven.'

'And there is no cure.' Steve's statement is not a question, but I hear desperation in his voice, as if, even in the face of all we have learned, the man sitting opposite may give us a ray of hope.

'I'm sorry. Andrew has had radiotherapy and if, and when, the disease progresses there are chemotherapy regimes that may delay progression. He is a fine young man who should concentrate on getting back to as normal a life as he can.'

He pulls a slender orange-covered volume from his desk drawer and furls the pages with his thumb. 'This is a book with much information about gliomas. It is written for health professionals and not something I would normally give to patients or their families. However, with your background I think it may be useful to you, but probably don't show it to Andrew. In your letter you mentioned the possible expansion of your business. That is a decision for you, of course, but I would think it unwise to rely on Andrew in your long-term plans.'

As if in a trance we thank him and retrace our steps through the crowded outpatients department, deaf to the noise of phones ringing, voices calling, the whirr and clicks of trolleys and wheelchairs. Outside the main door the chill air hits us, Steve grasps my hand and we make for the car park.

Shocked into silence we travel south to deliver the unwelcome news to our daughter, Laura, in Chichester. But my mind is turning over that 'blow to the head' comment and remembering too many blows.

Playground fights had resulted in more than one black eye and I have a picture of Andrew jumping from the minibus after a weekend at cub-camp, a slab of pink Elastoplast stuck to his right temple. I sighed, 'What happened this time?'

Grinning, he waved away my concern. 'A tent pole fell on my head, Mum. Shouldn't have such a big one, should I?'

A few years ago, he decided to have a go at body-building, causing great amusement in the family. Apart from cycling as a teenager and enjoying early morning swims in a local pool, fitness had never been Andrew's goal. Nevertheless, he invested in some dumbbells, golden in colour and very heavy. Proudly he flexed the beginnings of impressive biceps, but soon ran out of enthusiasm.

When he and Gosia were organising possessions in their new home he placed his dumbbells on a high shelf in the utility room and bent to pick up his cycle helmet. It was a pity he wasn't wearing it when a weighty dumbbell rolled silently from its place and landed on top of him, all but knocking him out.

And there was the Balinese banana tree; more blows to his head.

But the incident that presses most insistently into the forefront of my mind as we drive silently through the dreary afternoon, took place in July 1968.

I was sitting on a chair in a cage, feeding a baby. The cage was a wooden playpen designed to keep a toddler safe. But Andrew, then fourteen months old, was on the outside, crawling freely around the sitting room. Barricading myself with my six-week-old daughter was, I thought, an ingenious way of feeding her in peace. Newly home from hospital where pneumonia had taken her, she was tiny and had been diagnosed with choanal stenosis. Her nasal passages were narrow, making breathing and sucking simultaneously a challenge, so she fed slowly. At night she snuffled, coughed, screamed, rejected the bottle, and continued screaming until all seven pounds of her pulsed and juddered like a tiny engine running out of fuel. Then she'd quieten. When I whispered shushing noises and slowly lowered her into the Moses basket I silently pleaded with her to sleep. *Just an hour, sweetie – give me an hour, please?* If, when I collapsed into our bed, the clock read 2.30am, I knew that by three she'd be screaming. Once again, I'd haul myself out of bed, stagger down the stairs, boil the kettle and pour steaming water into a Pyrex jug. Like an automaton, I'd take one of the prepared bottles of Ostermilk from the fridge, plunge it into the jug to warm and carry it up the stairs to the box room we had rather grandly christened 'the nursery'. My eyelids were leaden, the effort of lifting them so great that I would attempt to feed my daughter like a blind woman, knowing she would squirm and yell all over again.

It was July, the nights were hot and sticky, the curtains by the open window hung listless in the still night. Holding this yelling bundle, I thought, *If I just drop her out of the window, she'll stop.* No problem opening my eyes then. How could I think that about this sick baby I loved so much? I practically hurled her into her cot and ran back to our bedroom and Steve held my rigid body, as, between shudders, I told him how I had thought of silencing our daughter. When the house was silent I drifted on the borders of sleep but was aware of him slipping out of bed to close the nursery window. After that he offered to do the night feeds more often, but I was irritable and felt he was inept. I snapped at him that he was useless. I'd manage by myself. Then he'd go off on the 7.45 train in the morning and I would face the endless day with my two babies.

If I tried to feed Laura outside my cage, sitting on the sofa like any normal mother, Andrew, becoming impatient, would clamber on to us, push the bottle aside and press his face to mine, separating the two of us from his new unwelcome sister.

At fourteen months Andrew was not yet toddling. Instead he crawled around the room inspecting table legs and cupboard doors, grizzling when the French windows were a barrier to his route into the garden. Then he saw the television. This was interesting – he'd seen it before – something inside it moved. Hands and knees scuttled across the olive-green carpet and he reached his fist to grab the edge of the low melamine table that made an ideal TV stand. He pulled his chunky little body up and stood on uncertain feet. The TV wobbled before him. I dropped the feeding bottle and, holding Laura in one arm, was in mid-hurdle over my enclosure when the heavy set steadied and became still. He had pushed the on/ off button and a black and white image appeared on the screen. He sat back to enjoy the show and I retreated to my place of safety. But his attention span was limited and so was mine. My eyes wandered to the window. Two of my neighbours were chatting on the corner of the street. Another cycled up to join them. I watched them laughing and gesticulating. What was all that about, I wondered? I wanted to join in the conversation and resented being isolated in my house, my cage, by two small people.

I heard the crash. Both babies screamed. I leapt over the play-pen, a hollering Laura over my shoulder and grabbed Andrew with my free arm. The television lay on the floor, emitting a continual whistling noise to feed my panic.

'Shush, shush, it's all right, you're all right, Mummy's here.' I could barely hear my words over the thump of my heart. 'Come on, now, let's have a cuddle.' We retreated to the sofa, I retrieved Laura's bottle and she quietened as her lips clamped around the teat. Andrew curled himself into me, the tremors of his body matching my shaking frame. His terror subsided into long, juddering gasps and, as I cradled my two children, I looked at the whining box on the floor, imagining the trajectory of its fall. It might have hit him. I lay Laura on the carpet and moved fast nurse's fingers through Andrew's blond hair, searching for swelling, bruising, tenderness. I took off his clothes, examined chubby limbs, tore off his nappy, palpated his tummy. No bruises, no injuries. My shoulders dropped. We had been lucky.

Guilt grabbed me by the throat and I fought for breath. Once again, I had proved to be a bad mother. Should I call the NSPCC? I had thought of dropping one baby out of a window and then left my other child unsupervised in the wide world of a living room full of hazards.

The playpen went to the village jumble sale.

Now that we have been told a blow to the head might have been responsible for his tumour, the scene has returned to haunt me. Could the television have hit his head? There was no evidence, no marks, but might that have been the beginning? Was my neglect thirty years ago responsible for this present trauma?

October rolls on into November. We have appointed a new member of staff to act as manager in the Tunbridge Wells shop. Keeping it afloat is a challenge and the sensible decision would be to close it. But that would be like pulling the rug of hope from beneath Andrew's feet.

'As soon as I've been fit-free for whatever time it says, and I can drive again, I'll be back there, so I hope you've made clear to her that it's a temporary job,' Andrew tells us.

Twelve months. No seizures for twelve months is the rule, before there is any chance of getting his licence back, and he is still having major seizures once or twice a week. Will he ever drive again?

The drug regime is a balancing act. The medical team is keen to reduce the high doses of phenytoin and sodium valporate he is taking to control the seizures. In addition, it would be beneficial to lower his intake of dexamethazone, the steroid that reduces the swelling around the tumour. This drug also causes Cushing's syndrome – moon-faced appearance, increased appetite and the weight gain that is becoming a problem physically and psychologically. Lowering the dose of dex would alleviate those symptoms but the pressure of increased swelling would cause more seizures. Discussing this with Gosia I mutter about being 'between the devil and the deep blue sea', but she shrugs her shoulders, nonplussed at our British colloquialisms.

Eighteen

The shores of Cumbrian lakes on a sunny day in mid November are a riot of colour. Amber oak trees, coppery beeches and yellow larches dip their toe-like roots into the shallows and use the tranquil surface of the water as mirrors for their beauty. The autumn sun shines through tumbling leaves, turning them into golden confetti that crunches beneath walkers' feet. Above the treeline, hardy Herdwick sheep munch on what remains of summer grass and amble across high mountain roads, only moving with haughty reluctance to make way for sporadic vehicles. High fells, still veiled with a faint purple heather-haze, are reflected in quivering lakes, inviting the energetic to don walking boots and climb to the top of Helvellyn or Striding Edge and look down on a wild landscape preparing to bed down for winter.

It has become routine for us and our close friends Ken and Wendy, with whom we have holidayed for so many years, to spend a few days here each autumn. This year Matthew joins us for a day. He crosses the Pennines from his base on Holy Island where he is researching the effect of wildfowlers' guns on the fragile bird population.

As if sensing our mood of despair, the leaden sky weeps, obscuring the beauty we have come to enjoy. Seeking shelter under flagging foliage, we decide on a woodland walk. Matthew grasps my elbow and we slow our steps, distancing ourselves from the rest of the party.

'What's the news, Mum?' He hasn't heard the latest.

'Not good, love,' I gulp, in a valiant effort to keep my voice steady, and I describe our visit to the Royal Marsden. 'So, it seems it has now progressed to a grade three tumour and, and –' My words fracture, my face crumples.

He squeezes my arm tighter. I can feel his shock, his love, and tears blind me so that I trip on a small slippery rock, nearly losing my balance.

He supports me, 'It's all right Mum, I'm here.'

I right myself and tighten my resolve to enjoy this brief time with our youngest child. 'I know you are, love, and I am grateful.'

How often, especially over the last ten months, Steve and I have felt thankful for all our three children, for their love and support. But each child is loved in his or her own way, each occupies its own space in our hearts, each gives back to us its own joy. If one is to be torn away from us, however many children we might have, none can fill the gaping void that loss will leave.

While we've been away Andrew's seizures have become more frequent and the weakness in his left side has increased. His dragging foot has caused him to trip and fall so he has arranged an appointment with Dr B.

'I don't know where is this place,' Gosia says, alarmed at the prospect of the journey. Neither she nor Andrew know of Steve's and my earlier visit, but I profess to know the way and offer to drive him.

As before, Dr B is cheerful and affable, listening carefully to Andrew's concerns.

'A small change in doses of the steroids and the anti-convulsants should sort your problems, Andrew,' he reassures, reaching for his prescription pad. 'You can pick these up from the pharmacy today.' He stands, walks to the front of his desk and perches there. 'Now, you don't want the long journey here more often than necessary, so I want you to know about our telephone clinic.' He calls through the open door of the small consulting room for someone called Frances and a dark-haired, motherly woman of about my age, wearing a pink uniform, greets us.

'Frances here is my research nurse and she'll take you for a coffee and tell you all about how the clinic works.'

'Just one thing, doctor,' Andrew asks as we rise to leave, 'my wife and I would like to have another baby sometime, a brother or sister for Alice. How soon do you think we should start trying?'

The doctor throws a meaningful look at the nurse. 'Frances will advise you about that, I am sure.'

We relax over coffee in the cafeteria and Frances explains to Andrew that whenever he has concerns he can phone her on this number – she hands him a card – and she will advise if she is able, or refer to Dr B for an answer. If necessary, she'll arrange an appointment at the hospital. 'That goes for all the family,' she adds, looking at me, 'I am here for all of you.'

I like this woman, her humanity shines out. She inspires confidence and when she talks to Andrew he is the full focus of her attention. I trust her.

'You asked about plans for another baby,' she says. Of course, that is ultimately a decision for you and your wife, Andrew, but I would suggest you leave it for a while, to see how you get on. Something to think about though, is banking sperm. If you should need chemotherapy in the future, that is likely to make you sterile. There's no urgency, but a little jar of your sperm in the bank could come in very useful.'

My son's irrepressible grin asserts itself, 'What? You mean I've got to produce a jarful?'

'Just a small one,' she says, 'I'll give you a container like this,' she holds up a plastic specimen pot, 'and you can bring it whenever you're here next.'

Frances laughs when he says, 'I'll need more than one container.'

These two are going to get on well.

'I think I'll do a Christmas letter, like you do, Mum, to send with the cards. If I dictate will you type it? You know my handwriting's rubbish.'

I agree – on both counts, and type:

Dear—

Sorry this is a general letter, but you'll understand the reason when you read on. Let's get the apologies behind us – we are sorry if you didn't get a card last year.

As you may know 1997 hasn't been a good year for the Dennys of 1 Military Road, with the exception of seeing our two-year-old daughter, Alice, grow into a cheeky little monkey. The night of 16 December 1996 was an eventful one. Not long after going to sleep I fell unconscious and had strong fits. They rushed me to hospital where I lay comatose for twenty-four hours. Having been transferred to a neuro-centre I then spent four weeks teasing the nurses while Gosia, Alice and the family tried to come to terms with what had happened. The muscle spasms during the fits were so strong (I've always had Mr Atlas muscles) I managed to break my shoulder into five pieces but a very clever surgeon managed to pin it back together. I left hospital with a half-hearted diagnosis of a 'funny sort of stroke' and spent two months rehabilitating. Then things went downhill, and I ended up having a hole drilled in my head to find I had a brain tumour. It was low grade benign (which really means malignant) so they made me a mask like an alien and I had six weeks of radiotherapy. Currently the tumour has neither grown, nor shrunk so only time will tell. If you have any suggestions for a cure they will be gratefully received.

On a lighter note, it has meant a year off work (on full pay), so we were able to visit my brother Matthew in Northumberland and friends in Holland. We are looking forward to hot, sunny holidays next year.

I hope this is the one and only Christmas letter to tell such a dramatic story.

Thanks for all your support – let's hope 1998 will bring better things for everyone.

HAPPY CHRISTMAS.

Love from Andrew, Gosia and Alice

Gosia's mother is coming for Christmas. The restrictions on Eastern Europeans travelling to the West have relaxed in the six and a half years since she was refused permission to attend her only child's wedding. Then, she had pleaded with the British embassy in Warsaw, but the feeling was that an impoverished single woman in her fifties applying for a visa to come to her daughter's wedding could only mean one thing – that she planned to stay. Despite protestations that this was not the case, no leniency was shown. It was Gosia's second cousin Magda who had a well-paid job and a family to return to in Poland who was permitted to act as stand-in mother. She brought with her a niece, Martinka, a bonny blonde with a wide grin that revealed the bare gums of a six-year-old awaiting grown-up teeth. The little girl charmed everyone as a bridesmaid in a simple white cotton dress, her head crowned by a ring of rosebuds, but understood not a word that was said.

Grandmother in Polish translates as *babcia* and this is Alice's *babcia's*, second visit. She was here at our granddaughter's first birthday celebration, clapping her hands with glee as Alice sat in her very own red and yellow plastic car, tooting the horn. That was when a healthy Andrew was his naturally social, enthusiastic self, charming his mother-in-law. Now the prospect of entertaining her is daunting. She has not a word of English and he can barely say more than *dzien dobry* (good morning), *dziekuje* (thank you), and, of course, *na zdrowie* (cheers) in Polish. Gosia has much translating to do, despite her own English being far from perfect. The effort is exhausting and the atmosphere is taut with anxiety.

Cinderella is the pantomime playing at the White Rock Theatre in Hastings and I have left work early to join them at an early evening performance. On the fifty-yard walk from our parking place to the theatre Andrew pauses to lean against the boundary wall of the ornamental gardens. His hand trembles and he squeezes his eyelids shut, breathing deeply.

Gosia and I exchange looks of alarm and she tells her mother to continue down the road with Alice, while we support Andrew, ready to lay him on the damp pavement if the seizure develops. Alice obediently holds hands with her *babcia*, but as the distance stretches between them and us she looks back for our reassuring wave.

'No worries, it was only a small one,' Andrew says when he opens his eyes. Slowly, very slowly, we catch up with *Babcia*, Alice and the carefree crowd streaming towards the theatre. Excited children wave wands with coloured streamers and tiny flashing lights. Andrew fumbles in his pocket for change to buy one from the street vendor, determined his daughter will not be left out.

Thankfully seated at the end of the row of seats, in case of a possible seizure, Andrew and I enter into the absurdities of British panto. We encourage Alice to join in the audience call of, 'He's behind you,' when the ugly sisters are laying their wicked plans, and respond to their 'Oh no he isn't' with a loud 'Oh yes he is!' – again and again. At first uncertain, Alice soon enters in to the spirit of the show, beaming up at Andrew as she joins in the excitement, waving her sparkling wand, delighting in their common enjoyment. Meanwhile her Polish mother and grandmother smile uncertainly, then pull faces at one another, baffled by the inane antics on the stage and in the audience.

Recollections of last Christmas Day are resolutely ignored as the whole family gather in our fifteenth-century home. Massive logs burn in the inglenook fireplace and under the twinkling tree the stack of parcels in festive wrappings grows as each party arrives and adds its contribution. Our two small granddaughters sit on the brick step that divides the levels of the kitchen comparing Alice's scruffy caterpillar with Katie's brand-new teddy, but Alice holds Pillar in a close embrace – he will always be the best. I open the door of the Aga releasing the seasonal aroma of sizzling turkey and silently congratulate myself. *It's done to a turn*, as my granny would have said. Familiar arms clasp around my waist, and a kiss from the lips I have known so intimately for thirty-three years is planted on the back of my neck.

'Well done, sweetie. Now come and have a drink with everyone. This is a very special Christmas.'

My shoulders sink and any euphoria over a perfectly cooked turkey is sucked out of me. 'I know. There might not be another…' But Steve silences me with another kiss, this one on my lips.

This year Alice is big enough, with her granddad's help, to bring in the flaming pudding and Andrew shouts, 'Hooray for the pudding' and claps the loudest of all of us. His expression is full of pride and love but his eyes glisten with sadness. My chest tightens; I know what thoughts he is trying to push away – of all those future Christmases when he may not be here to watch his beautiful daughter.

Nineteen

Nineteen ninety-eight begins quietly. Apart from a freak whirlwind the other side of Sussex, the weather is mild. January is uncharacteristically sunny. The brightness does not penetrate the cottage in Military Road, however. Gloom surrounds the little family. Even habitually sunny Alice is crotchety and Gosia's face is perpetually grim. Andrew doesn't have the energy to engage in conversation and berates his left leg for its weakness and propensity to trip him up.

Well-meaning friends bombard us with suggestions, stories and newspaper cuttings about miracle cures.

'I've heard of an operation in America.'

'What about the gamma knife I read about in the *Daily Mail*?'

'There's this wonderful man in China. The treatment's a bit unconventional but he gets great results.'

'We'll do some fundraising.'

I know most are either unsuitable, anecdotal or quack remedies, but if there is a straw, surely we should clutch it?

Steve and I have a long-awaited holiday planned in Sri Lanka with Ken and Wendy, beginning on the nineteenth of January. Should we cancel?

'Of course not. Just wish I was going with you,' Andrew replies when we moot the possibility. 'You'll only be away two weeks. I'll still be alive when you get back.' My stomach tightens when he adds a barely audible, 'I hope.'

Before we leave I write to Dr B:

We hear of many advancements in the treatment of gliomas and, although we have every confidence in the treatment Andrew is currently receiving, we feel we would be failing him if we did not at least begin to investigate them. We are therefore enclosing some pieces of information for your comments as we would not wish to proceed without your advice.

Generous friends have offered financial help and have plans to raise as much money as necessary, but we are conscious of the dangers of spending it unwisely.

Yours sincerely,

Janet and Steve Denny

Sri Lanka is a country full of gentle people, ancient history, intriguing wildlife and captivating beauty. Sweating our way through the rainforest, bird book in hand, we discover rose-ringed parakeets, paradise flycatchers and a chestnut-headed bee-eater in its rainbow plumage. We marvel at giant stone Buddhas lying peacefully, surrounded by camera-clicking tourists at the Temple of Dambulla. At the elephant orphanage, I experience mixed feelings of gratitude that the animals are being cared for and discomfort that they are gawped at by coachloads of visitors. My lasting impressions of the Temple of the Tooth in Kandy are gold and silver decoration, women in jewel-coloured saris, smooth-skinned children with wide brown eyes, and a great press of noisy people.

I feel Andrew with me everywhere, engaging with the locals, in awe of the beauty, feigning an ironic yawn as our guide proudly shows us yet another stupa – one of the hundreds of beehive-shaped mounds housing holy relics.

When we visit Sygirya, the massive rock fortress, we climb to the top, passing glowing frescoes of bare-breasted beauties, painted fifteen hundred years ago. On level ground once more, I break away from the party to sit alone. This enormous flat-topped volcanic plug rises out of a vast plateau and it feels like I could be at the top of the world.

Andrew will never come here, never have this, or many other experiences he had planned. 'I want to travel the whole world, Mum,' he'd said, as a teenager, 'and I've got a whole lifetime to do it.' So, how long is a lifetime? Tears prick my eyes, course down my cheeks and, without warning, I am rocked by uncontrollable sobbing. This is not like me; I don't do crying. I am the mother, the centre of the family and the centre must hold. I must stay strong. For now, though, the barrier is breached, and I lose control.

A figure shimmers into view through my tears. A wizened old woman in a green and gold sari, she wears round gold-rimmed spectacles, her grey hair is drawn back into a bun. Wordlessly, she sits beside me, reaches for my hand and squeezes it. Then she touches her lips to my cheek and sits with me until my sobbing subsides. I unearth a tissue from the pocket of my shorts, wipe my face and blow my nose. I begin to explain but the words stutter incoherently as my throat constricts and my body shudders. She indicates that she speaks no English, but she doesn't need to. She understands only that I am in distress and in need of comfort. We sit for a while – I've no idea how long, and when I am calm I look into her patient brown eyes. 'Thank you,' I say and as I walk back to Steve and our friends I turn and see her arm is held out in a gesture of blessing.

Cold winds whistle us to the car park at Heathrow on our return and the news, when we reach home, has no warmth in it either. Andrew has fallen several times. 'I keep tripping up,' he tells us, 'can't seem to lift my left foot.' He is gaining more weight because the steroids are increasing his appetite. He is tired and depressed.

Among the pile of two weeks' post that greets us at home we find a letter from Dr B suggesting we may be interested in coming to a carers' support meeting when alternative therapies will be considered. Gosia recoils at the suggestion and Steve has a council meeting he must attend, so I drive the familiar route – A21, M25, A217 to the Royal Marsden, with Sergeant Pepper's Lonely Hearts Club Band filling my ears with old favourites.

I feed the parking machine with several pound coins and the

lack of Andrew leaning on my arm feels strangely liberating. The meeting, when I locate it, is surprisingly crowded with carers, young and old. Sipping a welcome coffee, I wave to Frances, the research nurse who is such a support to Andrew. She is in conversation with a couple of about my age. The woman has her back to me but when she turns I recognise her. Thirty years ago, we did our nursing training together at Westminster Hospital. Since then we have met briefly at hospital reunions and now I recall that she lives in Surrey and is still in the profession. Frances moves off and I move in. 'Di,' I say, 'what a coincidence, I didn't know you were working here.'

Her look of surprise melts into a smile of recognition and she lays her arm on my shoulder. 'Janet, whatever are you doing here?'

'It's my son,' my voice is heavy, 'he has a brain tumour. Do you work on the oncology team?'

We move to occupy some vacant chairs near the window and when we are seated Di says, 'I don't work here, Janet.' She introduces her husband, Barrie, and her next words sound so unreal they might have been plucked from a novel. 'Our son also has a brain tumour.'

Simon, a few months older than Andrew, has been travelling a similar route, his parents experiencing the same anguished helplessness as Steve and me. During our training Di and I had never been close friends but now we feel bound together, fighting a common foe, endeavouring, and failing, to protect our boys.

We sit through a question and answer session on alternative therapies, many of which Dr B dismisses and urges us not to be tempted by 'miracle cures' reported in the press. He understands that families will do anything to preserve the life of a loved one but pleads with us to discuss any moves with him before spending money on unproven alternative remedies. I have had this conversation already. Andrew's schoolfriend, Mary, is the daughter of one of the Fab Four, and her dad has indicated that there is money available if there is anything that can help Andrew. But, like us, that family is living with the knowledge that there are things no amount of money can buy – like miracle cures for cancer.

Phone conversations with Linda McCartney have cheered Andrew.

He and this well-known woman are travelling the cancer trail at the same time, and Linda, with her belief in vegetarian organic remedies, has sent him an enormous parcel of green tea.

On my journey home from the Marsden, I try to process this surprising evening, buoyed up by finding an old friend in the same position as me, then ashamed of the feeling and wishing we hadn't met in such circumstances.

Andrew is cheered when I recount the story to him and is keen to speak with Simon. They never meet, but a friendship of sorts is forged on the phone.

Meanwhile a CT scan suggests a high-grade tumour and in the first week of February Dr B confirms the bad news of tumour progression. Andrew, Steve, Gosia and I discuss all options with Dr B who assures those of us who hadn't heard it before that there is no need to go abroad; in fact, he feels strongly that any further treatments are available here for free here at the Marsden. He has seen too many patients spend savings and submerge themselves and their families in debt to follow quack remedies in far-flung countries. We all believe him. Chemotherapy is the next recommended treatment and when we ask again about surgery we are told it is almost certainly not an option, but Dr B will forward Andrew's scans to Henry Marsh, a highly respected neurosurgeon at the Atkinson Morley Hospital, for another opinion.

Frances, Dr B's research nurse, takes Andrew and Gosia aside to suggest that now is the time to consider banking sperm and supplies a suitable container. On the journey home, our anxious concern is covered with ribald jokes about dirty magazines. Andrew maintains there is no need. After all, he has his beautiful, sexy wife.

When she drives him to Surrey for his first chemo dose Gosia has a full plastic jar tucked down her bra between her boobs. 'Well, got to keep our future children warm,' says Andrew.

He tolerates the first dose of chemical poisons well. He's tired certainly, but suffers no nausea and jokes that hair loss is no problem to a bald-headed man. Six weeks later, however, when I take him for the next treatment a young woman at the reception desk hands Andrew a letter and leaves us in a small airless treatment room to read it. It is a copy of Henry Marsh's reply to Dr B. In uncompromising terms, it states that although he (Mr Marsh) is known for his radical approach, in Andrew's case any surgical intervention would be disastrous owing to the position and size of the tumour. He writes that he has looked at the original MRI scan done at Hurstwood Park and has absolutely no doubt that the tumour had undergone malignant change by that stage and the prognosis from the start was necessarily poor.

So much for 'a funny sort of stroke.'

Another meteor has crashed into Andrew and rocked his existence with no preparation, no warning, but my son's stoicism in the face of this latest blow amazes me. He rolls his eyes, hands me the letter and says, 'Tear it up, Mum, I don't want to read it again. Let's just forget all talk of surgery and concentrate on the chemo.' He even manages a joke with the nurse who spears the vein in his arm. I, however, am furious and leave him to absorb the toxins while I seek out whoever is standing in for Frances, who is off duty today. When I find him, and show him the letter, the nurse hammers his head with his fist. 'I am so sorry, this should never have happened,' he says testily. 'I can only suppose that, as the letter had Andrew's name on it, it was handed to him without reference to the team.' A simple mistake perhaps, but the abject apology comes too late.

As we leave the hospital I am still a seething cauldron of wrath, ready to boil over, but Andrew calms me. 'Forget it, Mum, it's Majorca in a couple of weeks.'

During those two weeks Linda McCartney dies. 'She fought so hard, Mum.' My son thumps his hand on to the arm of the sofa. 'She tried everything, but nothing could save her. Fucking, bloody cancer.'

Twenty

It is May and Andrew's entire family – wife, daughter, parents, brother, sister, brother-in-law, niece, aunt and both grannies – are travelling with him for a week in Majorca. Thinking it would be a good idea to have a (I refuse to think *last*) holiday all together we have hired a large villa near Pollensa, a resort well known to us, in the less crowded north of the island. Steve's mother has never flown before and is terrified. But in support of her grandson she has gathered up her courage, obtained a passport and she giggles like a nervous schoolgirl as we go through security. Andrew is irritated to find that we have arranged wheelchair assistance at the airport, but grateful when the corridors at Palma prove to be even longer than those at Gatwick.

Mediterranean sun, sea and food is enjoyed by all of us and the week sees celebrations of Granny's eightieth and Laura's thirtieth birthdays. The little girls paddle and splash in the shallows then set to with buckets and spades watched by great-grannies on wobbly folding beach chairs, who applaud their castle-building efforts. Gosia stretches on the sand soaking up the sun while Steve and Matthew take Andrew on a birdwatching trip.

In the cool, cavernous kitchen of the villa the pre-prepared domestic rota (two cooks, two washers-up per night) runs smoothly and with the children in bed the adults enjoy evenings by the pool under the stars. Andrew is seizure-free, but his signature laughter is forced, animation all but missing, and his sky-blue eyes are clouded with sadness. The strain of pretending life is normal and jolly crackles in the air. Faces are plastered with fake smiles, teeth are gritted, eyes moist and tempers, controlled all week, flare on the final day.

Perhaps this holiday wasn't a good idea after all.

The summer rolls on in six-week segments, each marked by another chemo appointment. Andrew drags his leg like it's filled with lead, too heavy to lift from the ground, so the dose of dexamethazone is increased, and so are the resulting side effects. He avoids looking in the mirror at a flushed moon-shaped face or at his increasingly large naked body. Where has that good-looking fit young man gone?
A scan before his third treatment shows the tumour stable – no bigger, but no smaller either. Is that good news? We pretend it is.

He is proud when he and Gosia are invited to Linda McCartney's memorial service at St Martin's in the Fields. Celebrity spotting is diverting, but not enough to distract him from the sadness of the occasion. When he tells us about it, there is no excitement in his voice; his heart is heavy.

In July, a routine blood test shows his white cell count to be low but just about acceptable for his fourth treatment to go ahead. In August, he counts it as a triumph that the same applies but grand mal seizures are plaguing him – one about every ten days. Sitting outside the Mermaid fish and chip restaurant with Gosia and Alice when they visit the local seaside town of Hastings, he feels one beginning. Gosia lays him on the ground – she is used to managing these events now – but horrified onlookers rush to call 999. Andrew describes to us what happened next. 'When I came to, I looked up and saw Nick – you know, that guy from Northiam who was in my class at school. He's a paramedic now and when he saw I was okay, he said, "Might have known it'd be you, Andy, you were always trouble." Then Robert (also an old schoolmate whose family own the café) came up and said, "S'pose you'll want a refund on the bill now?" We had a real laugh. I always said I wanted to be a celebrity, but I hadn't quite envisaged lying on the ground being peered at and then applauded by Hastings holidaymakers.'

Another increase in medication means fewer and less severe fits but in October his final chemotherapy dose is delayed twice because of a low blood count.

Twenty-One

Occasionally Gosia drives Andrew the short distance to the shop, but he rarely stays for more than half an hour before his face is etched with exhaustion and anxiety and he admits defeat and reluctantly asks, 'Sorry, Dad, can you ring Gosia, ask her to pick me up?'

However much we try to include him, seek his opinion on new stock or ask him to do small tasks, he tires easily and feels like a spare part. Most of all he fears the indignity of suffering a seizure in public.

Spending inactive days at home, boredom, anxiety and frustration dominate our boy's existence. He dreams of a day when he will be driving again, back at work in his own shop, engaging with customers, negotiating with reps. He misses the competition between our branches, the sweet moment when, comparing takings at the end of the day, he finds Tunbridge Wells has done better than Rye.

'Going to Southwold any time soon?' Andrew enquires when Steve and I drop in to see them at the end of a busy day in the Rye shop. His tone is casual, but I know why he asks.

We hadn't intended an imminent visit to our cottage on the Suffolk coast. It's the tail end of the summer tourist season and in Rye we are busy seven days a week.

Andrew loves Southwold and a change of scene might cheer him, and also give Gosia a break. Secretly I relish the prospect of being just the three of us. Time to talk, time to enjoy our son without distraction, is appealing.

'Why not? Like to come with us, lad?' Steve reads my mind, as we enjoy a cool glass of wine and Andrew downs another tasteless non-alcoholic alternative without complaint. He is instantly alert, animated. 'Yeah. But what about the shops?'

Steve reassures him. 'Can't see a problem. Schools go back next week, so the staff will cope in Rye for Monday and Tuesday. It's a quiet time of year in Tunbridge Wells, Liz can manage on her own.'

So, after a busy September Sunday trading, we collect Andrew from the cottage in Military Road.

'Can I come to the seaside, too, Daddy?' pleads Alice.

Andrew bites his bottom lip and wrestles with the decision he and Gosia have made.

'I need you to stay here and look after Mummy, Booboo. And you don't want to miss any fun at nursery school, do you?' We all feel mean, but he hugs her, saying, 'Not this time Booboo, but I'll take you there soon – promise.' He knows that time alone with her daughter is precious to Gosia.

Steve breaks the tension. 'Got everything? Okay, let's go.'

In the late nineties, the Suffolk coastal town of Southwold has begun to appear more and more in the Sunday supplements and upmarket magazines, described as, 'a hidden gem'. Lying at the end of a two-mile dead-end road that branches off the A12, the only other access is to trek across the marshes or to sail into the harbour of the River Blyth from the North Sea.

Fishing, brewing and boat-building have sustained the community for centuries. Those trades survive now thanks to the support of an influx of second-home owners who spend money in the town, relax in front of their over-priced beach huts with a tray of tea, sail their yachts out of the harbour, or risk the polite disapproval of golfers as they walk across the greens on the common. Herring gulls screech as they racket over the rooftops, eager to pounce on fish and chip remnants or cast-offs from fishing boats. At times, the pungent aroma of malted hops from Adnams brewery pervades the town, inviting visitors into the Nelson, the number one hostelry.

To our family, however, Southwold is more than a pleasant, old-fashioned holiday resort. It is the place where the Dennys were planted two hundred years ago – and to Andrew those roots are a source of great pride. His great-great-grandfather founded the tailor's business in the market place, still in the family, still called Denny's. The little town has been a place of annual pilgrimage throughout his life. Our family have holidayed in hired cottages, spooky Victorian houses or what were once the cramped homes of coastguards and lighthouse-keepers.

In juddering old family cine-films Andrew appears as a tottering fourteen-month-old trying (and failing) to stay upright on chubby, cherubim legs. A few years later he is shouting at the waves, Canute-like, chuckling, then shrieking as they knock him off his feet and envelop him in the surf. My memory bank holds pictures of him burying his dad's legs in the sand, plastering his own face with ice cream and as a two-year-old standing solemnly in the churchyard as his Southwold-born grandfather's ashes were interred.

There were interminable arguments with his brother and sister over who had caught the biggest crab by dangling a hook baited with bacon over the harbour wall. Serious stuff; after all, Southwold is the venue for the World Crabbing Championships.

A few years ago, in advance of the explosion in house prices, we were able to buy our own small second home. Once the servants' quarters attached to the rear of a larger house, Stern Cottage is within sound, if not sight, of the waves.

Tonight, we arrive after dark and pause on the promenade to feast our eyes on the moonlit sea before groping our way down the unlit alley that leads to our front door.

A cup of tea and a snack later, Steve carries our luggage up the steep cottage stairs followed by Andrew in peg-leg fashion, his left leg incapable of lifting on to the next tread.

I am struggling to fit a duvet into its cover when Andrew calls from his room as he is unpacking, 'Uh, oh, no medication.'

My muscles tense, alert to danger as I cross the landing, to confirm his bag is empty and there are no drugs.

'I asked if you had everything before we left.' Steve sounds tetchy.

I rein in my rising panic. The important drugs are dexamethasone to control the swelling round the tumour and a cocktail of anti-convulsants to control the fits. Shall we turn tail and drive the three hours home now, or can we wait until the morning?

Andrew sits on his bed, head bowed, tears welling.

'No worries, as you would say, love. Which do you take in the evening?'

'I took the phenytoin before we left home, 'cos I was worried about a fit on the way. So, I think it's only the dex tonight.'

'Okay. I expect you can do without that until tomorrow.'

While Andrew is having a pee Steve and I have a whispered conversation. There is no phone in the house, so he will go to the call box around the corner on St James' Green, phone Gosia, and ask her to check the medication regime.

Surely there must be a way we can continue our short break, but the medication is vital. By the time Steve returns with a list of drug doses and times, I have looked up the number of the local GP. Is it too late to call him? Yes, but I'm going to leave a message to be picked up first thing in the morning.

This is an old-fashioned town in many ways and my call is transferred from the surgery number to the doctor's home where he is probably enjoying a glass of wine in front of the telly – *Men Behaving Badly* or *Jools Holland*, perhaps. I explain our problem in detail, with abject apologies for interrupting his Sunday evening, but he is remarkably unfazed and listens patiently.

'Poor old chap,' he says, when I pause for breath. 'He'll be fine without anything until the morning. I'll pop in around seven-thirty, before surgery.'

Save for toothbrushes and pyjamas our bags remain packed and we sleep fitfully, planning the homeward journey.

'Morning.' The doctor greets Steve when he opens the door just before seven-thirty the next day. We welcome a balding grey-haired man of about sixty sporting a red and black bow tie and a creased pale linen suit, in his hand a scuffed leather bag. He only needs a pipe in his mouth to complete the image of the family doctors of my childhood. He brushes aside our gratitude for this early visit and mounts the stairs to see Andrew. Sitting on his bed he peruses the notes Gosia dictated to Steve last night, then opens his bag to search through a muddle of packets and bottles. 'Ah, I don't seem to have the right dosages.'

I think, *So, we'll have to go home after all.*

I say, 'We can be home before lunch. Do you think he'll be okay until then?'

'No need for that. Jump in my car and we'll get some from the surgery. You don't want to go home, do you, old chap?'

Andrew grins, 'No way. Thanks, Doc.'

I travel next to the doctor in his very old open-topped Jag – it fits the picture – to the other end of town. 'How long are you here for?' he asks.

'Until Tuesday.'

'Wait here,' he instructs and disappears into a 1960s building. Casting my eyes over the jumble of objects on the back seat, I am amused – and amazed – to see a selection of drugs and needles. How does he know I'm not a thieving druggie?

He returns and jumps into the front seat beside me, bearing enough medications for Andrew's needs for two days. Carefully he explains the prescriptions to me and then offers to drive me home. I want to throw my arms round this kind man, but I resist temptation and thank him for his offer, which I decline, conscious of his busy day ahead.

I float home on a cloud of relief.

Two sunlit days, and we feel blessed. We revisit familiar places, like the Sailor's Reading Room where we once found a blurred photo of Great-Uncle Paul staring into a hole in the ground in about 1916. They're gone now – the hole, the photo and, indeed, Great-Uncle Paul, but we're here to remember. We take short walks past the colourful beach huts, noting that one, among a group with royal names, has *Andrew* painted on a plaque over the door. Fish and chips served in paper at the Harbour Inn, birdwatching at Minsmere, all these activities trigger memories. We wallow in a comfortable past, as if it might negate an unknown future.

Small birds scurry at the water's edge and Andrew lifts his binoculars to his eyes. 'Dunlin,' he declares.

'Let's see,' Steve takes the field glasses from him. 'Yep, you're right.'

'Course I am, Dad. Don't forget, I was the champion,' and he punches the air with his right fist.

'What started your interest in birdwatching, Andrew?' In 1976 the serious elderly members of the Sevenoaks RSPB group had asked the new nine-year old member of the junior section, impressed that he had won the bird-recognition quiz at the summer fair.

His grin disarmed them as he answered simply, 'Peanut butter.'

Steve couldn't resist explaining that on the back of the label on the peanut butter jar was an invitation to join the Young Ornithologist's Club, and our boy just loved to be part of a club, especially if he could be the star – or the clown.

Minsmere, the flagship RSPB Reserve, lies just along the coast from Southwold, which meant repeated visits by the whole family. Andrew's interest grew, as did Steve's, and especially Matthew's. I provided the sandwiches and sat for what seemed like many hours peering through binoculars and feigning excitement when, clinging to a trembling reed, was an indistinct shape which my boys identified as a reed warbler or a bearded tit. Laura covered her ears with her hands and declared, 'I hate birds. Can we go now?"

Between the peanut butter and Minsmere came Mrs Russell Smith.

At that time, our home was a new-build among a maze of new-builds occupied by commuters in North Kent. But Steve and I had a dream. It was of an old Suffolk farmhouse, moated perhaps, nestling among the gentle undulations, streams, wide skies and salt marshes, which surprise the visitor to the coastal strip of East Suffolk. This imagined home sat beneath a steeply gabled roof covered in ubiquitous East Anglian pantiles.

In anticipation of finding our dream house (which, some years later, we discovered in Sussex, not Suffolk), we had started to collect suitable period furniture and bygones. Not the fine pieces gracing the windows of elegant antique shops in wealthy villages, but country chairs and dressers, warming pans and milking stools to be found in rural barns or small ads.

By a series of recommendations and explorations of remote country lanes we located Mrs Russell Smith on her ancient Suffolk farm. She was a collector and dealer in such items. A gracious, mysterious lady of what seemed to us all a great age, she welcomed us as we poked around the treasure-trove of furniture and artefacts in her barn while the children grew bored and restless.

'Why don't I take the children into the house while you look, my dears?' she suggested. 'I'll make some tea. Come in when you are ready.'

'Great idea.' Andrew was always up for something interesting (and he thought an old house with an old lady could be interesting – and cake might come with the tea). He followed her across the yard with his little brother in tow. Laura frowned and tightened her grip on my hand.

Having selected a few items we were interested in, we too meandered through the clucking chickens towards the open back door of the farmhouse. The kitchen table was covered with a cloth embroidered with primroses and violets and, in the centre, a green and white striped jug held catkins and pussy willow. A fine bone china tea set was laid out and Mrs Russell Smith turned from the Aga, holding a silver teapot.

'Come in, come in. The tea's made and we've been talking about birds. My, your Andrew knows a lot about them – an extraordinary boy.'

He was sitting with a large book in his hands and a superior expression on his face. Behind our hostess's back, he stuck his tongue out at his sister. As we feasted on homemade bread, with churned butter, and honey from the beehives we had noticed in the fields, we negotiated the price of a washing dolly and a pine dough-bin. The children's stock of good behaviour was running low, so we settled our deal and went to load our purchases into the car. Before we left, the lady of the house insisted on presenting to Andrew the *Reader's Digest Book of British Birds* with its detailed illustrations.

For the remainder of that summer he studied every page. Each night, instead of a story, he insisted on us testing his powers of recognition by covering up the name of the bird while he triumphantly identified it.

The avian obsession only lasted a few months, however, to be replaced by Action Man, or Cubs, or maybe his new BMX bike. Nevertheless, two decades later, when Matthew was on his way to a PhD in Ornithology, Andrew was anxious to remind his brother that it was he who was responsible for introducing him to the joys of watching birds and he looked proud enough to have gained the qualification himself.

We leave Southwold with some reluctance on Tuesday after an early supper of scallops, bacon, salad and locally baked bread.

'What's next?' Andrew's appetite (and his weight) increases by the day, thanks to the effects of steroids. Ice cream with shortbread fills the bill.

The A12 isn't too busy – the rush hour is over. We've passed Ipswich and the Spice Girls on the car radio are exhorting the listener to *Spice up Your Life*. Steve would rather have Classic FM but Andrew prefers Radio One. We are crossing the bridge over the river Orwell when I feel Andrew kicking the back of my seat. 'Mum, fit...'

'Steve, pull up, he's having a seizure.' In my head I am screaming, but to my son, to my husband, I am in control as usual.

Steve squeezes his reply through tight lips. 'Soon as I can. There's nowhere on the bridge.'

I twist my body to reach out to Andrew. 'Try and lie along the seat, love,' I tell him, knowing the seizure will force him to extend his legs. If he has no room, will he break them?

At the end of the bridge Steve pulls sharply on to the verge. We leap out and pull open the rear door. Andrew's arms and legs are jerking, his eyes are rolling. Awkwardly, we lift our son from the car and lie him on the grass, kneeling beside him as vehicles swish past, headlights sweeping over us, then leaving us in the silent twilight. Steve says, 'It's all right, lad, you're safe, you're okay', while I hold his arm as the jerks diminish to twitches and gradually dwindle into trembling. The seizure is subsiding and his eyes dart around, puzzled at where he is.

'Bloody hell, Dad, is this the best place you could find?'

'Cheeky devil. I didn't have much choice, did I?' Steve's words are drowned out by the engine of a heavy lorry, but he is smiling.

For the remainder of the journey I sit in the corner of the back seat with my thirty-one-year-old boy resting his head in my lap – like a baby.

Twenty-Two

It seems like a lifetime ago that Alice and I sat in that little room watching the fish tank in Hurstwood Park Hospital. Then, I happily ignored the details of the Brain Tumour Foundation on the poster stuck to the wall. Andrew had just been told 'definitely no tumour' by the consultant surgeon and I was beginning to suspend my disbelief. After the diagnosis was changed and the dreaded 'T' word re-entered our lives, we were thrashing about in a fog of ignorance. On one of many sleepless nights I recalled the name of the charity and wondered why I hadn't contacted them. What may they be able to tell me? How could they support Andrew? I phoned the hospital early next morning and asked for the phone number. 'I don't know what you are talking about,' said the voice on the other end of the line. 'I've never heard of this organisation.'

Stupid woman. My anger at everything about Hurstwood Park still burned hot. Tight-lipped, I asked, 'Please will you go to that horrid little room with the fish tank and look for a curling, grubby notice on the wall. Then look down the list of phone numbers until you find Brain Tumour Foundation.' To my surprise she agreed and as I held on I wondered if the notice was still there, or even if it had been a figment of my imagination.

I was in luck. When she picked up the receiver the woman said, 'Oh yes, well I never knew about that,' and gave me the contact details.

*

Now, a year later, we know BTF to be a small 'kitchen table' charity set up by a young mother, whose husband has a brain tumour, and her occupational therapist friend. The information and support they've given us on our journey has been like a warm blanket of friendship. They know what we are experiencing. In the pages of their newsletter we meet others, hear their stories, read their poems, their jokes, and understand that we are not alone. There is a whole brain tumour community out there.

Autumn is approaching and Matthew, living in Newcastle, determined to improve his fitness, enters himself for the Great North Run and the Brain Tumour Foundation is his chosen charity. Andrew fundraises enthusiastically, gathering sponsorship from friends and indeed anyone he meets – and who can resist? On the day of the event Matthew and a friend who is based in the same city achieve very creditable times and raise several thousands of pounds.

Andrew is overjoyed and suggests to the charity that the money should be ring-fenced to provide small financial treats for sufferers. 'I know money is needed for research,' he tells them, 'but a few thousand pounds would be a drop in the ocean. Let's do something for people while they are alive.' And that is the beginning of The Denny Care and Relief Fund which, during the years it functions, provides many treats: holidays, driving lessons for partners, taxi fares to hospital appointments and Christmas dinners and gifts for impoverished families. Our family continues to fundraise and it gives Andrew a focus beyond himself – and the bloody tumour.

A BTF collecting box sits on our shop counter beside the cash register. Sarah, manning the till, notices a middle-aged woman with a young man beside her, push a five-pound note through the slot. She calls me over to explain why we support the charity. The young man tells me that he also has a brain tumour but is doing okay.

'Long may it continue,' I say with what feels like false optimism, but this may not be a glioma and other types of tumour have a much better prognosis. The woman locks eyes with me and I guess she is a mother experiencing the same pain as I am. They are probably some of the many tourists who visit our town and as I bid them goodbye and good luck I expect I will never see them again.

But I do. The district nurse, when she is taking Andrew's next blood test, tells him there is a young man in Rye who would like to meet him. He also has a brain tumour and he and his mother have seen the collecting box in our shop. Can she introduce them?

Richard is about Andrew's age with a young wife, Helen. When the two couples meet an instant rapport progresses to a firm friendship – four young people united against a common enemy.

In late October, another grand mal seizure leaves Andrew unconscious and he's blue-lighted to hospital. The drug regime is adjusted once more to control the fits but when he is discharged it is clear his general condition has worsened and there is no going back. Walking is slow and difficult, his left arm all but useless. A scan in November confirms further disease progression, but a glimmer of hope appears when Dr B suggests Andrew may like to take part in the trial of a new drug, temozolomide. He jumps at the chance, discounting the possible unpleasant side effects. 'I don't care if I'm sick, Doc. It's all in a good cause.' Then softly he adds, 'For someone – if not for me.'

I will not let my heart break. Like my son, I will cling to this raft of hope that the current has washed towards us as we are tossed in an ever-stormier sea.

Lelly, now his friend as well as his GP, visits regularly and convinces him to have a wheelchair for use when he's tired. It will be helpful for him – and for Gosia. He nods his head in reluctant acceptance. A pain in his leg proves to be evidence of a deep vein thrombosis caused by lack of movement, so he begins on a course of blood-thinning Warfarin and the district nurse, whom he jovially addresses as 'Miss Vampire', calls regularly to collect a syringe-full of blood for testing. Frances from the Marsden phones him each week for long, intimate conversations, a Macmillan nurse visits to advise on benefits and an occupational therapist advises on adaptions to the house – grab handles, raised toilet seats, railings along the garden path. The Conservation Society, eagle-eyed in our ancient town, object to the latter, saying planning permission must be obtained.

'Sod them,' says Andrew, and we go ahead with the installation.

At last, after a long, rocky road, a caring support network is in place, but Andrew finds it difficult to smile about. So does Gosia. However, in November, life is stable enough for the little family to enjoy a relaxing visit to friends who have moved to southern Spain.

The first dose of temozolomide produces no nasty side effects but we are aware that immuno-suppression is likely, so we watch for the slightest sign of cold or flu-like symptoms.

Another traditional family Christmas passes and in the days before the New Year we arrive for the next appointment at the Marsden to find it decked with Christmas trees and tinsel. The usual line of pale, emaciated dressing-gowned patients sit outside in the cold puffing on their fags. As ever, my horror at cancer victims dependent on the white tubes of tobacco that have possibly contributed to their disease is overtaken by compassion for those who need their comfort.

Andrew's blood test shows evidence of bone-marrow suppression which, together with the suspicion of a cold, precludes today's planned chemo treatment. An increased dose of steroids has reduced the swelling around the tumour, eradicating troublesome headaches and improving his mobility. But Dr B's registrar, a young man from South Africa who shares Andrew's sense of humour, is keen to gradually reduce the dose and, hopefully, his weight-gain. He tells us that if there's no further disease progression at the next appointment in early February he can continue on the trial.

January signals the start of the trade-fair season and we recognise that Andrew won't be up to the big Birmingham Gift Fair this year. Instead Steve tentatively suggests the smaller Torquay Fair in mid-January. 'Of course I'll come, Dad,' says our boy, 'anything to break the monotony.' When we wave goodbye to Gosia and Alice the little girl's lower lip quivers – 'I'll bring you back a present, Booboo,' her daddy says and hugs her as tightly as she holds her beloved caterpillar.

A night at Laura's home in Chichester breaks our outward journey. Brother and sister hug each other, all childhood rivalries forgotten. Andrew jokes about Laura's pregnant belly.

'Well done, sis. Never fear, we'll be catching you up soon.' Katie, at two, holds her arms up and, initially puzzled, runs to find a book when he explains that he can't pick her up but would love to sit on the sofa to read a story.

'Alice loves Pingu, Katie,' he says.

'So do I. And Winnie Pooh, but I like this one best.' Katie curls into Uncle Andrew, his good arm surrounding her, and they are lost in a Mister Men story.

Laura closes her eyes, clasps her father's hand and turns away. Later he tells me, 'She's got your genes, won't let her emotions show.'

The West Country in January is usually grey, often wet, and this year it's both. We've booked a family room in the hotel. Andrew will need Steve's help with showering and I'm happier that he doesn't sleep alone.

Hilly Torquay is a challenge to pushers of wheelchairs, but we try not to let Andrew hear our puffing breath as it takes the strength of both of us to push him up what at first sight appear to be gentle slopes.

The three-day exhibition is spread over assorted hotel rooms and marquees, thankfully heated – the winter winds are biting in the 'Tropical' Gardens. Andrew discards the undignified wheelchair in favour of a stick and his dad's support as we make our slow way around the stands. Familiar suppliers, many we would count as friends, having dealt with them for so many years, greet us warmly. Andrew's penchant for repartee is undiminished and the people we meet are unfailingly responsive and kind. But their words falter, their faces flush or blanch when they see Andrew's condition, and I can sense their discomfort as the situation becomes clear to them. Their expressions as they bid us farewell are full of compassion for all three of us.

Andrew's staying power is limited so we bow out a day early. We haven't found many new, exciting lines, but we're pleased we came – our boy is smiling, enjoying the world again.

But this has not been a business trip, it has been a last goodbye.

Twenty-Three

'So, where shall we go on holiday?' Andrew throws out the question on a January evening in our kitchen as he shovels down a second helping of chicken casserole with potatoes, carrots and broccoli. I watch with mixed feelings as he consumes increasingly gargantuan meals. There is not much, these days, to make Andrew smile but food is a highlight in long, frustrating days. He needs those highlights. Combined with the impossibility of exercise it means that when I take him shopping the slim, active young man who began each working day with a half mile swim, now sits in a wheelchair scanning the rails of outsize clothes for anything remotely fashionable. He doesn't complain, but witnessing his self-disgust is almost too much for me to bear.

'We? You mean you want us to come on holiday with you?' asks Steve.

'Gosia says she can't manage me alone.' Andrew's eyes and voice are downcast to hide the misery of helpless dependence. His wife pushes her food around her plate and stares into the darkness beyond the window as if she has not heard.

'We could go to Southwold,' I suggest.

'Aw, come off it Mum, he looks up, energized by disagreement, 'Southwold's fine but we need a real holiday – abroad – somewhere with a bit of sun.'

Gosia is a sun-worshipper. She likes nothing better than to lie on the beach toasting her body. Motherhood and a sick husband have curtailed such pleasures. Somewhere hot would suit her well. But

Andrew? He doesn't cope well with heat now, but he does revel in the relaxed atmosphere that goes with a warm climate.

'Where did you have in mind?' I ask, while a stream of problems ticker-tape across my mind: He'll never get insurance. Where will we find a wheelchair-friendly beach? Can Steve and I both be away from the business – we're already short-staffed. How will we cope if Andrew falls? Steve is not exactly Superman.

Our son casts a mischievous grin at us. 'Well, I thought about Australia.' At our horrified faces, he guffaws. 'Thought that would get you. No, I know Oz is a bit ambitious, but never fear, Gosia,' he looks at his wife who turns her gaze from the night, 'we'll get there one day.' Now it is her turn to lower her eyes.

He's still hanging in there, so who are we to burst his bubble of hope?

'France?' I suggest. It's quick and easy to get there and, more importantly, to get back home.

The corners of his mouth turn down. 'The best thing about France is the wine and I can't drink because of the meds. The next best thing is the nudist beaches where I used to show off my perfect body,' he flutters his eyelids and wiggles his shoulders, 'but, I ask you, is the world ready for all this blubber? I think not.'

We are all imagining the map of Europe and the lure of a favourite country is strong. 'Or Italy?' says Steve. 'After all I do speak the lingo.'

'Dad, I'd love to see the Ponte Vecchio in Venice,' ('Florence,' whispers Steve), but there's all those steps…and I don't think Alice is ready for the Forum yet – that's in Italy isn't it?' Alice looks up from her colouring book at the sound of her name, and her father continues, 'Pompeii? Been there, seen it, done that, probably got a tee shirt somewhere.'

'Hattie's been to America,' Alice chips in.

'We'll go there sometime, Booboo. I promise I'll take you to Disneyland as soon as I'm better. There'll be a great big Mickey Mouse and Donald Duck.'

'And Teletubbies?'

'Oh, yes, they'll all be there.' He is excited at the prospect of a future. Then, in an aside to the adults, 'But there's not a company in the world mad enough to insure an American trip for an obese cripple who's prone to the odd scary seizure.'

Steve fills the awkward silence. 'How about Greece? That might be a possibility as long as we go before it gets too hot.'

'Brilliant idea, Dad. I fancy a swordfish souvlaki. Maybe lay off the ouzo, though.'

His animated smile, his excitement at the prospect of a Greek holiday takes me back to 1984. We were in Crete with our friends, the Wilsons. Andrew was seventeen and was putting a great deal of effort into being 'cool'. He and David were intent on charming gorgeous young girls and feeling a bit hampered by a younger brother tagging along. At fourteen Matthew was only interested in watching birds of the feathered variety, but Andrew had been determined to teach him to appreciate of both kinds.

They ended up looking at all the birds from afar on that holiday. Ten of us were travelling in two cars up a tortuous mountain road one day when an arm waved at the sky from the front vehicle. We screeched to a halt and Wendy and I were deputed to hold tightly to the hand brakes of the ancient jalopies we'd hired to stop them sliding backwards down the hill.

'Not another bird,' the girls complained. Steve, Ken and the three boys jumped out with their binoculars and lay flat in the middle of the road staring at a couple of specks in the sky, high above the rocky crags. On the way up, we'd passed a pair of German cyclists and I'll never forget their puzzled expressions when they pulled up, gazed down at the prostrate figures and asked if they could do anything to help. 'Thanks, but no thanks,' was the reply, 'we're just watching griffon vultures'. They cycled on, muttering something that must have been German for 'mad English' – or worse.

I'm back there, basking in the memory, escaping from the here and now.

Was that the day we met that beautiful Greek girl in the village where El Greco was born? I bought a hand-woven rug from her.

Andrew described her later as having hair the colour of ink, deep blue eyes, olive skin, and he had fallen instantly and deeply in love. When I look at that rug I still see my handsome, blond son on the brink of adulthood, embracing the joys that life had in store.

'Cephalonia might be a good choice,' suggests Steve, and I'm back into the present, moving my thoughts from one Greek island to another.

'Mm, before it gets too popular,' I say. 'When that film of Captain Corelli's Mandolin comes out the tourists will be flocking there.'

'S'pose I should read that book before we go, but I can't concentrate very well now. Well, never could, really, could I?' Andrew says, throwing me a cheeky grin.

'We'll get a super-light wheelchair for travelling. The one you have was too heavy in Majorca.'

'Mum, don't be ridiculous, I'm okay. I won't need a wheelchair. You all seem to think I'm useless – well I'm not.'

'I know you're not Andrew, but it will be useful at the airport and it would be a good idea to have it with us – just in case.'

'Just in case of what, may I ask? In case I suddenly become paralytic? Only it won't be drink that causes it, it'll be a fucking brain tumour. No, I can still walk, with my stick, and I'll go on walking. I don't want a bloody wheelchair, okay?'

'Calm down, love. You know what Greek village roads are like, full of potholes and rubble. Yes, of course you can walk, but uneven ground can be a problem and the last thing we want is to have you in a Greek hospital with a broken leg.'

The thought of hospitals and broken legs is sobering. He sighs in defeat. 'Okay, you win. With my luck, I'd be bound to break the good one, wouldn't I?'

Greece – what sort of a health service do they have? Will he get insurance? What will Dr B think about it?

There is a general assent around the table that Greece is a possibility and Steve agrees to make some investigations. Early May would seem to be a good time for weather and it's a fairly quiet period in our shops between the two bank holidays. May is three months away. How will he be by then? Dr B is concerned about Andrew's weight gain and plans to reduce the dexamethozone again, which will make him more vulnerable to seizures. Suppose he has one on the plane while strapped into his seat. He could lose consciousness and the space won't allow for that automatic extension of his entire body when he lies like a rigid stick-man. He might break a leg, or his neck, even...

'Well, that's a good plan, as long as we get permission from Dr B,' I say, trying to sound positive. 'I'm looking forward to it already. Apple crumble, anyone?' I ask, knowing my boy will be the first in the queue.

Keep calm, protect, the centre must hold. The mantra drums in my head. How long can I keep this up?

'Of course, he must go.' Dr B is encouraging when we see him in February. 'A holiday now is important for all of you.' I know he is carefully avoiding calling it a 'last holiday'. I frown and bite my lip. He touches my hand lightly, but addresses Andrew. 'We'll review your medications shortly before you set off and I'll write a letter for the Greek doctors, should you need it.'

I am a little surprised at the doctor's enthusiasm, as Andrew has told him of the problems he's been having with his short-term memory and increased left-sided weakness. But he can see how much this means to Andrew and his policy is quality over quantity when it comes to lifespan. Does he believe we'll ever get to Greece?

Twenty-Four

The phone rings as I'm grabbing my coat, late for work. I hesitate but decide to answer – it might be Andrew.

'Hello, Janet, it's Frances. Nothing to worry about but have you time for a quick chat?' I always have time for Frances; work (and the customers) can wait. 'Dr B – Mike, has asked me to put something to you.'

I stiffen. Is this bad news or good? I know it can't be really good, singing and dancing good, but could it be that he has looked at the latest scan and it's better than his registrar thought, or even – ever more unlikely possibilities skid across my mind – a miraculous new treatment breakthrough?

'Mike's organising a sort of seminar of brain-tumour doctors and he wondered if you would consider speaking to them about your experiences.'

A moment's silence while I absorb her unexpected words before I make my obvious reply to her ridiculous question. 'Oh no, Frances, I couldn't possibly. First, Gosia is Andrew's main carer, not me. More importantly, I've never spoken in public and the whole idea terrifies me. Sorry, but Mike will have to find someone else.'

'I understand, Janet, but Mike thinks you would be the ideal candidate, and so do I. Doctors see patients in the consulting room and often have little idea of how life is for them and their carers at home. Mike wants them to hear it from you. We don't want to pressure you, but please consider it. Talk to Steve, Andrew and Gosia – see what they think. Ring me any time if you want to ask any questions.'

I smile to myself as I drive into Rye. 'What a preposterous idea – me talking to a load of doctors,' I say to Steve later as we munch our sandwiches in the office.

'Not at all,' he replies. 'You could do that, and you'd do it well.' I can tell from the certainty in his voice that he isn't just being kind, he means it. I turn the idea over in my mind while I spend the afternoon reorganising the stock room. At the end of the working day we call into the cottage in Military Road where Andrew is dozing, Gosia is cooking and Alice is watching Pingu on the telly. Quietly, Steve seats himself on the sofa beside our son and gently squeezes his hand until he wakes and attempts a smile. 'Hey, lad. Mum's got something to tell you.'

'Nothing important, love,' I say. 'It's just that I had a call from Frances this morning, making a rather strange suggestion.'

When I explain, he sits upright, animation flooding his face. 'Wow, Mum, what an invitation. Say yes, for goodness sake. Tell 'em how it is – you'll be brilliant.' I demur, but he says, 'Do it for me, Mum.' So, hesitantly, I agree. Right now, I'll do anything at all to cheer him up.

Mike, Dr B, is also encouraging when he phones to thank me for agreeing and gives me more details. The event is sponsored by the American drug company that produces temozolomide, the experimental drug Andrew is helping to trial. The conference will take place over two days at the Royal Marsden Hospital in Fulham and he's sorry that as I'm not a professional they won't be able to pay me. They will, however, accommodate Steve and me in a good hotel and give us a generous allowance for food and entertainment.

'Whoa, Mike,' I say, 'I thought this was a seminar, which in my experience is a small group of people sitting in a circle discussing a topic. Now you tell me it's a two-day conference.'

'Sorry, didn't Frances tell you that?' I can hear a chuckle in his voice and I say that they seem to have set me up nicely. 'But I'm sure you'll still do it,' he says, and there is no question mark at the end of the sentence.

I have a month to prepare my speech which, I have been told, can be as long as I wish, but preferably not more than thirty minutes. Half an hour? They must be joking. My first draft lasts only five minutes when I read it in front of the mirror, but after much thinking, rewriting and redrafting I manage to stretch what I have to say to twenty minutes and do my best to sound confident when I orate to the wall and later test it on my family.

For four weeks I practice speaking clearly, slowing and modulating my words, raising my head to look a non-existent audience in the eye, only glancing at my notes written on postcards when I allow panic to enter the game.

The day arrives, and we walk from Charing Cross station to the five-star hotel opposite the BBC in Langham Place. Mike greets us in the lobby as he removes his cycle helmet. He slips his rucksack from his shoulders, unzips it and hands me the programme for the conference. The names of delegates – about a hundred international brain tumour specialists – are followed by a list of speakers. My heart thunders and heat rises from my chest to my neck. 'Mike,' I say as I run my finger down the page, 'look at all these doctors and professors and look at this name near the end of the running order for the second day – just plain Mrs Janet Denny.'

'You'll be fine, Janet. In fact, I bet you'll be the star of the show,' he says, and Steve nods his agreement. My beloved, supportive husband; but what does he know?

The first item on the agenda is a welcome reception in the hotel. I don't want to go but, ever curious, Steve is keen to talk to the experts who have flown in from as far as Japan, Brazil and Canada to share their knowledge. I am nervous as we enter the lavish function room, lit by sparkling chandeliers. The ice clinks against the wine glass in my trembling hand and I am overawed by this assembly of men (they are almost exclusively men) at the top of their game. But I relax as I catch some of Steve's confidence and genuine interest as he draws out the humanity of burly Russians and intense Chinese.

With a blank cheque in our pocket we decline dinner in the hotel and dine instead at The Ivy for a try at celebrity spotting. If only Andrew could be with us. How he would enjoy identifying faces only vaguely familiar to his parents whose knowledge of music, film and celebrity gossip got stuck twenty years ago.

After breakfast the next day, a coach arrives to take the conference delegates to Fulham. I am not required to attend this first day, but although we know the presentations will be way beyond our understanding, we won't miss this opportunity to glean what knowledge we can. We flounder in a foreign land of techno-medical vocabulary, we gaze at a screen showing calculations of drug doses and the now familiar scans of brains with varying patches of dark or areas of paleness. We do our best to grasp a modicum of what the experts deduce from them. The overriding memory we take from the day, however, is that when we emerge to board our coach back to Langham Place newspaper hoardings scream that the much-loved TV presenter Jill Dando has been shot on her own doorstep. While we sat in a lecture theatre only a couple of streets away.

Oklahoma! the Rodgers and Hammerstein musical, is special to Steve and me. When we were teenage sweethearts he bought me the LP and *People Will Say We're in Love* became our secret song. On this first evening in London we sit in a West End theatre watching Maureen Lipman in a revival. Hands clasped, eyes glistening, we think of the happiness and sorrow that life has brought us since those carefree days. After the show, we walk hand in hand through damp London streets back to our hotel, grateful that our love has deepened over four decades and we have each other to lean on in these dark days.

'You'll be wonderful tomorrow, sweetie,' he says.

The lectures on the second morning are a little more intelligible so that I can push to the back of my mind the terror that awaits me in the late afternoon. When the time comes, Mike gives me a generous introduction and I walk to the podium with my notes and raise my eyes to a theatre full of the people I viewed with awe at the drinks party. *None of them knows what it's really like,* I think, *but I am going to tell them. I am going to make them squirm in their comfortable seats, shut their eyes against the pain. I am going to make them feel the horror of watching a beloved son being destroyed by a bunch of out of control cells eating into his brain, with little to even slow their progress. I will tell them just what it's like to be given a wrong diagnosis and told to go away and get on with your life. So that when they see their next patient with his or her anxious mother, father, husband, child – whoever loves them – they will understand and, feeling empathy, deliver bad news gently. And resolve to try even harder to find a cure.* I look at these people, think these thoughts and my heartbeat returns to its normal rate, my hands become calm, I open my mouth and my voice is strong. I deliver my words to a silent room and as I look at the faces in my audience they seem rapt. When I finish and thank them for listening there is a moment's silence before several delegates stand and clap their hands together. Others join in and as I return to my seat I am deafened by the applause.

Steve wipes his eyes and punches the air. 'Well done, my love.'

Worn out by emotion, we make a swift escape to catch our train. As soon as we reach home Mike is on the phone to congratulate me and tell us that many delegates had told him mine was the most useful talk of the conference.

When I report to Andrew the next day I watch his face crease with joy, I feel his hand grip mine and his kiss on my cheek. I am proud to have made him proud of me. But I can't make him healthy again. Mummy can't make everything better.

Twenty-Five

It is springtime again and I see soft lime-green leaves emerge from bare brown branches. Bulbs are blooming, eggs are hatching and lambs are gambolling in the field beyond the garden. And in the last week of April our family has its own new baby to celebrate when Laura gives birth to Joe. Steve and I manage to unwind the tension inside us and open our hearts to a new, precious grandson. Andrew is thrilled to have a nephew and is only half joking when he talks of his own son being safe in the freezer.

Two weeks later we fly from Stansted to Cephalonia.

The holiday is a nightmare in many ways but, looking back, the memories are precious. Matthew has arranged his work so that he can come with us. At this news Steve and I feel a burden lifted from our backs. His presence will relieve the ever-rising pressures that blow around all our heads. He will give physical and emotional support to his brother, sharing past experiences and jokes, and he will have fun with Alice. Matthew is to share one apartment with Steve and me, while Andrew, Gosia and Alice will have the adjoining one.

We check in at the airport with Andrew in his wheelchair. Steve, Andrew and I are directed to wait in a distant deserted room until we are called. Take-off time is approaching when Steve searches for someone – anyone – to remind them where we are. A young man dressed in airline uniform reassures him and we wait. With five minutes to go to take-off and no tannoy alerts I run through empty passages, up stairs, through doors until I am back at the enquiry desk. I elbow my way in front of a statuesque middle-aged woman with orange hair who harrumphs like an elephant when I apologise and tell her of the urgency.

'What?' The desk clerk's eyes bulge when I explain our position. 'You should have been loaded ages ago.' She makes a call, holding her palm up to the irate woman's gesticulations. Then she points to me and then to the door I recently emerged from and I hotfoot it back to our party. As I arrive, breathless, two flustered porters appear, and Andrew is nearly tipped from his wheelchair as they load us onto a minibus. When we are lifted onto the plane the captain welcomes us with a joke about the lost property having been found and a cheer goes up from the waiting passengers. Gosia closes her eyes and sighs. Alice copies her uncle and sticks both thumbs in the air and we are on our way to Greece.

The tiny resort is as expected unspoiled, beautiful and quiet, infused with laid-back rural Greek hospitality. The apartments are basic but adequate and although classed as ground floor, are, in fact, a number of steps up from the street. 'Sod's law,' says Andrew and wills his useless leg to climb, swinging it out to the left and trying to physically lift it with his right arm. This causes him to overbalance and he slides down the steps, with his customary laugh, which quickly turns to tears of frustration when Steve and Matthew haul him to his feet.

'Yeah, all right, I'll let you help me next time.'

Our younger son fills the gaps of fatherhood left by Andrew's incapacity, joyfully tossing his niece in the air, kicking a football with her, running races on the sand and teaching her to swim. Alice's adoration is absolute. This morning I watch from the balcony as they walk hand in hand in the fields adjoining the apartments. I notice Matthew bend low to point out a colourful insect or discuss a wild flower and then I see him pick up a bucket, fill it from a standpipe, and pour the water onto the baked ground. Alice lifts her face to the sky and, catching sight of me looking at them, she waves.

'Granny, guess what we're doing?' she shouts.

'Wasting water?'

'No, silly. We're making mud for the swallows to build their nests.'

Three days into the holiday it is Alice's fourth birthday. Matthew has risen early to tie a dozen balloons to the parapet of the terrace outside our front doors, accompanied by the frantic chirruping activity of swallows, some feeding new chicks in nests they have tucked into the corners under the overhanging roof, others adding last-minute additions to their homes. The cough Alice has brought with her from England is no better, and although she is unusually hot this morning, she still enjoys breakfast and lots of parcel-opening. Miska, the travel company rep who escorted us from the airport, arrives with a sickly, gaudy confection and sings Happy Birthday in Greek. Is this company policy, I wonder, to study the passports for evidence of children's birthdays? Or, recognising the tragedy of the situation, is it one kind young woman's effort to help?

Gosia is not having a good day. She doesn't want to be here, far from her home country, with a dying husband who depends on her for even his most basic needs. She doesn't want to be on holiday with her in-laws and she's worried about Alice whose cough has kept them awake most of the night. My daughter-in-law is frightened of the future. What will she do, how she will she cope? She wants to be in that other life, the life she expected, enjoying a seaside holiday with a healthy, active husband who would be building sandcastles and teaching Alice to swim. And, who knows, by now she might have had another baby. Exhausted, mentally, emotionally and physically, she can no longer summon a smile for anyone and she doesn't feel like coming out with us today. Her temper is so short she snaps at anyone near. Yet, this is her daughter's birthday. I know I should be offering her more support but I too, am weary – weary with buoying up my son, trying to hold us all together while we watch his decline.

I lay my arm on her shoulder, 'Why don't you stay here, Gosia? Have a rest and prepare the party. We'll be back about three.' She nods, and attempts a smile.

We visit the Blue Pool on that May birthday and Matthew shows Alice how to use her favourite birthday gift, a blue and red plastic camera, to take real pictures of her Dad. Andrew shares a joke of doubtful taste as his brother unobtrusively helps with an urgent unzipping of flies, (his bladder is less controllable now and when he has to go he just has to go). I declare the approach to the subterranean pool impossible for Andrew to manage, but Matthew and Steve support his weight and calmly pilot him down two steep flights of stairs. Getting a large man on unsteady feet from the landing stage into the small rowing boat on the lake is hazardous. With much laughter, anxiety and boat-rocking however, it is achieved.

I sit quietly smiling in the stern of the boat. Inside I feel a torrent of joy and pain. Hold this in your mind forever, I tell myself as I listen to Andrew telling his little girl fairy stories and a few inaccurate Greek myths while the boatman rows us around the tranquil, azure pool. A shaft of sunlight shines through a cleft in the rock above us and illuminates a host of dancing fireflies skimming the water.

When we return to the apartments Gosia is rested and smiling. The table is set with the cheap, minimal tableware provided and the paper hats, streamers and hooters brought from England. Gosia tells us the village shop is not big on cakes, but she has found a dry yellow sponge and plastered it with jam and something that passes for cream. Alice claps her hands when she sees it is decorated with candles and a big, multi-coloured number four made of Smarties. We play silly games and Alice blows out the candles countless times. No one notices the quality of the cake.

As the sun goes down we make for Spiros's taverna on the waterfront a hundred yards away. Spiros himself is a handsome man, expansive, and very 'front of house' – a bit of a go-getter, with his plans for an apartment building and another taverna up the street. His wife, known to all as Mama, and his daughter, Vicky, both toil in the kitchen.

Alice rides down the uneven stony road to the taverna in 'Daddy's buggy'. She pretends to be the Queen, waving to the locals who return her greeting. Children are always a social passport and this pretty, blonde, blue-eyed little girl elicits smiles and waves from even the most frosty-faced inhabitants. Andrew walks slowly, unevenly beside her, holding on to the frame of the wheelchair, as Steve pushes. A breath of evening breeze ripples the water in the harbour as we seat ourselves at our outdoor table and see that Spiros's family has done Alice proud. There is a beribboned parcel at Alice's place and an Americanised version of Happy Birthday crackles into life from the speaker inside.

'Who is the present for, I wonder?' Andrew asks.

'Me, of course – it's my birthday,' shouts Alice.

'Oh, I nearly forgot,' he laughs. 'You've had lots of presents, Booboo. Can't I have this one?'

By now Alice has torn the parcel open and found inside a sparkly tee shirt. Gosia wrinkles her nose at the tasteless design, but the gold fringe and jewel-laden princess on the front are magic to Alice. She holds it against her dad's bulky body and declares, 'Sorry Daddy, it's too small for you.' Amid the general hilarity I notice Andrew biting his lip.

We enjoy a feast of swordfish, calamari and stefado, and Mama invites Alice to a secret assignation by the ice cream cabinet for her to choose her favourite flavour. Our birthday girl is feted and kissed by the other patrons and Andrew is the proudest man on the island. The lovely Vicky (Andrew has not lost his eye for a pretty girl) appears from the kitchen bearing a luscious cheesecake dessert that glitters with fizzing sparklers. Alice invites the other diners to share it with us and the notes of Happy Birthday ring out again along the seafront.

At the end of a really good day, Alice offers to help push Daddy home in his buggy. He doesn't protest.

Meeting on the little beach next morning, I thank Vicky for their kindness. 'It is so little to do,' she demurs. 'Your son, he is very sick?'

'Yes, Vicky, he is very sick. I am afraid he will die soon. This holiday is very important.'

I am shocked at my words. Have I actually just said that he will die? Yes, I have. I have said it because it is easier to confront reality with a relative stranger; too painful, too dangerous to utter within the family. Vicky's eyes glisten and, as she reaches out her hand, I am suddenly aware that Alice, who had been searching for shells on the beach, is silently beside me. How long has she been there? What did she hear? How much does she understand? I berate myself – *no more careless words.*

Alice comes to our apartment one morning. 'Dad's got funny legs, Granny. Will you come and see?'

He certainly has got funny legs. They are covered in angry red weals, back and front. It could be an allergy, an infection or an unexpected response to his drugs. The miracle is that he hasn't had a reaction before to the cocktail of tablets he takes every day. Or could it be some sort of subcutaneous haemorrhage? He has been taking anti-coagulants for months now and his blood is monitored weekly at home. It's just his bad luck for it to happen now. We need a doctor. Where do we find a doctor?

'Spiros will know,' Steve decides.

'Alice, sweetie, shall we go and see Spiros?'

'I love Spiros,' she replies and skips ahead of her granddad down the quiet road to the harbour.

At this hour, the taverna is closed and lifeless. While Steve considers where to go next, the little girl presses her nose to the glass doors and spies Mama in the distant kitchen chopping vegetables for lunchtime customers. Alice hammers her fist on the glass. Mama turns, squinting at the sunshine and moves towards the doors. She beams when she sees who is knocking and slides the door open. '*Kalime'ra*, Alice, you come for ice cream?'

Steve interjects swiftly. 'Oh no, it's much too early for ice cream. Good morning – *Kalime'ra*, Mama. I need your help, please. Where can we find a doctor?'

Mama wrinkles her face and shakes her head. 'No understand,' she says. 'Sit moment, I get Vicky.' From the back of the kitchen she yells Vicky's name up the stairs, followed by incomprehensible

Greek. Then she returns bearing sweet pastries, a small cup of strong coffee and a glass of water.

'My daddy has funny legs,' announces Alice, eyeing the pastries.

Mama passes her the plate. 'Eat, Alice. Is good.'

'Thank you,' says Steve, and tries to explain. 'Andrew,' he says, frowning and rubbing his legs, 'he has bad legs, very red, very sore.'

Mama shakes her head, then says, 'She here now,' with some relief. Tousle-haired Vicky arrives clad in a long pink T-shirt. '*Kalime'ra*,' she greets them with a smiley yawn.

'*Kalime'ra*, Vicky – so sorry to wake you, but we need to know where we can find a doctor. Andrew has a bad rash on his legs and we are not sure what to do.'

'It's all red and nasty, but it doesn't itch,' adds Alice, enjoying her part in the drama.

Vicky locks eyes with Steve. 'Oh, I am sorry,' she says. 'There is a doctor in the next village. A green building, new. It is on the right as you begin the main street, a big notice with a red cross outside. Go now – I will telephone you are coming.'

Matthew takes Alice to watch the fishermen unloading the morning's silver catch from red and blue boats. The rest of us drive the short but tortuous route to the doctor's surgery, which we find to be unexpectedly bright and pristine. The young practitioner speaks some English. He reads Mike's letter, and on inspecting Andrew's bright red legs, he is cautious.

'I think you must go to the hospital in Argostoli,' he says. 'I will write a letter to give them.'

I feel the now familiar, fearful rush of adrenaline rising like fire through my body, then I find myself shivering. I open my mouth to ask why he can't help us. Doesn't he know what this is? What does he suspect? But I change my mind and simply thank him. The island's main hospital will have specialist staff to give trustworthy advice.

Letter in hand, we return to collect Matthew and Alice. Who knows how long we will be or what will happen next? We need to be together.

Two hours later, after a tense journey through the mountains in our ancient hired car, we are in the island's capital, Argostoli – a scrappy, workaday town. The hospital, when we find it, is built in the worst traditions of 1960s architecture and looks semi-abandoned.

'There's no point in us all being here,' says Steve. 'Matthew, you take Alice to find some lunch. There were a few decent-looking places on the harbour as we drove in.'

Gosia has been quiet on the journey while Steve, Matthew and I have been doing our best to jolly everyone into believing this is a good opportunity to get a look at the 'real' Cefalonia, the part tourists don't usually reach. Now she says 'I think I go with them, Janet. You can understand hospitals much better.'

We wave them off and, clutching the doctor's letter, we support Andrew between us and walk through the graffitied entrance, parents taking their son to a hospital appointment, reassuring, making light of the occasion. The cavernous vestibule is deserted. A single strip light buzzes, flickering on and off. The cracked panes in the grubby windows allow enough daylight to show the torn vinyl flooring, scuffed paintwork and an unmanned desk. A couple of traditional, blue painted chairs with the rush-work seats punched through stand against the wall.

Andrew's voice is flat. 'Oh shit. Let's turn round now, Mum.'

I look at Steve in despair. 'This is just reception, it's got to be better inside. At least they must have proper doctors. After all they're in the EU now. Come on, let's ring the bell.'

A middle-aged man in blue overalls appears in answer to the summons.

'He must be the boiler man,' mutters Andrew. But no, he is not the boiler man, he is the receptionist who shrugs his shoulders and shakes his head when we speak to him in English. We hand him the letter in its envelope. He glances at it but returns it unopened, pointing to the lift and giving us the thumbs down.

'I think he's indicating the basement,' says Steve.

'I thought it was a hell-hole,' replies Andrew, raising his eyebrows.

We emerge from the lift into a dark corridor. On one side are lines of closed doors once painted blue, and along the opposite wall a row of brown armchairs with stuffing pouring out of the split sides and unidentifiable stains on the seats. Four or five blank-faced souls are there. An old woman has a swab stuck with dried blood to her balding head. A man is racked with coughing causing his face to turn an alarming shade of red, then blue, and a young woman with terror in her eyes paces up and down holding a sleeping infant. Cold fluorescent light drains the life out of all their faces. They all ignore us newcomers.

'I'll try to find someone,' I say. 'Which door shall I try?'

'The one with the smoke coming from under it,' Steve suggests. I knock and wait. And wait. I knock again – and wait. Patience stretched to the limit, I turn the handle and push the door open. Peering through a fug of cigarette smoke, I make out six people sitting around the room, all dressed in coats that pass for white. Proffering the letter, I request attention. An unsmiling woman rises reluctantly from her chair, slowly reads what the doctor has written and, pointing me to the row of seats in the corridor, closes the door in my face.

Fortunately, we have had the forethought to bring a drink and some bread and feta cheese.

It is not until our lunch has become a distant memory that a dark-haired, overweight woman of about forty, dressed in blood-stained, green scrubs, invites us into what appears to be a treatment room. To our immense relief she speaks some English but doesn't respond to our tumbling questions as she does the routine tests – blood pressure, pulse and temperature. She makes no comment on her findings. 'A doctor will be with you soon,' she says as she leaves.

I run a practiced eye around the room. 'A druggie's paradise, this,' I pronounce as I note not only endless syringes and needles (thankfully in sterile packages), but also packs of morphine, heroin and drugs of all descriptions lying on the open shelves.

Half an hour later the door opens and a small woman totters in on six-inch stilettos surrounded by a cloud of exotic perfume. She has tumbling bleached curls and her thick black eyeliner has run into the wrinkles under her eyes. Her fingers, weighed down with rings, end in long red talons.

'I am the doctor, what is your problem?' Her voice is laden with tobacco.

By now, if we were not taut with worry, we would be helpless with laughter, imagining ourselves in a comedy film. We hand her the letters from Mike and the Greek doctor explaining Andrew's diagnosis, his medication, and the reason for our present concern. With a smile, Andrew covertly indicates the packet of cigarettes poking from the pocket of her off-white coat. When she has finished firing questions at him, she extracts a phial of blood from his arm and hands it to me.

'Take to the blood laboratory. You will see the sign. Return later for the result.'

'Where is the blood lab. . .?' I follow her to the door, but she waves her arm in an indeterminate direction and disappears into another room leaving me mid-sentence.

Steve and Andrew resettle themselves in the corridor and I set out on the Great Haematology Lab Hunt. There is a sign, in fact there is a profusion of signs, with arrows pointing every which way, all in Greek, a language that bears no relation to any I have even a nodding acquaintance with. I wave the blood at anyone I meet and plead for directions. A woman points heavenwards and holds up two fingers. Am I really that unpleasant, or does she mean two floors up? I try the lift and emerge to the usual row of closed doors. I try the first one and find a lecture in progress. I shake the tube of blood at the lecturer.

'Where the hell is the haematology lab?' I demand. He points down the corridor, while his students look in amazement at this wild-eyed, middle-aged English woman fizzing with anger and frustration.

On the left at the end of the corridor is a transparent panel, through which I see white-coated women looking through microscopes. I hammer on the glass. The brunette woman who opens it has wire-framed spectacles and a large mole on her sagging cheek. She looks at the phial of blood and accompanying form, points to the next window and slides the window closed. I move along four paces, hammer on the glass, and the same woman, having moved along four paces on the other side of the wall, opens the panel and takes what she is given. 'Come back, one hour,' she commands and shuts the window firmly.

I return to the basement. 'Let's get the hell out of here,' I hiss. Andrew refuses my arm but leans heavily on his dad. We negotiate the clanking lift and ignore the man in overalls leaning on the reception desk, puffing on his fag, as we make for the door. Matthew is waiting with the car and we join Gosia and Alice in a comfortable waterfront bar to de-stress. We sip our cold beers and Andrew does not complain at his lemonade.

A pelican on the seafront is a source of fascination for Alice so Gosia, Steve and Andrew stay with her while Matthew drives me back to collect the blood test results.

'Nothing wrong,' the moley woman declares when she opens her window and looks at me as if I have enjoyed burdening her with unnecessary work. She pushes the result form towards me, slides the glass shut and turns back to her microscope.

'What do we do now?' asks Matthew.

I am distraught. 'I'll have to go home with him. Who knows what this rash is all about? This result means nothing.' I wave the piece of paper I was given. 'I bet they didn't even bother to test it. He might be bleeding to death. We must get him back to the Marsden, they'll know what to do. We can get flights, I'm sure. I'll phone the rep.'

'No, Mum,' Matthew says. 'He won't go, you know. He's enjoying himself. He knows he's going to die and I think he'd rather die here, in the sunshine.' He slips his arm through mine and gives it a squeeze.

I slump against him, blinking away my exhausted anxiety. 'Come on, let's get the others and go back for supper at Spiros's.'

'What? You didn't go *there*.' Spiros is shocked and regales all his patrons with our adventures. The locals are incredulous. 'No one goes to the hospital in Argostoli unless they can't afford the fare to the mainland. Are you okay? What did they do to you?' Andrew

187

revels in the attention. Feeling heroic for braving the dreaded hospital, he sits talking and laughing long into the night with Spiros and his drinking friends.

The next morning his legs are lily-white again.

He has his last swim in Cephalonia. We set out to find that other bay, the one featured in so many travel brochures, a perfect white crescent of sand surrounded by steep cliffs lapped by a turquoise sea. A picturesque wooden wreck completes the picture of magnificent isolation. The road down to this paradise is twisty and narrow and I'm thankful Steve is driving. We reach the bottom and discover the beach has no shade at all and consists not of sand but of large white pebbles. Alice's bucket and spade will not be needed. A satisfied smile spreads across Gosia's face. For her this is what holidays are about. She spreads her towel and strips to her bikini. Steve unloads Andrew's wheelchair from the boot of the car and our son sits, unevenly enthroned at the top of the beach. Matthew shows Alice how to skim the flat pebbles into the water, seeing how far they can go, counting how many times they will bounce – two, three, even four before sinking with a final flourishing splash.

Andrew's bowels have been at work and he needs to go. Urgently. Distancing ourselves as far as possible from the only other party on the beach, Steve fashions a hollow in the stones and together we help Andrew to lower his heavy body. We make light of it, of course; jokes have become part of our armoury against the tumour. It is a difficult operation – humiliating for Andrew, emotionally painful for us. The sun is searing and after Matthew and Steve enjoy a cooling dip in the Mediterranean, it irritates the drying salt on their bodies. I sit beside Andrew who watches from his chair, baseball cap and a muslin scarf his only protection from the burning rays, and declare that we must move off the beach.

Gosia decides to stay, to soak up the sun alone. 'I will be fine here, don't worry.' She lifts her head as we give her our last bottle of water. We can buy more.

We load ourselves into the car and Steve is concentrating on the hairpin bends in the road when Alice lays her head in my lap. 'I don't feel well, Granny,' she whimpers.

I feel her burning forehead and think heatstroke. 'Sweetie, we are going to find a shop to get some water very soon. You need a big drink and then you'll feel better.' I hope I am right and am relieved when we reach the straight road at the top of the ravine. Steve puts his foot down. He understands the urgency.

When we reach the tiny harbour of Assos the sound of cicadas is deafening. Cicadas live in trees, and trees offer shade. Andrew rejects the wheelchair and leans on Steve as we seat ourselves at a wooden table beneath the spreading branches. I point to a dark cave in a building displaying a small picture of an ice cream. 'Water,' I say to Steve, 'surely they'll have some.' A few minutes later he returns under the weight of several two-litre bottles.

After lots of liquid and a sleep on my lap, Alice wakes to the smile of a toothless Greek Mama, dressed in black. Her long hair is drawn back into a grey tail snaking down her fleshy back. With her equally time-worn, toothless husband, the woman sits at a neighbouring table, which is stacked with pots of their honey, a price scribbled on a piece of cardboard propped against them. When we ask to buy one they insist we taste first and offer Alice a full spoonful, clapping their hands at her smile of approval.

Children recover quickly, and our granddaughter is now ready for some fun in the sea.

'I'll come in with you, Booboo,' Andrew says, fleetingly forgetting that he can barely walk on level ground, let alone on slippery pebbles in the water. Even with the help of his father and brother on dry land he quickly loses confidence, and they know that if he falls, lifting sixteen stone will not be easy for two slight men. Nevertheless, Matthew pilots him to the water's edge.

Alice stands in the shallows reaching out to him. 'I'll help you, Daddy. Hold my hand.'

'It's no good, Booboo. I can't do it.' He hits his useless palm with his other fist and wrestles with humiliating tears.

A large figure, chest hair glistening wet above his red trunks, leaps out of the water like a breaching whale. 'Yeah, you can, mate. I'll 'elp yer.' He indicates his wife sitting in a wheelchair under the trees. 'Used to this, I am.' And once again, as so often during these terrible, painful times, we experience the incomparable kindness of a complete stranger. Gently, patiently, the man helps Matthew and Steve lead Andrew into the water, pausing and supporting when he feels his balance deserting him, encouraging and joking when his confidence falters, until he is in deep enough to swim.

The salt water buoys him up and, taking his daughter's hand, he is triumphant. 'Come on, Alice, swim with Daddy.'

When we collect Gosia from her beach Andrew laughs at her disbelief when he tells her he has been swimming with Alice.

The next morning Steve, Matthew and I set out for an early morning bird-watch. On our return we call *'Kalime'ra'* to the family sitting outside the office where we hired our car. The black-clad old lady beckons animatedly, shouting, 'Your boy – here.' And, sure enough, his stick is propped against the wall and there he sits with a self-satisfied smile, drinking coffee and charming the socks off his companions.

'Andrew, how the hell did you get here?' I am amazed, worried, disbelieving. It must be fifty yards from the apartment. Where is his wheelchair? Who pushed him here?

'How do you think I got here, Mum? I walked, of course.'

It must have been a Herculean effort, staggering down the steps from the apartments to the stony unmade roadway, clinging to the walls of houses and the railings of front yards, then resting before screwing up his courage to step across open passageways to reach and grasp the wooden posts marking out a tiny vegetable garden. He is exultant. A conquering hero. He has triumphed over the fucking tumour.

Twenty-Six

We report our Greek adventures to Dr B when we see him on our return and he concludes the rash on Andrew's legs was probably a reaction to brushing past some unknown vegetation. When we describe the hospital in Argostoli he gives us a wry smile and congratulates Andrew on his survival skills. But he is concerned that the latest scan shows more solidity in the tumour and a cyst causing increased pressure.

'Are you sure you want to continue on the drug trial?' he asks, but Andrew is adamant, so he agrees. The doctor strokes his chin and looks into the distance. 'If you would like me to, I could ask Henry Marsh, the neurosurgeon we consulted before, if he can do a little operation to relieve the pressure around the tumour.' Andrew and I sit up a little straighter and I try to excise the last letter from Mr Marsh from my memory. Mike continues, 'It would mean putting a little bubble called an Ommaya reservoir under the skin of your scalp. Some of the fluid in the cyst would drain into it and we could syringe it away. What do you think?'

'Yep. You know me Doc, up for anything.'

'Okay, I'll write to him and his secretary will be in touch with you.'

The flame of hope in Andrew's eyes, which had been perilously nearing extinction, burns a little brighter.

The portrait is Gosia's idea. We've known Louis Turpin for years. A talented artist and musician, he plays at local gigs and is much in demand as a portrait and landscape painter. His reputation is nationwide, having had work hung in such illustrious institutions as the National Portrait Gallery and the Royal Academy. Consequently, Gosia's first suggestion that we should commission an oil painting of the three of them is beyond our purse, but an image of two people, Andrew and Alice, we can just about manage.

On a sunny June day, Louis arrives at the farmhouse with his camera and sketching materials and positions an excited four-year-old girl and her daddy on a wooden bench in the field beside the farm pond, against a background of the rolling pastures of the Brede Valley. The yellow flags growing at the margins of the water are echoed in the lemon daisies on Alice's sandals. Wearing a pink summer dress, she leans casually onto her father's shoulder. Their parted lips reveal identical gaps between their front teeth, and their blue eyes, echoing each other's, look directly at the viewer.

When Louis delivers the finished portrait, I want to hug these two painted figures, keep them close forever. This picture is priceless, the first thing I would save from any fire or earthquake.

I hear a vehicle pull into the yard when I am weeding the rockery at the back of the house. I stand and take off my gloves, wondering who might be arriving on a sunny summer afternoon. Footsteps run across the gravel and Gosia appears, red-eyed, her cheeks stained with old and new tears. Dropping my trowel, I run to comfort her. 'What is it, Gosia, whatever has happened?'

She is distraught, can barely force words between her sobs but I understand enough to know she has been speaking to Frances. 'She says he will always be in a wheelchair,' she stutters, 'that he, he won't get better. He is going to die.' She covers her face with her hands and is wracked with sobbing. She didn't know, she hasn't realised, hasn't understood the nuances of conversations with doctors, nurses, Steve and me. Terminal is a word we have all used, perhaps that is another mysterious English word she has not grasped the meaning of. *My fault*, I berate myself. I've been so busy keeping strong, hiding my emotions I've not been thinking of her.

I can't make amends. I can only make a cup of tea.

Alice attends a nursery school at Roadend Farm a few hundred yards further along our narrow winding lane. A converted oast house, recently retired from drying the hops that are still an important crop in the neighbouring valley, houses the children's indoor activities. Beyond its doors they can pet lambs, stroke ponies, search for eggs laid by the free-ranging hens, run races and play games overlooking the wide fields of the valley. An apparent rural idyll, but even idylls can have sinister shadows. In this small rural community many of the children, staff and parents associated with Roadend Nursery are friends and acquaintances of ours, or more likely of Andrew's and Gosia's. They are all aware of the Damoclesian sword hanging over the Dennys. The school, though, is a safe haven, a loving oasis of normality for a little girl who is feeling, but not yet understanding, the family stress that is the fallout of a terminal illness.

Louise (fondly known as Loopy) is the young farmer's wife who runs the nursery. Full of vibrant energy, she decides to hold a charity ball in a marquee on the farm and one of her chosen charities is to be the Brain Tumour Foundation. Andrew is energised by the prospect, inviting friends from far and near, selling numerous tickets for the Grand Draw. When the appointed evening arrives, friends who have gathered at the farmhouse earlier in the day are dressed to impress, and a convoy of cars assembles to drive along the lane. As always Andrew revels in the sense of occasion and he sets off from our house in a friend's bright red sports car, wearing a Noddy Holder wig of black tumbling curls on his hairless head, full of humour and apparent optimism. I wave him and Gosia off for an evening of fun, wondering at his courage. Steve holds Alice in his arms, cheering and joining in the jubilation. Then he looks at me and shakes his head slowly from side to side and we retreat indoors.

Still on a high after the ball, Andrew receives a letter asking him to report to the Atkinson Morley Hospital on the twenty-sixth of June for insertion of a reservoir to drain the cyst in his head. He is elated but a warning klaxon sounds in my brain. *He can't have a surgical operation while he's still on Warfarin* – the blood-thinning drug that had been prescribed following the deep vein thrombosis in his leg.

'Sod it,' he exclaims when I mention it. But after the dose is gradually reduced, he is admitted a week later than planned. The operation doesn't involve a craniotomy. 'No Black and Decker this time', he tells us. My guess is they went in through the old scar and he is discharged after only a couple of days. The operation is a success and Andrew swears the cherry-sized bubble close to the original scar on the top right-hand side of his head is already relieving the pressure. When we arrive to collect him from the once gracious old building, now nearing the end of its useful life as a hospital, he stands proudly beside the bed. 'Look, Mum, no stick.'

The thin strand of optimism doesn't last. On a visit to the Marsden five days later, Dr B aspirates only 15ml of fluid from the reservoir. To us this seems a significant amount, but Mike writes in his notes that Andrew has difficulty standing and his hemiparesis is worse than before surgery. He suggests that his GP, Dr James (Lelly), can do the aspirations in future to save us a long journey, and asks again if Andrew wants to continue with the temozolomide. When our boy nods his head vigorously, Mike agrees but looks at me with a slight frown and turned-down mouth. He writes in the notes: *Treatment to be continued for psychological reasons.*

How much longer can this go on? Andrew is going down fast now, drifting visibly in conversations of any length. I call in to the little cottage after work in mid-August.

'He's in there.' Three words and an inclination of the head from my exhausted, tight-lipped daughter-in-law.

As I put my arms around his swollen body and kiss him I feel the wet tears on his cheek.

'Hi, Mum.' Now there is a sigh instead of his customary smile.

A discussion about the forthcoming total eclipse of the sun animates him a little. Steve and Matthew are going to France to get the best view, but Andrew is not up for joining them.

'No, Dad, I'll only be a nuisance and anyway, I'm too tired. I'll come over to the farmhouse and we can watch it with Alice.'

So, when the day comes, Gosia drops them off and returns home for an afternoon to herself. Father and daughter fool around with the special plastic specs we have all been warned to wear to protect our eyes when we look at the disappearing sun. Andrew wonders why we didn't stock them in the shop. 'Everyone's been buying them – we could have sold hundreds.'

'Maybe', I reply, 'but we couldn't have sold the remaining stock until the next eclipse – in God knows how many years' time.'

'Yeah, see your point. Maybe I could have started a hoax campaign, put up a load of notices next August when all the tourists are around to convince them there's another one due and we're the only shop with stocks of protective goggles.' His mischievous grin, absent for a while, spreads across his face and Alice laughs – because he laughs.

I place garden chairs on the wide grass verge that separates our house from the narrow lane. Alice skips beside us as Andrew leans heavily on me, swings his near useless left leg in a wide circle and limps to a seat. We wait with excited anticipation. In the mid-afternoon of a sunny August day the skies begin to dim, the bleating of the sheep falters, and then ceases. Birds roost in the trees and fall silent as apparent night approaches. Through darkened lenses we watch our planet's shadow encroach on the golden orb in the sky and the eerie silence adds to the atmosphere of expectation. Then, at the very moment when the sun is about to be totally obscured, our neighbouring farmer starts up his noisy tractor and pauses to load some haybales from the barn opposite, blocking our view of the sky.

'Oh bugger. I bet he did that on purpose.' Andrew hits his floppy left palm with a strong right fist. 'Come on Booboo, let's go in and have a cup of tea. You might see the next one, but Granny and I have had it now.'

The Rye Christian Lunch Club is an ecumenical venture, meeting every few weeks at the Community Centre. A simple bread and cheese lunch is followed by a speaker, sometimes well known, such as Delia Smith. Having experienced a reverse Damascene moment some years ago, I have attended only once, when I was interested to hear that old atheist curmudgeon turned proselytizing Christian, Malcom Muggeridge.

Christian friends urge us to join them for a talk about faith-healing that has achieved miraculous results. I decline but Steve thinks it can do no harm to listen, to turn over every stone, a last-ditch attempt to unearth a miracle. While maintaining his scepticism, he can't entirely subdue a tinge of hope in his voice when he describes the event to me. He has heard the testimony of a ballet dancer who was confined to a wheelchair after losing the use of her legs. However, after prayers for healing (and conventional treatment) she was able to dance again. I scoff, but look up from my newspaper when I hear the words 'brain tumour'. The young daughter of the speaker had received this diagnosis.

'What kind of tumour?' I ask, but he can't tell me. My knowledge of the many different types of these invasive demons is now extensive and I know a few, a very few, are curable.

'They were told it was terminal five years ago and the girl was there today in full health and about to sit her GCSEs.'

'And that was achieved by prayer?'

'The doctors have no other explanation. There's this place called Burrswood at Groombridge where she was treated, a proper registered hospital that offers physiotherapy, hydrotherapy and what they term reablement care. It's a Christian foundation and has its own church, dedicated to the Ministry of Christian Healing.' His voice falters and he smiles, self-conscious at his own enthusiasm. 'I think we should talk to Andrew, not push the praying side but suggest it as a possible help with rehabilitation.'

Late summer has produced a blaze of colour in the immaculate grounds of Burrswood. Pink and white Japanese anemones, flaming monbretia, zingy blue ceanothus, hydrangeas like blobs of pastel-coloured ice cream line the long driveway to the mansion that has become a hospital. We are here to 'case the joint', gauge whether a short stay here would appeal to Andrew. Kindness pervades the atmosphere. He is helped from the car, we drink coffee with others – patients, staff, volunteers and locals who are here to attend the service. A short tour introduces us to the facilities and treatment on offer. The church is light, bright and full of people. We seat ourselves near the back – 'So we can escape if I feel a fit coming on,' says Andrew. The singing is lusty, the sermon uplifting, the prayers moving. While others go to the altar rail to receive communion, music plays softly. Our heads are bowed and when I glance sideways at Andrew I notice his shoulders are shaking. I reach for his hand, he raises tear-laden eyes to me. The organist is playing Elgar's *Nimrod*. Andrew whispers, 'Play this at my funeral.'

A short stay at Burrswood is not a success, however. Despite much care and kindness Andrew finds it difficult to maintain a train of thought or make conversation. He is lonely in his little single room dreaming of being back with his family.

But there are few smiles when he returns home. The strain sparks in the air like a live electric wire ready to ignite an explosion. Incontinence is an increasing problem.

It has been one of those damp, gloomy November Tuesdays. The shop wasn't busy with customers, but with bulky deliveries, staff off sick, and a stream of reps anxious for orders. After watching the ten o'clock news we sink gladly into a warm bed, scan what remains of the weekend papers and are about to switch off the light when the phone tears through the silence.

'He's on the floor. I can't move him. Will you come and deal with it?' Gosia's voice is flat and expressionless. She doesn't elaborate and hangs up.

When we open the unlocked door, we find her sitting on the blue sofa, pale and dishevelled, smoking a cigarette. Her blue eyes are blank but behind the façade the anger that has become her constant weapon against despair, is bubbling. She stares into space and points to the ceiling.

Our boy is lying naked, his bloated body curled foetally in a pool of poo on the wooden floor of the bedroom. He screws his eyes shut in a vain attempt to prevent tears spilling out. I cover his shivering form with a blanket and hold his hand while Steve fetches a bowl of warm soapy water, flannel and towel. As I clean between my son's buttocks and under his thighs I gag at the stench, not so different from the smell of all those terry-towelling nappies I had changed with equanimity decades before. It is not the stink making me retch but the sickening horror of the situation.

'Mum, you shouldn't be doing this. I'm thirty-two and I can't even go for a shit on my own.'

I make light of it, trying to normalise our abnormal lives.

'Nonsense, love. Remember, I was a nurse. I've done this for plenty of other thirty-two-, fifty-two-, even eighty-two-year-olds. I did it for you thirty years ago. There's not much difference really.'

'Only about fifteen stone difference.' His eyes are still tight shut.

Between us we manage to lift him from the floor onto his knees and thence to a standing position. He leans on us so heavily as we cross the tiny landing to the bathroom that I voice my fear that I will collapse under his weight. Even in such a desperate, humiliating position Andrew's humour is not far beneath the surface and he describes a picture of us all falling in a heap, a naked Andrew pinning his helpless parents to the floor. The tension is broken, and it is laughter that threatens to disable us.

Steve is showering him as I return to the bedroom to find Gosia manically scrubbing the floor. 'I'll never get it out from between the boards.' Her face is hard. She dare not smile, lest smiling should open the floodgates and allow her tears to flow. She is not trying to scrub the shit from the floorboards – she is trying to scrub the tumour from their lives.

We are silent on the journey home, silent as we get into bed. 'Gosia's under terrific strain, she won't cope for much longer,' says Steve.

The medical director of our local hospice comes to see Andrew. A gentle man, he explains all the facilities on offer: respite care, counselling, social events, alternative therapies. Andrew doesn't physically cover his ears, but this is the impression he gives. He says that he still wants 'to fight the bugger,' not to spend his time with a lot of old people who have given up. Gosia agrees. The doctor writes in his notes that Andrew is reluctant to discuss his incontinence. He is aware that his diagnosis is terminal but refuses to discuss the prognosis.

Is this when I should intervene? Give him the opportunity to be honest? I don't. Instead I accuse myself of cowardice, being lily-livered, chicken, gutless. But I still can't open the conversation. I know it will bring him even lower – I want him to believe there is still hope. I want to believe it myself.

Another chest infection, another deep vein thrombosis, take him into hospital. The aspirations of the reservoir have ceased. There is nothing to drain – the fluid in the many cysts now appearing in the fast-growing tumour obstinately remains in his head, pressing harder and harder on to his healthy brain tissue.

Lelly, his GP, is supporting us all. She looks me in the eye and asks me how I am. 'I'm fine.' It is my stock reply. I have to be fine. I must not fall apart.

'Janet, you can't be. How are you coping?'

'I just get up each morning and put on another layer of emotional armour-plating.'

'You know you are going to have to take that off at some point?'

'Yes. But don't ask me to yet. I need a buttress against the world.'

She squeezes my hand. 'I understand, Janet. Remember, I'll be here if you need help.'

I thank her and can feel the plates of armour against my eyes preventing a waterfall of emotion from spilling over.

Twenty-Seven

An invitation drops through the letterbox of 1 Military Road. The postman hands a similar envelope to me as I pass his red van in the lane. I open it to find a formally printed card inviting Steve and me to a wedding. David, Andrew's lifelong friend, is getting married – again.

His first marriage had been short-lived and unhappy, and the boys have felt each other's pain, pouring their troubles into their shared pool of friendship, drawing strength from it. Andrew has seen them as partners in adversity, holding one another up, unburdening sorrows onto someone outside the family but with an intimate knowledge of the other's history – a past in common that needs no explanation. Now, soon after a painful divorce, David has found love again. Andrew has watched as his friend's life has opened up once more. Like a plant that has withered for lack of nourishment, in the sunshine of love, it is blooming once more.

He is happy for David but is painfully aware that his own life is shrivelling and the chance of it rising healthy from the toxic soup of cancer cells and poisonous drugs is remote. He's not sure he can face a joyous wedding. Gosia certainly can't. She is worn out with caring, wearied with mothering, sapped by fear of an unknown future.

'No need to go, Andrew, if you'd rather not – everyone will understand,' Steve tells him.

'I know, Dad, but I want to go, and take Alice, as long as you can drive us. Gosia needs a break from me and I won't let my oldest friend down.'

Alice is excited about our little holiday. Her bag is packed with her prettiest dress. Andrew, however, curls his lip, despising his new trousers with the XXL label. Gosia's face is etched with grey misery as she straps Alice into her car seat and retreats indoors as soon as Steve starts the engine. Andrew lowers his gaze and Alice waves forlornly at her mother's back. But once on the open road the atmosphere lightens. Steve, a 'mapaholic', has carefully researched the route to the Lake District, and has marked all the scenic spots and places of interest. He's also marked all toilet stops on the way. I never thought I'd be so reassured by knowing the position of lavatories. The inevitable miles of motorway are accompanied by tapes of nursery rhymes and we all join in enthusiastically. We pull into a faceless service station for a coffee and loo-stop but are overtaken by a souped-up black Ford Capri with white skull and crossbones painted on its bonnet. Music blares through the open windows as it swerves into the only empty disabled parking bay.

'Bastards,' says Andrew.

Steve backs into a free space opposite and Andrew can't wait to get out of the car. Leaning on his stick he crosses the tarmac as three youths jump out of the Capri.

'Excuse me.' Andrew's tone is polite.

'Wha'?' snarls the man with the three-day growth of beard and a roll-up stuck to his lower lip.

'Did you realise that this is a disabled space?'

'So what?' The man's multi-pierced companion, clad in black, leers and thrusts his menacingly large head close to Andrew's face. I move my foot forward, but Steve holds me back. 'He's okay, love, he can cope,' he says with pride.

'I was just wondering if your friend here is suffering from cancer? If so, I wanted to offer my sympathies.'

The third youth grimaces and reaches to touch the spider tattooed on to his shaven head and the dark-chinned man grinds his fag end under his boot. 'So, what the fuck's wrong with you, then, apart from being fat?'

Andrew indicates the little balloon on his own head. 'Just a brain tumour that's slowly depriving me of my life.'

'Likely story,' the man in black sneers. But he avoids eye contact. The aggression has been sucked out of him.

Stubble-chin has his hand on the driver's door-handle. 'We was just goin' anyway, so you better have this space.' All three climb back into the car, the driver fires it into action, screeching the tyres as he reverses, and they drive off at speed scattering frightened pedestrians. The noise of the engine drowns the words Andrew tosses after them but then he looks at his dad, sticks his right thumb in the air and beckons our car into the disabled parking space, victory written all over his face.

Birmingham suburbs finally turn into green space until we reach our planned lunch break at a National Trust property. A weak October sun filters through falling leaves onto the empty disabled parking spot close to Packwood House. Middle-class National Trust members clearly know how to behave.

Andrew pauses on the stone bridge crossing the stream. He refused the wheelchair and has been leaning on Steve's arm, shuffling, and needs to rest. Mallards are dabbling in the water, causing Alice to jump up and down and ask if we have any bread for them. Her daddy, however, is gazing at the building ahead of him. 'God, that's beautiful,' he whispers, 'I do love old houses.' Tall ribbed Elizabethan chimneys stand high above the cream, gabled front and sunlight reflects off the ancient window glass. On the way to the barn restaurant where we lunch Andrew picks up a leaflet on the history of the house.

'It's quite new, really,' he reads, 'not begun until the 1550s, it says here. So not as old and interesting as our lovely old Float Farm. That's nearly a hundred years older, Booboo.' Alice looks quizzical and then returns to her beans on toast. Andrew tucks in to steak and kidney pie with potatoes, carrots and cabbage. We have not yet reached the Lake District, scene of Beatrix Potter's stories, but Andrew buys his daughter a large volume of the collected tales in the National Trust bookshop. 'You're going to love these stories, Booboo, just like I did.'

When we tour the house after lunch, the friendly guide tells us about the sixteenth and seventeenth century furniture and points out to Alice the cat following a tiny mouse in the corner of a tapestry. From the window, we admire the fine topiary gardens. Seeing the need, the guide finds a chair for Andrew. Alice is keen to search the first floor for more cats and mice so I suggest that Andrew and I wait at the bottom of the stairs until she and Granddad return, but Andrew is having none of it. Slowly, painfully, one side supported by Steve, he holds on to the Tudor banister rail and drags himself to the top, where, triumphant, he sinks on to the chair the kind lady has carried up behind him.

'My daddy's got a poorly head,' Alice explains pointing to Andrew's scar, 'That's his injury,' and she climbs on to his lap to kiss it.

Back in the car Andrew and his daughter both fall asleep as we drive on to Preston where we have arranged to call on an old friend. Gill had been a receptionist in the hotel in Rye, the scene of Andrew's misdeed when he was a breakfast chef. In the small social circle of the young of Rye, they had become good friends and we had often entertained her at the farmhouse. At Heathrow, when he'd set off on his travels, Gill had kissed him goodbye and presented him with a single red rose. Did either of them ever have hopes that friendship would develop into romance? I don't think so, but they enjoyed a loving friendship. The lure of home had been strong, and Gill had returned to Lancashire. Married now, with a small daughter, she welcomes us to their home with a delicious supper. She masks her shock at Andrew's condition and holds him close in a whispered conversation before she says goodbye.

The hotel is just off the M6 north of Lancaster. One of a national chain, we have chosen it for its ground-floor room with disabled facilities. Matthew and his friend Richard have arrived before us. They are not coming to the wedding but will share a room with Andrew, help him with showering and dressing and no doubt add some hilarity to his stay.

The wedding is traditional: church, formal dress, white-clad bride, complete with bridesmaids. I watch Andrew's inscrutable face and wonder what he is thinking. Is it of that sunny April day eight years ago, when he stood at the door of a country church with his own bride, before they scrambled amongst the daffodils to find the silver coins family and friends had tossed towards them, following an ancient Polish tradition? When endless life stretched out before them?

A reception at a Lake District hotel is followed by a dusk cruise on Lake Windermere, then guests gather on the hotel steps to wave off the bride and groom into their new life together. Steve offers Andrew his arm to join them, but he declines. 'You go, Dad. Mum, take Alice to enjoy the fun. I'll sit here with Arthur.'

As soon as the bridal car has left, tin cans clattering behind, its occupants smiling under a confetti storm, I go back into the hotel to find Andrew sitting with another guest, nonagenerian Arthur, whom I have known since I was a teenager. In response to my concern the old man chortles, 'We're just fine, Janet. Two old crocks together.'

Andrew, at thirty-two, is not amused.

Twenty-Eight

'Mum, I'm going into the Care Centre – just for a few days, to give Gosia a break.'

With the phone to my ear I mouth the news silently to Steve who is toying with his shepherd's pie at the table. He sighs, closes his eyes, pushes his plate away and slowly nods his head. Another big step on the downward path has been reached, but we are relieved that the rising tension at home will be diffused. Andrew has been having severe headaches and more focal fits causing raised anxiety levels and straining family relationships. Lelly, knowing the situation, and aware of Andrew's misgivings about the hospice, has arranged a respite bed at the Care Centre a few hundred yards away from Military Road.

None of us realise that a few days will extend into the last four months of Andrew's life.

I push open the door of the modern, comfortable, friendly building that will become so familiar. The old Cottage Hospital was built as a memorial to the fallen of the First World War. Past its useful life in 1992, it was scheduled for closure, but the community rose up in protest. We held jumble sales, fetes, appeals, deputations, to try to save it. All to little avail until our trump cards came on board. Paul and Linda McCartney were local residents, they shopped in our shops, their children attended the comprehensive school in town and are friends of Andrew's. Like us, the McCartneys had reason to believe a hospital was an important facility for the town. They would not let it go. The publicity they lent the campaign by lobbying the politicians, leading thousands on a protest march through the streets and, not least, pouring in some of their own money, meant our hospital was saved and rebuilt as the Rye Memorial Care Centre.

'I've come to visit my son, Andrew Denny,' I tell the nurse whose face, like most in our small town, is vaguely familiar. Her smile broadens into a giggle.

'He's in room six,' she points to the end of the short corridor, 'but you enter at your peril – it's all vindaloo and testosterone in there.'

As I open the door of Andrew's room, strong aromas of the sub-continent (or, more accurately, the Ghandi Tandoori Takeaway) pervade the air, and gales of bawdy male laughter meet my ears. His mates have got there before me with a 'better than hospital lunch' and a fund of dirty jokes.

Our family quickly develops a new routine. The Care Centre is en route to the small village school where Alice has begun full-time education. Gosia can take her to see Daddy most days, on the way home from school. Steve and I pop in daily – often twice or thrice daily. My mother appoints herself as self-styled 'washerwoman', glad of the opportunity to help by collecting, laundering and returning Andrew's soiled clothes. Wider family and friends throng his room, take him out for pub lunches, wheel him into the garden for one of the cigarettes he smoked only occasionally before he fell ill, but which are now becoming more important. *Like the patients lined up outside the Marsden*, I think.

He is occupying a respite care bed and after three weeks the time for respite is running out. Andrew would like to go home but Gosia shudders at the prospect. He can barely walk now and there are steps to their front door, more to the back, narrow stairs to the basement and first floors where the only loos are situated. There is nothing I would like more than to have him at the farmhouse, but the same restrictions apply – there is no possibility of installing a shower on the 'ground floor', which is on five different levels in our medieval house. The step or two between rooms are an unremarkable fact of life for the able-bodied, for Andrew each one is another Everest. Lelly petitions the health authority for a 'continuing care' bed. They refuse. Lelly fights. They cave in. Andrew can stay. But it is a pyrrhic victory. He will never sleep at home again.

He moves into room one, which has an en suite wet-room with facilities for a hoist. We make it as homely as we can with pictures on the wall, a television, his own phone line, a CD player and a stock of his favourite music.

It is December and another Christmas season is upon us, three years since a violent night-time seizure brought normality tumbling around our ears. The third anniversary of our boy's death sentence. We only have one shop to worry about now, having closed in Tunbridge Wells. It felt like a betrayal, an acceptance that there was no future for him, but we needed to spend time with Andrew, rather than tearing ourselves apart managing two establishments.

Gosia, Alice and I join good friends with young children to take Andrew to a performance of *The Snowman* in Eastbourne. He delights in watching the children's entranced expressions as the magic unfolds, but I think he enjoys even more the knickerbocker glory in the café afterwards.

Rye has one pre-Christmas Saturday when the shops stay open until nine pm. Santa enters the town on a sleigh, (or mini train, or boat, or whatever mode of transport the Chamber of Trade can conjure up). Crowds flock into the town, shop assistants dress up as angels, fairies or Santa's elves to serve mulled wine and mince pies to their customers. The illuminations on an enormous tree on the balcony of The George Hotel are switched on by Father Christmas and the small trees that line the High Street twinkle with myriad tiny silver lights. It is a traditional, convivial evening for all ages and Andrew will not miss it. We bring him to the shop, but he doesn't venture onto the crowded pavement. Instead he sits at the door, chatting to friends, soaking up the atmosphere and wishing he could soak up some of the mulled wine. He downs an extra mince pie instead.

The next day his headache is unbearable despite the usual medication, and the doctor orders a syringe pump to inject a constant, controlled dose of diamorphine. It is strapped to his thigh and the drug is delivered via a cannula that sits just under his skin.

'It's magic,' he tells me, 'black magic. Mum, I need to do some shopping – a present for Gosia.'

'Have you any ideas?'

'Maybe some jewellery? Do you think she'd like that?'

The thought of trailing around shops with a sick, heavy man in a wheelchair among the press of pre-Christmas crowds is alarming. 'Would you like me to get something?' I offer.

'Please.' His shoulders sag with relief.

Our fellow traders in Rye are more than happy for me to take a selection of items for Andrew to choose from and he selects a necklace and earrings hung with silver glass hearts.

On Christmas day Steve collects him and brings him to the farmhouse. Everyone he loves is there, his whole extended family. We follow the usual rituals of a family lunch. Steve's mum says grace and makes her usual call for 'a clap for the cook'. We pull crackers, don paper hats and groan at bad jokes. Roast dinner smells waft from the kitchen, mouths water in anticipation of the traditional turkey and trimmings. But this is unlike any previous Christmas day. Andrew's voice, his laughter, his enjoyment of life is missing. His face is blank, eyes glazed as he sits silently eating the food Gosia has cut into bite-sized portions for him, now that his left hand has grown so weak. Alice, with Granddad's supervision, brings in the flaming pudding and at last, her daddy summons a weak smile, attempts and fails to clap his hands.

The logs flame and crackle in the inglenook as Alice and Katie distribute the presents. Andrew drifts in and out of slumber, to the sounds of parcels being unwrapped, exclamations of joy and appreciation, the sound of the Queen's voice, the rattle of teacups. Then he is propelled into wakefulness by Alice climbing on to his lap to kiss him goodnight. Gosia has decided it is time to go home to bed.

He lifts his hand weakly from the arm of his chair, but it falls back before he can wave. His eyelids drop, and he snoozes on and off for the next hour.

'You're tired, lad. It's been a big day. Would you like to go back now?' Steve asks.

'Like to go home, see my house again.'

Matthew offers to go with them, to help negotiate the wheelchair on the uneven steps, so I phone Gosia. Her words when she answers are weighted with hopeless despair. 'No, it's not a good time, we're tired. We'll see him tomorrow.'

I relay her words as gently as possible to Andrew who narrows his lips and nods his head in resignation and Steve drives him back to the Care Centre.

It is the eve of a new millennium. The world is alive with excitement and optimism for what it may bring. Kind friends have invited Andrew, Gosia and Alice to spend the evening with them, to watch from the cliff at the edge of the town, the fireworks that will see the beginning of the year two thousand. Knowing this arrangement is in place, Steve and I spend Millenium Eve with our friends, the Wilsons, in our little cottage in Southwold. The night is dry and starlit. As darkness approaches, the occupants of houses fronting the streets and surrounding the many greens in the little town leave their windows uncurtained to reveal to passers-by glowing fireplaces and tables set with cut glass and fine silver for once-in-a-thousand-year celebratory dinners. Black ties, dinner jackets and the best of best dresses can be glimpsed on animated figures flitting in and out of the rooms. We, too, have made an effort to lift our hearts out of the black hole that has become their default residence, to don our emotional armour and join in the jubilant mood. After a gourmet meal which our friends declare delicious but which I pick at randomly, we join the crowds in the square. The local corps of pipes and drums heralds the appearance on the balcony of the town hall of the town council and Mr Mayor, complete with robes, maces and tricorne hats. It is toytown come alive. The lady vicar says a prayer about a man who stood at the gate of the year and the crowd follow the band up to Gun Hill where the beacon is lit in response to the one further along the coast. I watch six-year-olds partnering ninety-year-olds as the band strikes up, and when the dancing is over, fireworks fizz and bang all along the beach and soar into bursting flowers of light against the sky, reflecting off the sea and illuminating brave young skinny-dippers. Strangers, champagne glasses in hand, embrace each other with wishes for a happy new year.

Steve grasps my hand and we flee to the cottage. We know what this first year of the new millennium will bring. It cannot be a happy new year.

Twenty-Nine

It is mid-January and today there is an important trade fair at Earl's Court. Andrew wishes he could go with his dad – he will miss the banter on the suppliers' stands.

'Sniff out some good lines, Dad,' he said last night.

Steve is reluctant to travel to London, but I encourage him. 'He'll love to know all about it, see what you've ordered, hear who has been asking about him. You go, love, and visit this evening.'

I am at work in shopkeeper mode, arranging the sale, preparing for the Birmingham gift fairs in February and March, answering the phone, paying invoices, smiling at customers, wishing them a happy new year. Many of them have no idea that my son is dying. Why should they? How many of us consider the personal lives of those anonymous people we interact with in the course of every day? Some of the customers are locals, acquaintances, friends, who ask hesitantly, self-consciously, 'How are things?' – wary of personalising the situation by uttering his name. They fear breaking my protective shell and causing an embarrassing emotional incident. A few are unable to look me in the eye as they fumble in their purses and mutter about being in a terrible rush. One or two glance obliquely through the door from the pavement and seeing me at the counter avert their gaze, quicken their pace and hope I haven't seen them.

Sarah is manning the till this morning. She raises her eyebrows when I come out of the office and inclines her head towards a figure, back towards us, standing in front of the card display. I can see the corner of his signature cravat poking above his jacket collar and recognise a friend and fellow trader. Sarah whispers, 'Have you heard? They say his son has committed suicide in New Zealand.' Her face has an expression of tragedy tinged with paparazzi excitement. I walk to the back of the shop, mercifully devoid of customers, and lay my hand on his shoulder.

'Is what I hear true, Malcom?' I enquire gently, willing him to turn, grinning, to ask what nonsense is going around.

He doesn't look up as he mutters, 'Yes, Janet, I am afraid it is.'

Staring with unseeing eyes at a line of 'congratulations' cards he tells me that no one has an inkling of why his clever son, who had a good job at Canterbury University in Christchurch, as well as a young family, had kissed his wife goodbye before she set off to drop the baby at nursery on the way to work, while he drove their daughter to school, why he then had driven into a disused industrial estate, attached a hose to his car exhaust, threaded it through the chink of open window and let the engine run until he met oblivion.

Bruce had been a contemporary of Andrew's. They had shared riding lessons, played football and grown up in the same small community. I feel a crater of grief and sympathy for his parents opening up inside me. But I do not expect the anger in Malcom's face when he turns to look at me.

'How could he do this?' He spits out the words. 'There is your boy fighting with everything he's got to hold on to his life, and my son just throws his away.' He buries his quivering face in my outstretched arms.

What agony it must be to never know why, to always wonder, *Was it something we did or didn't do?* It must be the worst legacy a child can leave. The same question nags at me. Is it my fault? Was it that time the television was knocked off the rickety coffee table? Could it have hit my baby's head? There was no evidence it had, but... Could it have been then that some cells in his brain were traumatised, lay dormant, and twenty-nine years later awoke in a mad frenzy of multiplication? I left him to crawl unsupervised by that telly, so is it my fault his brain is now being consumed by itself?

The day wears on and I know Andrew is waiting for me. I dread going to see him, constantly finding just one more thing I must do before I leave work. I am two mothers now, a split personality. I am the mother of a beautiful boy, who still feels that rush of maternal devotion and pride welling up at every sight of him, who wants to hold him in this world forever. I am also the mother of a man experiencing a slow, painful and inevitable death and I feel this death reflected in myself. Every time I put my arms around his bloated body with its useless arm and leg, see the bubble on his bald head, hear his slurred voice trying to find words, a little more life drains out of me.

I phone Frances. 'How long will this go on? I can't keep strong for much longer.' I am outraged as she confirms what I already know – it could be weeks, months.

No, No, No.

The gremlin in my head torments me. *So, you want your son to die then?*

Yes, I do.

Oh God, how can I think that? I should be thinking, *I wish it could be me instead of him.* That is what devoted mothers should think. Why can't I?

I put on my coat, switch off the lights, lock the door of the shop behind me and walk up the hill, glad of the darkness to hide me from familiar passers-by. I am a jumble of emotions: love, anger, frustration, grief. Of all my children Andrew has always been the one who has tested my patience to the limit, the most frustrating to bring up. Yet he has always made me laugh, made my heart leap at the sight of him, and I know he has always been devoted to me and Steve, the most needful of our love. I am wretched with guilt. As I near the hospital I lift my head and my pace quickens. Suddenly I feel desperate to see his face, hear his laugh, and hold him in my arms again. How could I have wished for his death? He is fighting like a tiger, and I will fight with him just as long as I have breath in my body and he has breath in his.

The first mother is back in charge.

'Hi Mum.' His face is glum, his shoulders slumped against the pillows.

I bend to hug him, hold my face to his. 'Sweetheart, I brought you some snowdrops from the garden, first flowers of the year.'

'Last ones I'll see, probably.' There is a long pause before he continues, 'I'm going to die, Mum.'

How do I reply? All my insides contort in panic. I know this is the moment, the moment we should confront reality together. But he said 'probably', he still has hope. Can I take that away from him? Once again, I take the coward's way, saying, 'We all have to die sometime, love.' He says nothing but his withering look shames me.

'Been trying to write –,' He glances towards the bed-table where a pen and a piece of lined paper torn from a spiral notebook, lie abandoned, '– to Alice, just in case.'

'Would you like me to help?'

He nods his head and I pick up the pen and paper. 'Just a few points,' he says, 'you'd better put it into proper sentences.' We both smile.

Following his instructions, I type up the notes at home and next morning he reads it through and seals his approval with a wobbly signature.

My Dearest Alice

It seems I may not be around to guide you through your growing up so I want to put on paper my love for you and my hopes and dreams for you.

Alice, I love you more than anything in the world. You have brought such happiness to me and Mum. You are beautiful, intelligent, loving and so very precious to me. During my illness you have accepted my disabilities with good humour and love, helping whenever you can and frequently kissing my 'injury' (the scar on my head). I have fought so hard to stay alive for you – I desperately want to see you grow into a beautiful woman and make your way in the world – but life can be cruel and end too soon, however hard we fight.

You only have one life, Alice, so make the most of it. Grasp every opportunity and (here comes the boring bit) work hard at school – harder than me! Education is the key that opens the door to all your dreams. Always be interested in other people and put them before yourself, you will be happier for it. But pick your friends carefully. I sometimes made mistakes and have found that, in times of adversity, your true friends are not necessarily the glamorous or wealthy ones. Money is not the most important thing in life, people are. Millions of pounds couldn't help me now, but my family and friends are priceless.

Always remember you are part of a close and loving family. You have a wonderful mother and although, like all parents and children, you will have many differences, you are everything to her and she only wants the best for you. Granny, Granddad, Laura, Tony, Katie, Joe, Matthew, Grangay, Great Granny, Auntie Mary, David, your Godfather, and all your Polish relations will always be there to love you, listen to you, help and support you through difficult and joyful times.

You live in a wonderful world of beauty, grandeur and mystery, interesting people and cultures and sometimes all too much injustice and unkindness. Explore it, enjoy it and do your best to make it even better for others.

Alice, I would like you to know what sort of a person I was (by no means perfect, I'm afraid.) Please ask friends and family about me, they will be happy to tell you – warts and all.

Whatever life has in store for you – whether you become a vet (your current ambition), or a poet or a nurse or an office worker – enjoy it and retain your sense of fun. Always keep a smile on your face – I hope that is what I will be remembered for.

Love as always

Daddy XX

'Well done, my love.' I slide the precious document into a plastic folder.

'I'll leave you to decide when to give it to her.'

'I hope I'll never have to.' I know this is another cowardly lie.

He wants to go home for a night, 'for a cuddle with my wife', but he knows the difficulties are insurmountable. The idea of arranging a double bed in his room is discussed and seems possible, but Gosia dismisses it. A loving night with her overweight, disabled husband in a hospital room is unthinkable.

When he attends his January hospital appointment for his eleventh cycle of temozolomide, Frances explains with tact and tenderness that it seems now to be having little effect. But he is insistent, grasping at an almost broken thread. The injection is given, reluctantly. The dose of the steroid, dexamethazone, is reduced to cut down his weight gain, but this results in fits of vomiting so anti-emetic drugs are added to the cocktail of chemicals in his syringe driver. The site of this is frequently changed – from his thigh to his upper arm, from his stomach to his shoulder – but soon after each move painful ulcers appear around the cannula.

The weather is cold and miserable. A heavy grey blanket divides our part of the earth from the sun, but we try to liberate Andrew from the Care Centre as often as possible. On the thirteenth of February Steve and I take him to a wheelchair-friendly supermarket where he relishes a full English breakfast and buys a big bunch of red roses for his valentine.

However, the fourteenth of February, despite Gosia's gratitude for the roses, is a harrowing day. It is his final visit to the Marsden for his last cycle of temozolomide – which Mike, Dr B, refuses to give. He writes in his notes that Andrew's condition is considerably worse. He is completely wheelchair-bound, unable to sustain a conversation and in the terminal stage of disease. Further active treatment is of no use.

I was not there, I don't know how he put this to Andrew. I'm sure he would have been sensitive, tactful, but when I hear the news and witness Andrew's utter dejection, I am angry. If only I had been with them. Surely, I could have pleaded with Mike not to snip this final strand of hope. Maybe I could have persuaded him to give a placebo dose? I was not there, however, and the deed is done – or not done. I encircle my son's ballooning body with my arms, kiss his damp cheek and I know he has given up.

It is only a short walk from the Care Centre to Rye Cemetery. Lying on the hillside overlooking the town and the Brede and Tillingham valleys he loves so dearly, it makes a good brief outing. Sitting muffled in thick winter clothing, a woollen hat pulled down over his ears, with Gosia on the wooden bench beside his chair, he says, 'This is a good place to be buried.'

Thirty

A new member has recently joined our team of part-time shop assistants, a charming, Belgian woman who belongs to a charismatic Christian church. She waylays me as I am locking the shop one wet and windy evening, anxious to be on my way up the hill to see Andrew. 'Janet, could I have a quick word, please?'

We shelter in the doorway avoiding a soaking by the wheels swooshing through the deep puddles in the gutter. 'What is it Leis?' I ask, conscious of the impatience in my voice.

'I would like, with some friends from my church, to visit Andrew and pray with him.'

I did not expect this, and I'm touched by her concern (she hardly knows Andrew), but doubtful about her suggestion. His experience at Burrswood was traumatic and ultimately unhelpful. I am not sure that this won't be the same. 'It is kind of you to think of him, Leis, but he is extremely weak now. I will put the idea to him, but the decision will have to be his alone and I trust you will understand if he turns down your offer.'

'Of course.' We hurry in opposite directions along the street, battling with our umbrellas in the wind.

'All right, Mum,' he says, when I tell him. 'Nothing else seems to work so there's no harm in giving God another go, is there?' He shrugs his shoulders and looks at the wall.

So, they come with their bibles and their prayers. When I ask him about it he tells me it was a bit of a mistake, then changes the subject. I let it rest but when I arrive a couple of days later, Anne, a mature staff nurse we have come to know and trust during Andrew's four months in this place, beckons me into the office.

'Those people, the Christians, came again last night – about nine o'clock – so rather late. I sent them away. I hope I did the right thing.'

'Of course, Anne. Nine is far too late.'

'It wasn't just that, Janet. Andrew was so upset after their first visit, I thought he wouldn't want to see them again.' In answer to my questioning frown she continues. 'He said that after all the praying and speaking in tongues, they pestered and bullied him to lay his hand on the bible and declare he accepted Jesus as his Lord, and that if it is God's will for him to die, he is ready for – I think he said it was – ready for glory. I sat with him for a long time afterwards, calming him, talking it through. He asked me not to tell anyone, but I think you should know.'

Fury bubbles up from my stomach to my ears. How dare they bully a vulnerable young man into accepting their belief in saving souls for the Lord? Then, the little gremlin who still lies somewhere deep in my mind, taunts me. It was you who didn't refute the idea in the first place, you who didn't protect your son from this.

The gremlin is correct. I have let him down again.

A cold March wind blows me up the hill to the Care Centre. Most of Andrew's time is spent sleeping, now, but the click of the door latch pierces his slumber and he opens one eye. 'Hi Mum.' He inclines his head towards the bedside locker. 'Paul brought me some, some –'

'Shortbread, how lovely.' I help him to find the word, which, like others, deserts him now that the tumour is encroaching on his language resource. Several fellow restaurateurs and colleagues from his cheffing days in Rye bring him foodie treats, increasing his weight more and more. But, at this stage, who cares, if it brightens his day? I sit with him as he slips in and out of sleep, playing his favourite CDs. As so often when I kiss him and rise to leave, he whispers, 'Take me outside, I want a smoke.'

Please, Andrew, I think, *not tonight. It's raining and I'm tired,*

I must go home, cook dinner, make phone calls, prepare for tomorrow. Please don't ask this of me now. But he can't go home and cook dinner, he can't chat on the phone and he knows there is no tomorrow to prepare for. So, with the help of one of the kind, willing nurses, I dress him in fleecy jogging trousers, thick quilted black jacket and pull a woollen beanie hat down over his ears. We hoist him into his wheelchair and, armed with cigarettes and matches, I push him through the deserted reception area and out into the chilly night. I light his cigarette and sit on a low wall next to him, watching the point of red glowing brighter, then duller as he puffs. When the ash threatens to fall I catch it in my cupped hand. He may smoke a third, even a half of it, before muttering, 'Enough,' and I grind the remaining stick of poison under my heel, pick up the remains and wheel him back to bed.

On the fifteenth of March, Laura and Matthew are staying overnight at the farmhouse. We plan to visit this evening – my mum, Gosia and Alice having been earlier in the day. Andrew is fading fast now, sedated with ever increasing doses of morphine, no longer eating and barely drinking. I know he can still appreciate smells and sounds, however, so Steve and I plan to take in smoked salmon and champagne to celebrate us all being together – a last supper for our nuclear family of five.

The pleasure on his face when he sees his siblings forces us into false jollity, suppressing our dismay at what is coming. We play CDs of the music they all enjoyed as teenagers: Paul Weller, Joy Division, Blondie, and hope the sharp aroma of the salmon is reminding him of past pleasures. 'Wow,' he murmurs when the pop of the champagne cork rouses him from morphia-land.

Steve pours a little into a glass and holds a straw between Andrew's lips. 'Here, lad, try a sip. It's the real stuff. No cava or prosecco tonight.'

Matthew has a new girlfriend and we are all curious to know about her. He pulls a photo from his pocket and Laura leans to get a glimpse. 'No, no.' Her brother snatches it away. 'I want Andrew to see it first – I need my big brother's approval.' He fixes it with a blob of Blu-Tack to the wall close to Andrew's eyes. 'Whaddya think?' The corners of his brother's lips twitch and there is a slight nod.

Laura asks him if he remembers when he put a banana down his Lycra jogging shorts to shock us. We laugh as I recall her white-faced embarrassment and my initial dismay until I got the joke and told him not to be so childish. He opens his eyes and attempts a wobbly grin.

We recall holidays on the farm in Cornwall, rain-sodden tramps on Dartmoor, picnics on the beach, and he screws up his face, pulling himself out of a drug-fuelled haze to utter one word, 'Bim.' We all applaud, as if he is a small child attaining the first word of language, and then we fall into reminiscing about our beloved dog, adopted from Cornwall twenty-four years ago.

He's only just below the surface; can he hear the strain in our high-pitched voices? We know this is the last time. Does he?

Laura's tears dampen his cheek when she bends to say goodbye. His face relaxes into a fond expression, not a smile, more a look of contentment, acceptance that after all that childhood fighting and competition, the sibling bonds of affection are transcendent.

How can we leave him? In my head I hear him crying, 'Don't go, please don't go.' I hug his unresponsive body and know the morphine has claimed him again, eased his pain, taken him from us. 'I'll see you tomorrow, my love,' I whisper in his ear.

Thirty-One

I am wearing that purple top with the tiny roses and the velveteen jeans I bought in the John Lewis sale when Laura took me on a shopping trip to re-taste normality, and the laced black boots I have worn every day this winter. It has been an unsuitably grey and damp season to herald in a new millennium.

I won't stay long. The dinner is keeping warm in the bottom of the Aga, so I will leave the Care Centre about nine when Steve is due home from a visit to a London supplier. Then we'll eat before returning together to say goodnight to Andrew.

I press the buzzer to announce my out of hours arrival and the door catch is released remotely. Wearily, I sign in. A whole page of family and friends' names precedes mine and this is the third time I have signed in today: 8-8.45am, 1.15-2pm and now 7pm. Staff nurse Anne Snow meets me in the corridor. Her face tells me things have changed. She touches my elbow as I open the door of his room.

'Oh, I see.' He is lying perfectly still, his eyes are closed, but I know this isn't sleep. Neither is he unconscious. Life seems to flutter intermittently across his face like a feather in the breeze. I've watched others in this near-death stage but never someone I love.

No longer is my body made of composite parts – head, trunk, limbs, stomach, heart – but a black, amorphous, heavy blob of despair in which I am trapped with no hope of escape. The demon that invaded Andrew's brain, masquerading as a stroke, has shown its true colours and grown, over three years, into a monster. It is hungry for its victim.

Not tonight, please don't gobble him up tonight. Metaphorically I am on my knees, stretching out my arms, contorting my face into a desperate, final plea for mercy. In reality, though, I am calm, controlled.

'When was the change?' I ask Anne and my words are steady.

'About ten minutes ago. I was about to phone you. Should I phone Gosia?'

'I will,' I reply. 'She'll have to find someone to sit with Alice.' I stoop to kiss his warm cheek, but he shows no sign of response. I lift the receiver of the phone in the room and punch in the number.

'But I took Alice in on the way home from school,' she says, when I tell her. 'He was sleepy, but he opened his eyes and tried to speak. Alice climbed on the bed and gave him a hug – but I think she was, well, a little bit frightened.'

'I think you should come, Gosia, as soon as Alice is in bed. Didn't Simon offer to sit with her?'

Andrew is still lying with his head to one side when Gosia arrives and bends to kiss him. His right ear is buried in the pillow, his steroid-swollen young body resembling a beached whale – his last description of himself.

Gosia and I sit on opposite sides of the bed concentrating on avoiding the pain in each other's eyes, while we stroke his body and whisper to him.

'*Kochanie,*' Gosia begins and continues in her native tongue so I know not what she says to him before she falters and stops. Silence blankets the room until my daughter-in-law rises and inserts a CD of Paul McCartney's *Working Classical* into the bulky machine – a 'ghetto blaster' past its glory days. The volume is low. The only ghetto to be blasted here is on the other side of the River Styx. Charon is preparing his oars in the hope of a new passenger.

I know something about ghettos. I've seen the pictures on the TV and in films. I've read the stories of poverty, fear, separation. I've been there, to Belfast where Catholics and Protestants built barricades to isolate themselves from each other. I've seen the places – in Venice, Warsaw and Kracow – where the *alien Jews* were incarcerated in walled spaces and slowly starved or shot. In the ghetto of death, however, on the opposite shore of the Styx there is no distinction of race or religion. They're all dead there. However loud the music, nothing will stir. Ultimately all life is herded into that unbordered space. A fortunate few escaped the Warsaw ghetto; no one escapes the ghetto of death.

As I sink into blackness I force myself to recall the comfort of Christian teaching – those words that upheld my optimism in a previous life, words that promised heaven, paradise, a joyous afterlife. I clutch at the possibility that I was arrogant and deluded to reject them; perhaps they're true after all. Maybe, just maybe, this is not the end. My mouth relaxes into what may become a smile and I feel myself rise from the underworld towards the light. Then the sun is covered by a cloud as I realise that whatever *undiscovered country* Andrew is destined for, it is *a bourn from whence no traveller returns.* Wherever he is bound, be it Hades, Paradise or, as common sense tells me, extinction, my boy is leaving me. These are our last hours.

I press my cheek to his. I curl my fingers around his as they lie motionless on the sheet and grip them tight as if I might hold him here for a little longer.

The door creaks open, and Anne enters the room. We look up and make to stand. We are used to moving out of the way when she gives Andrew his medications, changes the bed, lifts him into a more comfortable position. Now she pushes the air with downward palms. 'No, don't get up. I just want to say goodnight. I'm going home now and tomorrow's my day off.' She touches my shoulder and then crosses the room to press Gosia's hand. All our eyes turn to the silent figure in the bed.

'He looks peaceful, doesn't he?' Anne says and forces a smile. She bends low and brushes her lips over his brow. 'Goodbye, Andrew,' she whispers.

As the door closes behind her, Gosia jumps up and grabs the phone. She jabs her finger at the buttons, keying in her home number.

'Simon? Is everything okay? Is she still asleep? Sure you can stay?

Don't know how long... No, no change. Make yourself a cup of tea. Thanks.' Andrew's school friend is babysitting Alice.

My call greets Steve as he arrives home. He is back in the car before the engine has cooled and is with us within minutes. *Please don't kiss me*, my eyes plead, and he understands that if he does, my emotional armour will crack and allow a grief-laden arrow to undo me. Always awkward in the face of illness, he keeps repeating 'Oh, lad, oh lad...' and his dear face is a picture of helplessness. Mummy can't make it better, Daddy can't mend it. We are failed parents unable even to attempt to rescue him from whatever blackness he faces.

Steve has fended off sleep for nights, knowing that if he lets it overcome him the creatures that stalk him in nightmares will attack and he'll scream and disturb me. He won't give in. I know how my husband copes with illness and trauma. He juts his chin forward and just keeps carrying on. It's the only way he knows. Every day he has been in the shop, greeting customers, seeing reps, listening to the worries of staff, doing the books, paying bills. All the while, inside, he has been collapsing into a barely functioning pile of angry grief, and today has been long and tiring, visiting suppliers in London. My strength, my love, my life.

'Go home, sweetheart. You are done in and your supper is in the Aga.' He grimaces – supper is the last thing he wants. 'And we have no idea how long... I'll phone when you need to come. Simon is happy to stay with Alice.'

He protests.

I insist.

Alison is on duty tonight. Quietly compassionate and calm, she inspires confidence in us all. Her son is in Alice's class at school and Andrew has described how he and Alison have talked long into the gloomy hours when it has seemed dawn will never lighten the sky. She has told me how he shared with her his despair, his grief, his anger, and kept his bright-faced optimism for us.

'I'm glad I'm on tonight,' she tells us.

So are we.

We talk to Andrew of good times, fun times, laugh about embarrassing moments. We assure him that Alice is okay – Simon is with her. My boy's finger twitches, he licks his lips, and we blink, jerking ourselves back into the moment as if, as if he might be… No. He's not waking. We keep talking. You never know if he can hear.

At midnight Alison brings us cocoa. I never drink cocoa but tonight the sweet, chocolate creaminess of it feels like an elixir comforting me from the inside. Gosia's eyelids droop as she sinks back into the pillows in the big armchair.

'I'm sorry we don't have another comfy chair for you, Janet,' Alison looks anxious, 'but we do have an empty bed in the room over the corridor. I've put a blanket and pillow on it so why don't you try and get a little rest?'

I shake my head before she has finished speaking. 'I must be here.'

'I'll call you if things change. He'd want you to rest.'

Reluctantly I assent, and she shepherds me to the room, unlaces my boots, eases them from my feet, and tucks me up like a baby.

Do I sleep? Maybe. Do I dream? I think so. I think I dream of a baby vomiting up his milk. I think I dream of hospitals, operations, dogs, seashores, chefs' hats, girl-friends; but maybe I'm not asleep, maybe I'm just running his life across my mind, grabbing at memories before they disappear.

All at once my chest tightens as if I am in a straitjacket. I am wide awake now and I jump from the bed, kick my boots away and meet Alison as I open the door. Her smile is as gentle as ever, but there is a suspicion of urgency in her words. 'I was just coming to call you.'

When I burst into Andrew's room, Gosia's face is devoid of expression. She stands by her husband but is looking at the blackness outside the window or some imagined space beyond.

I take in the sights and sounds in the room and control the lump of panic rising from my chest to my throat. 'Ah,' I say, and reach for the phone. 'Come now,' I whisper to Steve when he picks up at the first ring, 'and hurry.'

Andrew has not moved. He lies, as before, propped by pillows, staring with closed eyes at Alice's painting of a smiley face high on the opposite wall. The calm, regular breathing I left him with has changed. Now, as his chest inflates, it rattles, not with the familiar sound of congestion, but with the otherworldly sound of death. 'Cheyne-Stokes respiration,' I say to Alison, my nearly forgotten nursing training coming back to form a film of professionalism between my panic and the horror before me. Alison nods.

It won't be long. Will Steve get here? *Please, Steve, drive fast.* We stroke Andrew's hands and I whisper in his ear, plucking my words from all those books I have read about death.

'Don't be afraid, love. It'll be all right – I promise. See that light? Go towards the light, Andrew, go towards the light. Everything will be okay.'

His chest rises, then falls with a harsh vibrating noise. All is silent for what feels like several minutes and I think he is gone, until he seems to make one more enormous effort. His eyelids quiver as he inhales like a giant about to blow a house down. The sound that follows is like metallic fragments and shards of glass being shaken in an empty oil drum. It repeats – the long silence, the next gargantuan breath, the sound of debris. And then it happens again. Each time the delay between breaths is longer and I am reminded of those long silences between screams when, as a toddler, he fell and banged his head. The more it hurt, the longer the pauses.

Another rackety breath pierces the air. We wait, and we wait.

He is still. Alison feels for a pulse then pulls the sheet over his wrist. Three silent women, we stand, for what feels like a long time, looking at one young man. Tears slide from our eyes.

My firstborn is dead.

It is only then that I realise I had been whispering my comfort into his deaf ear.

I do not scream or wail. I feel only a blank acceptance of the inevitable, followed by relief that his suffering is over. Then I am overwhelmed by guilt that I haven't done more to stop this monster taking his life, and anger that no one took it seriously early enough, then terrible regret that I didn't tell him more often how much I loved him. It is only when my eyes meet my husband's as he enters the room that my lip falters and I sob quietly.

Steve stands at the end of the bed staring in disbelief until his face crumbles, he removes his glasses and fists his tears away.

'What do we do now?' Gosia's voice pushes up through the miasma pressing down on the room.

'The doctor will come to see him in the morning,' says Alison. 'Then you can decide what you want to do. Stay with him for as long as you like.'

Gosia's startled eyes move from one to the other of us. She is shaking. 'I don't know, I don't know what I want to do, I've never...'

I know.

I know what I want to do. I brought him into this world and I will prepare him to leave it. I am no longer his next of kin, he has a wife to fill that role, so I must be careful.

'Gosia,' I choose my words warily, I speak them slowly, 'we need to wash him, make him look how he would like to look, dress him in his favourite clothes.'

She throws a look of panic at me as if I have asked her to perform a post-mortem. 'Would you like me to do that for you, with Alison's help?' I say.

She nods her head vigorously. 'I'll get the clothes. I must go anyway, I need to be with Alice, Simon has to go home. Sorry.'

I hug her. 'Of course, you must. It's okay, Andrew would want you to be with Alice.' She is scrabbling in her bag, looking for her car keys.

Steve takes her arm. 'I'll drive you.' At the door, she hesitates and looks back towards the bed.

Alison says, 'Don't worry, he's not going anywhere yet, Gosia. He'll be waiting for you when you come back.' When they have gone she looks me in the eye and says, 'You don't have to do this, Janet.'

'I've done it for complete strangers so why would I not want to do it for my own son?' I hear the snappiness in my voice.

'Why not have a cup of tea first?'

'I don't drink tea.' I spit the words out too harshly. 'Sorry,' I say. Alison hugs me. 'It's okay, I understand.'

'I haven't laid out a body for over thirty years,' I tell her.

'It's different these days,' she says. 'It's much simpler now – no cotton wool…' Her voice trails away as I nod. No need for her to remind me of packing body orifices. Gently, reverently, we wash his bloated body. Alison reminds me that he may sigh as we turn him and the last air is forced from his lungs. I assure her that I remember also about the bruising where the no longer circulating blood will have pooled in his back. All very professional. I see the scene from above as if through a camera lens, two women laying out a body, quite calmly, in the dead of night.

Who am I? I ask myself. Am I a mortician? Am I a nurse? Am I a mother? Or am I a mother pretending to be a nurse, putting up that barrier again, distancing myself from emotion? Yes, I am all of those and I can do these things. I can still care for and love my boy even in death. I am not just any mortician, nurse, mother – I am Andrew's.

'Do you think he needs a shave?' asks Alison and we agree that, being blond, he has no five o'clock shadow so there's no need.

'But we should give him a squirt of Fahrenheit, Alison.'

'Oh yes.' She reaches for the after-shave. 'He used to tell me the girls couldn't resist it.' We both attempt a laugh.

A tap on the door announces Steve's return with Andrew's clothes.

'They're not your favourites, lad, but Gosia thought they'd be comfy.' Steve speaks in the upbeat encouraging tone that is natural to him. *This isn't really happening, Andrew, Daddy will make it go away.* He falters at the sight of the pale face and the shock of the cool arm beneath his touch. He squeezes his eyelids closed, forcing the pain and the tears back, out of sight.

I want to wrap my arms around my husband and around my son. I want us to be the threesome we were in the delivery room nearly thirty-three years ago. I want a future for us together. But I cannot move, I cannot cry, I cannot believe our son is dead.

Andrew fancied himself in cream chinos and a fashionably unmatched linen shirt but the steroids caused him to outgrow those months ago. These comfy clothes are jogging pants with an elasticated waist and the tee shirt made by a designer friend. A panel on the front shows a black and white Border Collie, a dead ringer for Andrew's beloved dog, Bim. A picture of a plate of fruit is superimposed onto the dog's body. The slogan beneath reads, *Still Life in the Old Dog*. Andrew appreciated the humour and wore the shirt proudly as his health declined.

I shake my head and wince at the irony as I pull it on to his lifeless body.

Thirty-Two

'Can you tell her, please, Janet?' Gosia whispers into her untouched mug of tea when we hear the creak of floorboards in Alice's bedroom above our heads.

Steve's eyes search my face. 'Are you all right with that, love? I'll do it if you like.'

I shake my head and turn to my daughter-in-law. 'If you're sure, Gosia.' She nods.

Alice bumps her bottom down the stairs into the kitchen – a favourite game. She rubs her little fists into her eyes. 'I don't want to go to school today.'

'You don't have to go today, *kochanie*,' Gosia says. 'Granny has something to tell you.' Alice sweeps her puzzled glance over the three of us and it's clear she knows this won't be good news. She stands clutching her soft one-eyed caterpillar, its bright colours already faded by love.

I open my arms and she climbs into my lap. Her chubby body is warm under the pink pyjamas covered in pictures of little bears enjoying their picnic. She smells of sleep and I bury my face in a cloud of tousled blonde hair.

She wriggles and turns her father's open, blue-eyed gaze on me. 'What, Granny?'

I hug her a little tighter and don another layer of metaphorical armour. 'Alice, sweetheart, the thing is, you know Daddy has not been feeling well for a long time?'

'That's why they're looking after him in the hospital.'

'Yes. And you know when you saw him yesterday he felt so ill that he couldn't even open his eyes?'

'Mm.' Her baby teeth shine like pearly beads when she stretches her mouth into a yawn and shows a gap wider than a pound coin between the front two, just like his.

'Well last night he was so tired that he…'

Alice's mouth snaps shut, and her soft body becomes rigid in my arms. Avoiding my eye, she clutches caterpillar close and asks, 'Did he die?'

My stomach feels full of stones. I am so weary. Why do I have to do this unnatural thing – tell my granddaughter that her daddy, my baby, is dead? Hugging her a little closer I screw up my courage and deliver the words. 'Yes, my darling. He died.'

She is off my lap, out of my grasp, running towards the door. 'I don't believe you. You're a liar. I'm going to see him.' Cold morning air blows in from the garden, the door stands wide and she is gone; around the side of the house, up the stony path, along the pavement, with three adults in pursuit. Gosia scoops her up and Alice buries her tears in her mother's shoulder.

Back in the kitchen she drinks some warm milk but refuses to eat. 'I want to see him. I want to see him now.'

Gosia twists her face into a question mark and looks at Steve and me. '*Kochanie,* he won't be able to speak to you. It's like he is asleep.'

'I'm going.'

'Well, you're not going anywhere in your pyjamas, so let's get you dressed first.'

When they go upstairs, Steve chews his lip, 'Is this a good idea, Janet?'

I rest my elbows on the table, hold my head in my hands. 'I don't know, I don't know, I don't know.'

We walk the few hundred yards up the hill to the Care Centre. Fresh air and a bit of exercise revive us. The working day is beginning and someone in a red car toots and waves. Steve raises a hand in acknowledgement.

'Who was that?' Gosia asks.

'No idea.'

Alice is skipping now, as if the initial shock of the villain entering the story has been assimilated and now we are on the next stage of the adventure to see off the wicked interloper and arrive at the familiar happy ending of her storybooks.

'Alice, sweetie,' I jump forward to catch hold of her hand, 'I need to tell you something.' She tries to pull away, but my grip is firm. 'You will find that Daddy is very pale now, and when we touch him he is rather cold.'

'He doesn't like being cold. They need to give him more blankets.'

'He doesn't mind the cold now, you see, because it is just his body that's still here. The real daddy we love, the daddy who can feel cold, is going somewhere else. That's why we're going to see him – to say goodbye.' Oh shit. How do I explain something I don't understand myself?

'Like the dragonfly?'

'Yes, yes, Alice. Just like the dragonfly.' My dear, dear, little girl, not yet five years old, has rescued me from my floundering attempts to describe the indescribable.

I had found the little book about the dragonfly on the sales table at the Royal Marsden Hospital as I was casting around for things to occupy my time while Andrew was trapped in the tunnel of an MRI machine. On the cover was a brightly coloured dragonfly emerging from a pond populated by jolly animals, flowers and insects. Frogs, marsh marigolds and water boatmen waved merrily as the splendid creature took flight on gossamer wings.

About four inches square – a perfect size for four-year-old hands – the book told the story of a little egg which turned into a nymph. The nymph lived in the water for a long time and made lots of friends. All the time he grew and grew, until spring arrived, and he climbed up the stem of the plant he lived on into the fresh morning air. He told his friends that he didn't want to leave them, but he had to go to somewhere even more wonderful. The creatures of the pond watched him change into a beautiful iridescent thing and fly away.

At first, they were sad, but they always remembered him, and they were glad he was well and happy now.

The book had lain in my 'Andrew' drawer with all the hospital correspondence, all my notes about gliomas, their grading and their inevitable progression and the slim, orange volume Mike B gave me – the definitive medical reference book that has guided me through this journey. I had read *The Dragonfly* many times and wondered when would be the right time to introduce it to Alice, always replacing it in the drawer with the thought, *not yet, there still might be a miracle*. I knew all along that the miracle wouldn't happen but that little worm called 'maybe' kept wriggling up through my desolation and I replaced the little book in its hiding place. As winter closed in I realised that the worm was dead and accepted that the same fate awaited Andrew before long. Most four-year-olds have no conception of what death is. They are at the beginning of life's adventure, they don't need their optimism brought low with the thought that their world and the people in it may change or disappear. Alice is not an average four-year-old; she has witnessed Andrew's seizures, watched as he has leaned on Gosia to steady his laboured, erratic steps, sensed the strained atmosphere in the house, overheard worried conversations and tenderly kissed her daddy's injury.

It was time for us to read about the dragonfly. Teletubbies and Bananas in Pyjamas had demanded her attention and she squirmed on my lap as I read the book to her. Now I know she was listening all the time. The dragonfly had done its job.

We peer through the glazed door when we reach the hospital and see that, this morning, Maureen Getley is the volunteer manning the reception desk. Andrew's history teacher at school, she had been one of the many staff for whom he exerted little effort, but on whom he bestowed much charm. Like all of us, not least Andrew himself, she had been amazed when he attained a B grade in O-level History. Since retirement she had moved to a bungalow in a neighbouring village, forsaking the house where she had been Andrew's near neighbour in Military Road. When he'd first met her at the hospital, Andrew had flung his arms around this rather proper spinster and told her how glad he was to have her near him again. Like his father, he was always good with old ladies.

When we push open the door Miss Getley rises to her feet, a confused, anxious expression on her face that she rearranges into a sincere, compassionate smile.

Tentatively, she touches Gosia's hand when we arrive at the desk and she greets Alice with an uncertain, 'Hello, dear.' Her eyes are moist as she addresses Steve and me. 'I am so sorry. Do go on in.'

We ignore the visitors' book where we have signed in and out hundreds of times and Alice skips ahead.

Mandy Martin is at the nurses' station. Dear Mandy, whom we have known since her teenage years. We celebrated when she married Phil, the apprentice builder who helped us restore our fifteenth-century ruin into a home. More recently he has done the same for Andrew and Gosia's Georgian cottage. Mandy and Phil now have three growing boys and we are thankful for her loving care of Andrew.

'Whoa!' Mandy catches Alice in her arms. 'Hello, sweetheart.'

'I've come to see Daddy.'

Mandy bites her lip and looks towards the closed door of room one.

'It's okay, Mandy,' I say.

Gosia holds tight to Alice's hand and we enter.

For a moment the child hesitates, then runs across the room. She climbs onto the bed in the way she is used to. Steve reaches out to restrain her. 'Gently, sweetie,' he says, although she cannot disturb Andrew now. Behind us Mandy sniffs and blows her nose, but we are out of tears. We stand watching.

Alice hugs the motionless body. 'Bye, bye, Daddy,' she says in a sad, puzzled voice. She draws her face back from the familiar, yet unfamiliar figure and stares at him.

The moment is frozen, endless, until Mandy asks if we've had any breakfast.

'No. And I'm hungry.' Alice slides off the bed and runs from the room without a backward glance. The rest of us follow her lead, closing the door behind us, leaving him alone. My grief is dry-eyed, tears too buried to be summoned.

'Dr James is here,' the staff nurse says.

Lelly embraces us one by one. Steve and I go with her to see our dead son. Gosia is busy with her living daughter.

After a cursory examination, to officially ascertain death, Lelly whispers her goodbyes to a patient she has become fond of and turns to me. 'He's at peace, Janet. Now you can begin to take off those layers of armour-plating.'

'Not yet, Lelly, not yet. I have to hold myself, all of us, together.'

In the kitchen, Mandy is ladling porridge into white bowls. 'Alice tells me you all like porridge.'

'With lots of brown sugar on the top,' says Alice.

'Say please, Alice.' Gosia reminds her of her manners as if this is any ordinary day.

Mandy sprinkles the bowls with demerara. 'Why don't you eat this in the quiet room where you won't be disturbed?' Carrying the tray of steaming bowls, she leads us across the vestibule of the rebuilt cottage hospital. There is a buzz of conversation – a few early patients are arriving for their outpatient appointments.

The quiet room is small and multi-purpose, a place to break bad news, a place to absorb it, a place to meditate or pray, and a place to discuss a difficult case. Today the March morning sun shines through the high window, dappled by the shadow of emerging leaves. A blackbird on a branch of the tree outside gives its all in a full-throated, exuberant spring song.

Mandy sets down her tray on the table with the simple wooden cross. 'Would you like tea or coffee?'

We don't want either.

'I'll leave you in peace, then. Let me know if I can do anything else for you.'

She knows this is just a form of words. She knows she can do nothing, so she closes the door quietly behind her.

There are two rows of four chairs.

'Sit there,' Alice instructs, 'and I'll be the cafe lady. She hands us each a bowl of porridge and a spoon and sits herself on the floor. 'Right, now. You are the three bears and I am Goldilocks. Now eat your porridge.' The smell of sugar melted into the bumpy, creamy oatmeal is tempting and we begin to eat. 'Granddad, you are daddy bear – so what do you say?'

We are back in her safe world, the world of games and fairy tales.

Steve adopts a deep brown voice. 'Who's been sitting in my chair?'

'Me, Goldilocks,' she squeals. 'Mummy, now it's your turn.'

'Ask Granny, Alice, I don't know these English stories.'

Alice looks expectantly at me.

'Who's been eating my porridge?' I ask in what I judge to be a suitable mother-bear voice.

With perfect logic, Goldilocks informs me that I am the only one who's been eating my porridge and I had better finish it before it gets cold. Applause and merriment fill the room.

How can her father not be here to join in this game? In healthy days, he would have revelled in the role of daddy bear, loping around the room, chasing his prey, then tossing her in the air, catching her in his arms and nuzzling his love into her. Instead he lies still and lifeless in a silent room only twenty yards from us.

I concentrate on the traffic and Gosia stares out of the window as we drive in silence to Hastings to register the death. The last time we made this journey together was to register Alice's birth.

In the waiting room of the multi-purpose 1960s building next to the police station we find ourselves in strange company. An untidy-looking couple in their twenties are looking glum. He shrugs off his shabby leather jacket and says something to the girl. 'Don't understandya,' she replies and continues to stare ahead and chew her gum.

The door to our left opens and a red-haired, middle-aged woman in a dark suit scans the room and approaches the couple with a smile. 'Miss Jenkins? And Mr Pavlo...?' The young woman nods. 'I understand you would like to arrange your wedding. Please come this way.'

I am not sure whether my Polish daughter-in-law takes in the situation, but I realise this marriage is a business transaction and wonder if the registrar does too.

A couple sit close together gazing at their newborn baby. At the slightest movement of their precious bundle they look up and smile proudly at each other.

The notice on the door reads, REGISTRAR OF BIRTHS DEATHS AND MARRIAGES, and she has to deal with all three this morning.

When we return to the farmhouse we see Steve and Alice sitting beside the pond. Ducklings swim across the water towards the woodland on the other side. Under the trees, primroses and white windflowers shine in shafts of sunlight. Alice looks up as my tyres crunch on the gravel and she runs to greet us.

Gosia lifts her daughter into her arms and Alice says, 'Me and Granddad have been sitting by the pond and crying together.'

Thirty-Three

The cardboard coffin has a wood grain design printed on it. Gosia accepts this was what he would want, given his care for the environment, not to mention that he would deem anything else to be a terrible waste of money. She is used to Polish Catholic funerals, however, so I wonder if she would have preferred something more ostentatious. Except for meetings to discuss the order of service and visits to the vicar to arrange the time and place, for the past ten days we have hardly seen her or Alice. Gosia has taken comfort from her friends. We have all been inundated with flowers and condolence cards and letters. I don't know if Alice has been to school, but trust that her young teacher would have handled the situation with sensitivity. There are balloons in the window of their cottage in Military Road and Alice has said that her daddy is a star now.

The day is here, March the twenty-seventh, and I am relieved that the sun is shining. Rain wouldn't have reflected Andrew's personality. Coincidentally, Laura and I have chosen yellow outfits and Matthew wears the jade-green jacket he sported at his sister's wedding. We know this will be shocking for some, but Andrew loved colour and today is all about Andrew. Yellow and green are the colours of spring and we need the birdsong, primroses and lengthening days to remind us that there is a future. It is a future I cannot yet envisage, a future without his grin, his infuriating lack of organisation, his tasteless jokes, his understated adoration. I know how much he loved us, his parents, and I know how much we will always love him.

'He didn't just love you, Dad,' Laura had said as she and Steve stood together, hands clasped, beside their unconscious brother and son, 'he wanted to *be* you.'

I recall the school parents' evening when Mrs Bygates, his French teacher, had told us in her continental accent not to worry about his poor grasp of a foreign language, he was a lovely boy who would always be with us. Now he is gone, but not gone.

Two nights ago, I had a vivid dream. I was visiting him at the Care Centre and he wanted to get out of bed. I drew back the covers and saw he wasn't wearing the outsized boxer shorts and tee shirt to cover his distended body, but was slim, dressed in his favourite cream linen shirt and chino trousers. He took my hand as I helped him from the bed but, as he opened the door and walked out of the room, he shook free of me saying, 'Let me go, Mum. It's okay, I can walk you know.' A psychologist would probably say it was my subconscious self, weaving a healing scenario, perhaps indicating an afterlife I do not believe in, but I take comfort from it all the same.

Steve and I stand at the door of the small medieval church where Gosia and Andrew were married nine years ago, where Alice was baptised. We greet the three hundred or so people who cram in. Those who haven't arrived early are obliged to stand three deep in the side aisles. Family, friends from far and wide, teachers, fellow shopkeepers, suppliers, customers, shop staff, nurses from the Care Centre just across the road – his home for the last four months, Lelly, the doctor... They are all here to honour and bid farewell to our extraordinary son.

Richard, his fellow brain-tumour sufferer, hobbles through the door, his face gaunt and pale. He leans his weight on a stick, supported by Helen, his pregnant wife. His mother gives me a moist-eyed hug as Steve evicts three people from the nearest pew who, when they see the need, are happy to help the family into their seats. Helen passes me a paper bearing the story of the foursome's unlikely friendship, which Richard had intended to read from the lectern, were he well enough. It is headed:

For a man with a great sense of (t)humour

It ends:

I have decided that I must now take the baton and fight the good fight for both of us. We will prevail. Be forever happy, Andy, and thanks for all the guidance and help you gave me.

We'll all be seeing you again someday.

Richard died in 'Andrew's' room at the Care Centre six months later, the day after his son was born.

The service is about to begin, and we are moving to take our seats when Paul McCartney arrives and stands modestly just inside the door. We are shocked to see him, knowing that at this time his house in a nearby lane is besieged by paparazzi prying into his private life. Steve shakes him warmly by the hand. 'Thank you for coming, Paul. How did you escape?'

Paul taps his nose, smiles, 'I have my ways.'

Gosia, her Polish cousin, Greg, and Alice, sit in the front, left-hand pew surrounded by friends. I smile at Alice, but she has her head bowed and doesn't see me. Gosia is talking to an old friend of Andrew's. I wish we were together, I wish I could gather them to me, but we are on separate islands of grief. I hope we aren't drifting away from each other. The rest of our family sit on the right-hand side of the church.

The elderly lady organist breaks into a faltering rendition of our chosen music, Elgar's *Nimrod*, and I recall listening to it at Burrswood, when Andrew wept and said, 'Play this at my funeral.'

Now, in his cardboard box decorated with flowers, he is escorted up the aisle by his brother and his closest friends. We sing his favourite hymns – *All Things Bright and Beautiful* and *Amazing Grace*. A friend reads from Corinthians 13, as she did at their wedding – *Love is patient, love is kind…love never fails.*

I have tried to be patient with those I love and how could I not be kind to my child? I have loved him, so much, but my love has failed. I have failed to make it better.

I put on my actor's face – a hard face, some would say. It is like that Perspex mask that protected Andrew's healthy brain from lethal rays directed at the tumour. It is part of my emotional shield.

A picture of composure, I mount the pulpit steps to read a favourite poem: *How long does a man live?* I have admired Brian Patten's poetry for years. I never imagined myself reading this at my son's funeral. But my voice doesn't waver.

Matthew follows me to give a loving tribute, saying that Andrew has always been and will continue to be his big brother. As such, he taught him how to deal with life's pitfalls and, in his own inimitable style, disentangled the myths and pains of adolescence.

He continues: 'The life skills I have gained through Andrew have stood me in better stead than any O-level or degree.

The last three years have been terrible in so many ways, but they have also been a gift of time to appreciate, understand and forgive each other for those inevitable but unimportant sibling disagreements – and to be so very proud of him.'

I am envious of the way Matthew's voice is cracked by sadness, the tears welling in his eyes.

Next to me Laura stares impassively ahead but I feel her body stiffen.

We both need to shed our armour.

Supported by his friends, Andrew leaves the church to his chosen music, *The Long and Winding Road,* and I catch a wistful smile on Paul McCartney's face.

Traffic stops as we process across the road, past the Care Centre, where nurses peel off to attend to their living patients, and we walk down the daffodil-lined path to the hillside cemetery. Alice is held high on the tall shoulders of her mum's cousin.

When we are gathered around to watch Andrew being lowered into the ground, John, our reverend friend, says a few words. He recalls Andrew's words when he visited him in the hospital in the early days of his illness; when, disturbed from sleep, Andrew had opened his eyes and joked, 'Blimey, I must have died and gone to heaven – it's the old Vic.' John is sure our boy is now in heaven and says that if he is lucky enough to get there himself, he looks forward to Andrew welcoming him with the words – 'Hello, old Vic. So, you too, have died and ended up here.'

We requested no flowers, but Alice holds a plastic ice cream container full of primroses and windflowers, gathered from our patch of woodland this morning. She offers them to everyone, invites them to throw them into the grave. One of Andrew's mates tosses in a tin of tobacco and a packet of Rizlas, saying, 'Here you are, old man, you'll need these.' And we know there is a full jar of Marmite tucked in beside him.

I feel a tap on my shoulder, hear a soft, 'Hello, Janet,' and I turn to see Gill from Lancashire. 'I promised him I'd come to his funeral,' she says, and adds a single rose to the flowers, the tobacco, the Marmite. It is an echo of her poignant farewell at Heathrow as Andrew set out on his year of travels.

Afterwards, at the nearby hotel, my disembodied consciousness watches myself greeting mourners – 'How good of you to come' – offering sandwiches, drinks, smiling, even laughing.

For God's sake, this is your son's funeral, your beloved child's farewell. You will never see him, hold him, again. How can you laugh? Why aren't you a pale figure sitting weeping in the corner?

Because this is his last party and he wouldn't want tears at his celebration. He isn't here to entertain his friends and family, to enjoy the occasion himself. But he is still the focus of attention and we must do the laughing for him.

Across the room I notice Steve sitting with Alice on his knee, her arms around his neck, now the man at the centre of her life. Perhaps Andrew is his dad after all. I blink my eyes, blow my nose and turn to comfort a young lady next to me who is shaking with sorrow; a stranger to me but clearly not to Andrew. Another life touched by him.

Postscript

Soon after Andrew's death I felt compelled to write this book, to put on record the life of a big personality who is and would want to be remembered, to show Alice her father in health as well as in sickness.

I began to type through my tears, but when my husband, Steve, was diagnosed with motor neurone disease only four years after Andrew's death I put the manuscript away. I couldn't live through two tragedies at once. But the urge to write remained. I wrote another book – about my father, whom I never knew.

'Now you've written about your dad, Granny,' said Alice when it was published, 'what about that book about mine?' So, I started again, although progress has been slow and intermittent. I am completing this manuscript in 2017, the year that would have seen Andrew's fiftieth birthday. Alice has recently turned twenty-two and graduated from University with a first-class degree. So, this book, completed more than seventeen years after her dad left us, is a belated birthday gift for them both.

Panic struck when I failed to remember the chronology of his illness: when exactly was it we first met Dr B? Was that big seizure on the A12 in May or July? My memory, mislaying this information, made me fearful that it would mislay Andrew.

He was just an ordinary guy, but like every mother's son, an extraordinary ordinary guy. I have committed my memories to paper so that he will not be lost. Not to me, nor to his wife, family, and friends. Most importantly so that he will not be lost to

Alice. Her recollections of her dad are almost certainly garnered from films, photographs and stories. Not entirely, though. On a sleepover at Granny and Granddad's at the age of nine she delayed bedtime by making great play of drinking from the tap to rinse her teeth, then sluicing her face and dampening the front of her hair. My heart somersaulted. How often I had seen Andrew perform this trick – moulding his wet hair in the fashion of the day; a Mohican coxcomb from crown to forehead, or a scalp covered in short, punky spikes.

'Hurry up, Alice. Whatever are you doing that for?'

'It's what Dad used to do, Granny. He showed me.' She'd never seen this on a video.

I want to put his life into print. But, even as I type the words, he slips away, squeezing past the text and disappearing into the air like a will-o'-the-wisp. I know, though, that it is my own inability to capture his spirit in words, which causes him to fly. He would want to stay – close to the bosom of his family in his cherished corner of Sussex.

Retrieving memory is like peering through ancient window glass in an abandoned house. I push aside the cobwebs and wipe the dusty pane with my tear-dampened handkerchief. The sunshine streams through and I see the detail clearly in full colour. Then, as I search further, the glass becomes thickened and striated, the contour lines get closer, so that the picture becomes indistinct and distorted and I strain to find the memory I seek. Sometimes, perhaps, I add a little imagination to complete the picture, but the essence remains.

Every personality is multi-faceted, presenting a different face to different people, and, as they interact, the facets reflect off each other like crystals. So that everyone's memories of Andrew are unique and personal. This book is about *my* memories.

In life he was laid-back, smiling, good-humoured, memorable, and would hurt no one. Like us all, he had dreams and limitations, irritations, fears and worries. I have tried to portray this and understand that others may not remember exactly the same man.

I'll be famous one day, you know, he chuckles in my ear.

Andrew, my love, I doubt you'll be that, but your head would certainly swell at the thought of a book written about you.

My layers of armour-plating have come off very slowly over seventeen years, and there are probably still more to shed. As my wounded spirit has been exposed more and more to the light and air I have cried more and more with the pain.

On better days, I cannot believe it all happened. He is not dead. He appears behind me in the mirror, grinning. Grasps me round the waist with, *Hi Mum, I'm back.* His proud laughter rings around the Christmas table as his daughter bears in the flaming pudding. He pronounces Dad's new car to be boring or Mum's new haircut cool.

When we holidayed in Australia, a year after his death, he seemed to greet his parents each morning with a cheery *G'day* and we remembered his descriptions of the fun he had in this place or that, or the strange incident on the coach to Alice Springs; how hard they worked fruit picking for a pittance, or the vengeful tricks he and his mates played on their mean employer. Then our tears overtook our smiles. *It's not fair.*

He was there in his little girl's school reports. 'Alice has a great big personality, but she must learn to display it in the right place at the right time'. Oh yes, he was there all right.

He was there when Alice showed her friends around our farm-house, insisting proudly that they look in every room, admire every historical feature, just as Andrew had done.

At the school pantomime, *Ali Baba*, we searched the chorus line of forty thieves for our granddaughter, long blonde hair drawn back under a tea towel, big, dreamy, blue eyes scanning the audience. She caught sight of us and grinned, revealing the inherited gap between her front teeth. Steve reached for my hand. 'Andrew', we whispered, glad of the darkness to hide our watery smiles.

As I walk in the Lake District, on the Dorset coast or in his beloved Brede Valley where he grew up, he is on my shoulder, revelling in the beauty, loving his world.

'Wow – what a view. Cor, look at that sunset – aren't we lucky to be alive?'

He is at my elbow, licking his lips, in food markets and delicatessens in Italy, discussing the varieties of mushrooms or seafood as he jokes with the stallholders in his fluent language of gesture and laughter.

'There's still a fortune to be made in a good deli Mum. I'll make my million yet, just you see.'

Frequently he appears in my dreams. One night I was on a ship when Laura bounded up to me laughing, eyes bright with excitement and tears. 'Mum, Andrew's here! Have you seen him? He is so well.'

Andrew lives on in his beautiful, now grown-up daughter on the verge of a career as a documentary filmmaker, combining her artistic ability, social conscience and endearing sense of humour.

The inscription on Andrew's rough, fossil-laden headstone reads:

A man lives for as long as we hold him inside us,
For as long as we hold the harvest of his dreams.

Alice, you are a rich harvest.

Acknowledgments

I am grateful to my family for allowing me to write this book. I could not have done it without the valuable input of my workshop colleagues and beta readers, Kim Hope, Jane Venn, Yvonne Phillips and Jill Treseder. I value greatly the advice I have been given by the writers Blake Morrison and Mark McCrum. Thanks also to Andrew's friends for generously sharing their memories with me. My thanks to Brian Patten and his agent for permitting me to quote from the poem, *So Many Different Lengths of Time*.

Some names and initials have been changed, but the events described in this book are my true memories; in as much as memories are ever true...

Lightning Source UK Ltd.
Milton Keynes UK
UKHW01f2350040918
328354UK00001B/91/P